BAD NEWS FOR YOU IS GOOD NEWS FOR ME

MIKE DEESON

ST. PETERSBURG PRESS

Due to the autobiographical nature of the content, all attempts have been made to preserve the stories of the events, locales and conversations contained in this collection as the author remembers them. The author reserves the right to have changed the names of individuals and places if necessary and may have changed some identifying characteristics and details such as physical properties, occupations and places of residence in order to maintain their anonymity.

Published by St. Petersburg Press

St. Petersburg, FL

www.stpetersburgpress.com

Design and composition by St. Petersburg Press

Cover design by St. Petersburg Press and Pablo Guidi

Print ISBN: 978-1-940300-12-2

eBook ISBN: 978-1-940300-11-5

First Edition

CONTENTS

DEDICATION

I want to dedicate this book to my best friend and wife Laurie Garrett, my biggest supporter and toughest critic.

My kids, Andrew and Megan who learned to eat dinner very late, because we always tried to eat dinner together and I was rarely home at a decent time.

To my grandkids, Ariana and Carter White, just because they inspire me every day.

To my parents, Marge and Jack Dissen, who always taught me with hard work you can accomplish anything.

To my in-laws Barbara and Murray Garrett who were a second set of parents and always supportive.

And to my Niles East Highschool Guidance Counselor, Aune Toivola, whom upon learning I wanted a career in Journalism insisted I go to the University of Missouri, which changed my life forever.

Special thanks to my editor, Hilary Crist for keeping my manuscript in line and making sure that all the stories in the book make sense and that I never begin a sentence with "However."

Thanks to Amy Cianci for making this project happen, I could not have done it without her.

PREFACE

THE FUTURE OF TELEVISION

Real news.

Fake news.

Facebook, Twitter, YouTube, Broadcast TV....

This is the new information age and it's changing so quickly that I have whiplash. In fact, in the time it took you to read the last 20 or so words on this written page, they have become old news. Words and pictures on TV become obsolete the moment they are written.

Nowadays, everyone is a "journalist", or so they think. Their journalism degree is a Smart Phone and they know how to operate a "camera" because their new iPhone can provide the world with live coverage. It's a fact that people are posting more than 300 hours of video on YouTube every minute and that number is rising.

Me? I'm old school.

I was fortunate enough to come up and then work during the Golden Age of local television news. I started long before we worried about memes, postings and social media. When I was a rookie reporter, we didn't even worry about competition from cable, any cable. There were three major networks, PBS and some cities had one or two independent stations not affiliated with a network.

This book traces the wild ride I've had in television for more than six decades. By the way, I've enjoyed every moment and I hope you do, too. As a warning, the language used in TV stations is coarse and rough and I know if my Mom were alive, she would be uncomfortable and perhaps even chastise me for so much profanity and dropping so many "F" bombs. I have tried to be completely honest with every story and the raw language is part of the TV landscape. Sorry Mom.

One more thing: This is what I call a great bathroom book. You'll be able to pick up and read stories (all true) while finding real insight into local television and the times they defined. You can do this by reading one story at a time, move on and come back again when you have another chance.

A BRIEF HISTORY OF TELEVISION NEWS

WHAT FOLLOWS ARE my experiences from Day One to Right Now. We begin when I shot my first TV news story in 1968 at KOMU-TV while I was a student at the University of Missouri hoping to have a career as an on-air journalist. We've come a long way from that first time when I shot my piece on a wind-up Bell and Howell three-turret camera in black and white and on silent film. It was ugly, but the good news was You could always tell in those days when good things were going to happen. The camera wound down and you had to wind it up.

If I was winding, news was happening.

We edited the film on a contraption called a Movie-O-La, which meant you hand-cranked the film from one reel to another with a viewer in the middle. Then we spliced it together by cutting the actual film with straight razor blades. In those cave man days, we finished the process with a glue pot, located at every editing station (which might explain why I am like I am today). We simply stuck it together.

Eventually, things got high-tech and the glue pot went away and was replaced by "high tech" Scotch Tape for a "cold splice" as opposed to a "hot splice" with the glue, which was indeed warmer. Time passed and soon we were able to get a camera that had actual sound. The only thing was the first ones involved finding an electrical outlet to plug into to get the machine to work. We did the interview on one camera and then shot the accompanying film to fit the narration on another camera. That meant when the films were played back during the newscasts, there had to be two different projectors − one for sound, the other for the reporter's narration. The terms A-roll (for the sound projector) and B-roll for the second one evolved. To this day when TV stories are shot, anything that isn't part of an interview or standup (where you see the reporter on camera) is still referred to as B roll. Proving that as much as things change, there are certain touchstones that remain.

Within a few short years, TV news evolved to using one camera that shot sound on the film, usually through a magnetic strip (that looked like the old-time tape decks), that ran along the bottom side of the film.

In order to do a story, we would go out, do the interview, shoot a stand up, and then shoot B-roll to accompany the narration. The most common camera was a CP-16, which had two attached film canisters on top that looked like Mickey Mouse ears. A nylon cord moved the film through the camera and it often squeaked very loudly as it was running. I remember in the '70's covering Virginia Governor John Dalton when unfortunately, our camera began to squeak extremely loudly. When we got a sound bite that would work, I told the photographer he could turn the camera off. At that point, the Governor looked at me in the front row and said, "Thank You, Mike, now everyone can hear what I have to say."

Film was expensive and usually each photographer and reporter's "film budget" was 400 feet for the day, or 12 minutes. Quite often, we had to do "pre-interviews" before we started the film rolling. That could be frustrating because when the camera started you might have to say, "Remember that emotional story you just told me before we started filming where you had tears running down your cheek? Could you tell it again? And I wouldn't get upset if you got upset again on film." Actually, the good photographers would listen to the pre-interview and would start rolling the moment it got emotional. Of course, some photogs would look at you after someone had just poured their heart out and say," Did you want me to roll on that?"

It's also worth noting that back in the film days, the 400 feet of film came in canisters that made their way to almost every reporter's desk because they made a perfect ashtray. Back in those days almost everyone smoked in the newsroom. Some drank, but we didn't do drugs. At least not until the 80's. But I'm getting ahead of myself.

THE PRESIDENTS BY THE NUMBERS

I'VE HAD the privilege of covering every President since Gerald Ford commissioned the USS Nimitz in Norfolk. And each time I've been with the President of the United States it always has been a special event. How can you describe being with the most powerful person in the world? To me, I always felt like I was etching my way into history, one broadcast at a time. As a journalist, however, a presidential experience is also another story, which is why some of the visits were more memorable than others. Although all left lasting impressions. One even involved Starbucks with the Leader of the Free World.

NUMBER 39

Jimmy Carter came to the Norfolk area during troubled times in 1980. The Iran hostage crisis was weighing on his mind along with a country that was facing bleak economic times. Interestingly enough, this was long before the kind of ramped-up security involved with presidential visits since September 11. That's why when a scruffy looking man walked towards the press platform before the Carter visit, I didn't think twice about it. Neither did the other reporters who were jockeying for position on that cool autumn afternoon. When he approached my photographer and me and asked to look inside our bags, we looked at him (and both indignantly) said, "No way!" (Can you even imagine saying that now and at a presidential event?) Once he flashed his Secret Service badge, however, our mood changed and we became extremely cooperative.

It was a foreshadowing of security that was going to be a natural part of presidential visits in the future. Sadly, for Jimmy Carter, the Secret Service inspection was the most memorable part of the appearance. Carter, not known for his great oratory, didn't wow the crowd or say anything memorable. It begged the question: how do you go home and tell your friends that being around the president wasn't really a life changing event?

NUMBER 40

Luckily, for this reporter, when Ronald Reagan became the 40th President of the United States, the events were far more memorable. The first occurred at the White House where there was some kind of news conference that would have significant impact on the Norfolk area. It's not surprising that any national issue affected Norfolk with the huge military presence in the area. In my congressional district, at least 50 percent of the registered voters worked for the Federal Government.

At this news conference, local reporters were invited into the White House, and I was one of them. Once we cleared security, we were taken to a waiting area and then called cattle-style to the Rose Garden where the press conference was to be held. It wasn't like in the movies where you just wear a nice suit and stroll around the "home of democracy". As we walked in, I was my own roadie as I carried the tripod while my photographer had the camera and a ton of other equipment. A quick walk through a glass doors and we would be in the famed Rose Garden.

I was walking and schlepping along when the reporter in front of me, who was holding the door just let go. It was on a spring and what followed seemed to be happening in slow motion. I saw the glass door moving towards the legs of the tripod and all I could think was: "This glass is going to shatter and I'm going to have to explain to our news director how I broke a window at the White House." Thankfully the windows were thick, probably bullet proof and I think they did more damage to the tripod than the tripod did to the window. To this day I have no idea what Reagan said that day. Instead, I focused on how thankful I was not to be led away in handcuffs for damaging federal property.

The next encounter with President Reagan occurred when I was in Richmond, VA and he was in D.C. It was March 30, 1981 and I was a political reporter for the NBC affiliate in Norfolk, WAVY TV. I was covering a committee hearing for a major issue coming out of the Virginia General Assembly when a reporter for the CBS station in Richmond, Ed Hazelwood, a good friend of mine who had a booming, resonant voice, rushed into the committee hearing.

"Boys we're not going to be the lead tonight," he announced, breathlessly. "The President has just been shot." Within seconds, the committee room cleared, and reporters all ran to the Press Room to call our assignment desks. At the time, there was no such thing as a cell phone. We were live, at the scene, and our jobs were to track down political leaders in the Capitol to get a comment on the shooting.

Back in those days, satellite feeds and live trucks were not a common part of the broadcast landscape, so we had to do our interviews, cut a quick stand up and write our narration track to record.

We had to put it on the Greyhound bus to ship back to Norfolk, so it could be developed and edited at the station for the 11 p.m. news.

Believe me when I say, it was even worse before the "modern" days of videotape. Way back in the day, when I covered the General Assembly on film, you had to have your film shot along with a standup in time for transport on the 12:15 p.m. Greyhound, which would arrive in Norfolk somewhere around 2:30 p.m. and then the film had to be picked up and rushed back to the station for the 3 p.m. film run. Back in those days most stations had a film processor in the building. The processor was usually adjacent to the newsroom and the smell of the chemicals would waft into the noses of the reporters and photographers who were nearby when the film was being developed. If we were sending the film back to the station via Greyhound bus, we would sometimes cut our narration over the telephone, but that sounded like crap.

Meanwhile, on the day that President Reagan was shot, the idea of getting anything at all on the Greyhound in time seemed like a fantasy. I'll never forget going back with my crew to the Holiday Inn in Richmond. We did the right journalistic thing by gathering in the bar (what you've heard about reporters and drinking is true) and met up with most of the members of the Norfolk Legislative Delegation. All of us were stunned as we watch the events of the day unfold on national news.

Before this historic night, I had learned an important lesson. You get the really good political stories at events where liquor is served vs. the dry gulch of a boring committee meeting. I can't count the times a well lubricated legislator or staffer would tell me something about an upcoming piece of legislation that would cause me to run to the men's room so I could write it down in the reporter's notebook I kept inside my blazer.

It amazed me when a few days later I would ask questions about a particular issue, sometimes to the same legislator who told me the information under the influence of alcohol, and he (there weren't many female legislators in the 70's and early 80's) would be astounded that I had found out about it before it became public. I found out about it before that first twist of lemon hit the glass.

Perhaps my favorite Reagan moment was an appearance he made when I was already in Tampa. In the 80's when the President came to the Tampa Bay Area, we would pull out all the stops including a special live report when the Commander in Chief landed at the airport. Of course, we would cover his speech and even track him back to the airport for another live report of the president re-boarding Air Force One and leaving the city limits.

On this day, my assignment was to cover the arrival and departure from the Clearwater-St. Petersburg Airport, a smaller and easier to access place than the craziness and snarling traffic of Tampa International Airport.

As the President arrived, our station broke into regular programming and I did the play-by-play as Reagan descended the steps of Air

Force One and got into his limousine on the way to his speech. It came off without a hitch, but now we had two or three hours to kill at the airport while we waited for the President to return. I would also be doing a special report of his departure.

Even before 9-11 security for the President could sometimes be extremely tight, but other times it was surprisingly loose. This was one of those loose security events and the reporters who were waiting around for Reagan to return had pretty much free run of the tarmac where Air Force One was parked. As we were killing time, I walked up to the stereotypical secret service agent (dark suit, sunglasses, short hair, earpiece and stiff pose) and asked him, "What are the chances...."

Before I could get out another word he said, "Stop. Do you personally know God?" I thought that was a strange question and figured he was a religious zealot. Yet, I still tried to answer the best I could by saying, "Well maybe not personally, but I do believe." He looked at me and said, "Then the answer is no!" I was a bit puzzled and he could tell by the look on my face that I had questions.

"You were going to say, 'What are the chances I could stick my head inside Air Force One, right?" he asked.

I had to admit that was exactly what I was going to say. His response: "Unless you personally know God, you can't get inside the airplane." Then the agent added, "I've been on this detail for more than six months and the bottom of these stairs is the closest I have been to being inside the airplane. I think the only people that get on beside the President and his staff must personally know God."

While the agent clearly shot down my chances for getting into Air Force One, he was a decent guy and offered to take a still picture of my photographer and me in front of the plane. By the time President Reagan returned to the airport and I did the play-by-play it was anticlimactic compared to my attempt to get onto the most famous plane in the world.

NUMBER 41

When George "Papa" Bush succeeded Reagan, I covered him several times as he came often to the Tampa Bay area. I remember that he gave a speech at the national headquarters for Tropicana orange juice in Bradenton. The most memorable event from that speech was, before the President arrived, I ran to the men's room inside and saw they had orange juice machines instead of water fountains in the office outside of the bathroom. I told my fellow reporters and there was a run on the freshly squeezed orange juice.

My best encounter with Papa Bush was in South Florida after he visited the devastation from Hurricane Andrew, a Category-5 hurricane that slammed into south Florida on August 24th, 1992. The effects of the storm were visually and emotionally mind boggling. The majority of Homestead, Florida looked like an atom bomb had exploded in the town and all South Florida was in complete chaos. I spent 4 weeks covering Andrew in South Florida and I've detailed those experiences under my storm coverage stories, but it was under this backdrop that I had my exclusive interview with the 41st President of the United States.

Bush, who was in the final months of the presidential campaign against Bill Clinton, had been criticized for not doing more for South Florida. There were signs on roofs begging, "President Bush Please Help Us" as well as "President Bush! Where Are You?" To complicate matters for the President, candidate Bill Clinton was visiting families and turning on his well-known charm for the victims as well as the cameras.

One night about a week after Andrew hit so hard, photographer Gene Yagle and I were working on a story when we got a beep on our beepers. Our producer needed us to check in so he could tell us that President Bush was visiting Homestead, and we should be there, and pronto.

There were a few particulars that separated us from the Leader of the Free World. First off, driving to any location during Andrew was crazy, treacherous and sometimes next to impossible. There were no traffic lights or streetlights. Trees and power poles that had been uprooted during the storm blocked the access roads and the street signs to find them were no longer standing. This was in the days before GPS and we had absolutely no idea where we were until we hit the main drag of US 1, which is also called the Dixie Highway.

By the time we got to the strip shopping center where the President would be, there was already a gaggle of hundreds of reporters following Papa Bush. I looked at Gene with dismay, refusing to go to the back of the pack.

"There is no way we will get even close if he keeps walking in the direction he is going," I said, figuring we'd get our feed from our affiliates at ABC News.

Or maybe there was another plan?

"Gene, if we stand where we are in front of the blown-out stores of this complex then the president might turn our way. If he gets close enough, I can put a microphone in Bush's face and ask him one question before the Secret Service tackles me." We were ready to get a few bruises and waited there.

Sure enough, Papa Bush turned our way and I shouted to him as I walked up. "Mr. President, it's heartbreaking isn't it?" I said. The President, who had been criticized for not empathizing with the regular people in South Florida the way his Democratic opponent Clinton did, was more than happy to talk to me and get an opportunity to show how much he cared to Floridians who would see the story.

As we walked and talked with Gene back peddling, camera on his shoulder, I could see out of the corner of my eye (and maybe hear) the sphincter muscles of the Secret Service Agents and some of the President's handlers puckering tighter than someone who has taken a bite of the sourest lemon on earth.

Miraculously, we kept walking and talking, and after I was able to ask about five questions, I felt a very strong hand on my left shoulder as a huge Secret Service agent said, "That's enough." (He was worse than any Hollywood publicist!) I understood and didn't try to push my luck, but said, "Thank you Mr. President."

He was on his way and I had my exclusive – impromptu, serendipitous and extremely rare.

NUMBER 42

Bill Clinton was a personality larger than life... and one of the personality traits that contributed to that is that Clinton was a profuse schmoozer and talker. I met him during the normal airport presidential fanfare that didn't seem out of the ordinary. He was off to make a speech and I waited until he returned to the Clearwater St. Pete Airport around 11:15 a.m. where the plan was to do a live cut-in of Mr. Personality In Chief waving to the local crowd before stepping back onto his ride, Air Force One, to leave town.

Clinton being Clinton began the return journey with one of his famous "schmooze fests" where he started talking with every Democratic politician who raced to the airport for their photo op. Fortunately, I had worked in Tampa Bay so long I was able to give some background to my viewers when it came to each of the politicians. There was 16-time elected Tampa Congressman Sam Gibbons who was a paratrooper on D-Day. Instead of a gas mask, he was supposed to keep in a pouch in his flight suit, he replaced it with two Schlitz beers. Why? If he was going to get shot, he wanted to have a beer before he died. Obviously, he made it and shared the two beers with his friends before they invaded a town. He told me they left the empty cans in the middle of the road as a sign of the first two Schlitz beers consumed in France since the war began.

Then there was Tampa Mayor Sandy Freeman who was a junior nationally ranked tennis star, a fact few knew. Believe me, I was able to tell stories about each of the politicians who were there to see and be seen with President Clinton.

The President continued to work the crowd, talking to each person and making each individual feel as if *they* were the most important person in the world.

My quick live "cut in" shot turned into 45 minutes of waiting and Clinton was STILL schmoozing. The noon news, in fact, had already started, and I continued to talk on air. I was doing a 50-minute live shot as we waited for him to step onto Air Force One.

I learned about the Clinton magic first-hand in 2002 when Florida Governor Jeb Bush was challenged by Bill McBride. McBride a liberal Democrat who was the managing partner of one of the state's largest law firms, Holland and Knight, was an extremely likeable bear of a man who served in the Marines in Vietnam. However, he was a terrible candidate.

During the last week of the campaign, I followed McBride around the state while one of my best friends and colleague Bill McGinty did the same thing with Bush. A major part of the last weekend of campaigning was flying around the state to various airports for a rally with all the Democratic candidates for statewide offices, along with singer Jimmy Buffett who opened each event with a couple of songs and a pitch for the Democratic slate.

I flew on small propeller airplanes with 6 other reporters from airport to airport and soon it became a big blur. You lose track of where you are because each airport and all the speeches suddenly start to look and sound the same. We were at West Palm airport when I got off the tiny aircraft. The first thing I always do is head right for the bathroom to pee. As I started to push on the door to the men's room, it flew open and standing on the other side was none other than Bill Clinton.

"Mr. President!" I said.

Clinton, who was enjoying my shock at seeing him, smiled and gestured with his free hand. "Come right in," he said with that smooth southern accent. "There's plenty of room."

That was only the beginning of a long day. Buffet sang his popular songs and then Clinton delivered a rousing speech followed by U.S. Senator Bill Nelson who also spoke to the crowd along with McBride and the other Democratic candidates. When it was over, we were quickly off to Miami for another campaign event.

The only thing significant about the flight to Miami involved another friend of mine, Samara Sodos, who everyone called Sam. She was working for the NBC affiliate in Tampa, WFLA, and doing the same coverage. But let's back up a moment. On the previous flight into West Palm, I was sitting up front in the small plane next to the pilot and thoroughly enjoying the ride. We had a box lunch, a lovely view, along with a pleasant conversation over the headset.

What I didn't know was that my pal Sam was in the back of the small plane tossing her cookies. Cut to our landing and my bathroom encounter with Clinton. It was clear that Sam was having a rough time as she looked as green as the Chicago River on St. Patrick's Day. She decided it would be best to close her eyes on a couch in the terminal before the next flight. Sam's discomfort was so obvious that McBride's wife, Alex Sink who later became Florida's CFO suggested that instead of flying in a prop plane, Sam join the candidate and other VIPS who were flying in a small jet. There was an open seat for the last leg. Sam jumped at the chance!

When we landed in Miami, Sam said flying on the jet with the campaign team was one of the worst decisions she had ever made. The campaign jet had rows of seats that faced each other. Sam got on board and sat in the first row of aisle seats. Senator Bill Nelson sat across from her.

As the plane taxied down the runway, according to Sam, Nelson took off his shoes and placed one leg on the armrest on her right and the other on the armrest on her left. At that moment, she was staring into the crotch of Florida's junior Senator.

As the plane became air bound, the nausea returned, and Sam was convinced she was going to puke into Nelson's crotch in front of the entire Democratic ticket. Somehow, she made it to Miami without losing it, but told me it was the most frightening plane ride of her life.

The next stop was an appearance at South Dade Community College. Although Bill McBride was the candidate, the true star of day was Bill Clinton who wowed the crowd with his speech that he gave with no notes and no teleprompter, but just flowed as if he were reading it word for word off written text.

After the speech, we all piled in vans to head for another appearance in South Beach or Florida's French Rivera. Although Clinton was no longer President at the time, we got the same type of motorcade with police stopping traffic thus allowing us to move ahead of everyone. I loved it. As we arrived at South Beach, the motorcade stopped in front of a Starbucks and those of us in the media van had no idea what was going on. When we opened the doors to our van, there was Bill Clinton smiling as he told us, "We're a little early for the speech here, so I thought I'd buy the traveling media some coffee." If we could have done it, we might have elected him president again – right on the spot.

Bill Clinton was our middleman when it came to us and the baristas. With the Secret Service in tow, we stormed the Starbucks scaring the hell out of everyone inside. Bill entered last after the "all clear," and led us inside where he started taking orders.

I was first one in and Clinton said, "What do you want? I'm paying!" "Just a regular coffee," I said to the former President of the United States who also handed me my Starbucks and pointed me towards the back as he said, "Cream and sugar right back there." "Mr. President," I said. "I drink it black." "Hope you enjoy," he said.

As we walked outside the Starbucks, I learned firsthand about the real Bill Clinton magic people had talked about for years. I was drinking my coffee and ended up in a circle with Senator Bill Nelson to my right, another reporter, photographer Gene Yagle, actor Chris Tucker and then Clinton on my left. Immediately I started playing reporter, it is instinctive, when I asked the former President a series of questions.

He just waved his hand.

"You know all about me," Clinton said. "I want to know all about you."

The tables turned and President Clinton asked me several questions: How long had I worked at the station; what were my favorite types of stories; what was the difference between local news and national news when it came to covering politics. He was extremely engaged in everything I said.

Then Clinton went around the circle we were standing in asking questions or telling stories about the people in our group. When he got to Chris Tucker, he chuckled and said he went with him on a trip to Africa and that's when it hit home. Clinton said in Africa everyone was impressed and knew Tucker from the Jackie Chan movies. Then his chest heaved with a big laugh as he said all he could hear from the crowd in Africa was, "Who is that old grey-haired guy with Chris Tucker?"

Clinton continued to talk to the entire circle and then it got back to me. It had been fully 15 minutes since we had our initial conversation when he said, "Mike, you said something a few moments ago that I want to know more about." He then asked me about something I told him more than 15 minutes earlier, meaning not only did he listen, but he also remembered what I had said. Almost everyone who has ever met Clinton says he has the ability to make you feel as if you were the most important person in the world. I certainly learned that during our encounter in South Beach.

I learned an important lesson that day. You must make sure to pay attention to someone when they are telling you their story. Ask their name; listen to what they have to say; ask follow-ups. You can learn from everyone – presidents and civilians.

The Election and Beyond

And then there was the vice president. On that same trip, Al Gore, the man who famously had lost the presidency to George W. Bush in 2000, was campaigning for McBride. I got to meet him, along with a small group of reporters, at a small airport in South Florida.

I found Gore to be witty, charming and completely likeable. In a semi, bold and possibly over the top move, I said, "Mr. Vice President I covered you at least nine times during the campaign." Of course, I included the morning of that election as he came to Tampa for an early morning rally on the day when many believe he actually beat George W. Bush. I said to the man-who-wouldn't-be-president, "To be honest, each time I covered you, I liked you less. Where was the guy that is here today?"

Gore took it in stride and in a moment of complete candor said, "The biggest mistake I made during the entire campaign was listening to my consultants instead of my gut." Gore agreed that the guy on the campaign trail wasn't the same guy he really was and the guy that I saw that day as he was campaigning for McBride.

By that time, almost two years later, Gore seemed to get over the fact that he might have been sitting in the White House if it wasn't for the complete breakdown of the vote count in Florida. Jeb Bush was Governor of that state and Kathryn Harris was the Secretary of State who certified the election results proclaiming that Bush defeated Gore by 537 votes out of six million cast - even though the recount wasn't completed. Once that happened, the U.S. Supreme Court stopped any further recount.

That decision gave Bush Florida's 25 electoral votes and gave him 271 votes in the electoral college -- one more than he needed to become the 43rd President of the United States.

Ironically, George W.'s brother Jeb helped him become President, but the family plan was for Jeb to be the 43rd President because he was known as a deeper thinker, harder worker and more interested in politics than W.

Clearly the family carefully plotted out their political plans when Jeb and George were growing up. Their grandfather, Prescott Bush, George H.W. Bush's father, was a U.S. Senator from Connecticut from 1952 until January 1963. When the Bush boys were growing up instead of calling him Grandpa or Gramps. they were required to refer to him as Senator, which was telling about the family's political push.

That takes us back to the family plan for Jeb to be President. Both Jeb and George W. ran for Governor in 1994. George W. was considered a longshot to defeat popular and outspoken Texas Governor, Ann Richards, while Jeb was expected to defeat incumbent Governor Lawton Chiles.

W. was able to upset Richards, as many Texas Democrats voted Republican and Jeb somehow lost to Chiles. The Governor was a former U.S. Senator who gained the moniker "Walkin' Lawton" when he ran for the Senate in 1970 and embarked upon a walk from Key West to Pensacola. It was a major publicity move and putting foot to pavement helped the relatively unknown state legislator become a U.S. Senator.

Chiles became fed up with his inability of being able to get anything accomplished in Washington and retired from politics in 1989. However, friends and the Democratic party convinced him to run against unpopular Governor Bob Martinez. In turn, Martinez, who was elected Mayor of Tampa in 1979, reelected in 1983, resigned in 1986 to run for Governor.

Martinez, a lifelong Democrat who had been heavily courted by the Republican Party, was called to a meeting at the White House.

President Reagan helped seal the deal and quickly persuaded Martinez to change parties and join the GOP. Yes, that's how it is done.

The election to replace popular Governor Bob Graham came about after Graham resigned. This happened a few weeks early from end of his second term, after he was elected to the U.S. Senate. Graham was an amazingly popular politician who was also a little quirky. I knew it wasn't the norm to keep detailed notebooks of almost every minute of every day, which is exactly what Graham did to keep a record.

These notebooks also helped Graham endear himself to the media. When he was Governor, if I did an interview with Graham on a Friday then by Monday, I would *expect* to get a letter on Official Stationary with the seal of the state and Office of the Governor embossed on it. There would be a detailed note such as: "Mike, thank you for asking me a question about XYZ (whatever I had asked)." And then, he would explain how it was something he really wanted to talk about and later wrote it down for the record. He always signed, "Sincerely, Bob Graham, Governor."

While all of us in the media realized it was a huge public relations campaign, you couldn't help but be impressed that the Governor would send out a personal letter about the specific question you asked him a few days earlier.

However, there was change in the air as Graham headed for D.C. and the U.S. Senate. Florida was becoming a red state, which was an amazing turn around, because when I first moved here in 1982, the Democratic primary was tantamount to being elected. Then there was an abrupt change in state politics. In 1986, the Democrats nominated professor-type candidate Steve Pajic a man with horned rimmed glasses and a bow tie. He just couldn't connect to the electorate, which is why Republican Martinez waltzed in at an almost ten-point victory.

It wasn't exactly a cake walk for him. Martinez made a series of huge missteps that made him essentially a lame duck Governor from the beginning. In order to make up the need for revenue, particularly because Florida doesn't have an income tax, Martinez championed a service tax that actually passed the legislature.

The plan was to tax lawyers, accountants, and even the advertising industry. There was an immediate outcry and the biggest problem for

Martinez was that national advertising agencies started boycotting Florida because of the tax. When that happened, Florida newspapers and TV Stations went completely ape shit! There were editorials on TV and in newspapers. Within a matter of weeks, Martinez and the legislature caved and repealed the tax.

That move basically emasculated Martinez. His popularity sunk to an all-time low afterwards when he called the legislature into special session to tighten restrictions on abortions. This came after the U.S. Supreme Court said states could do so. Florida wasn't having it and the bill never got out of the committee debates.

All of the above set the stage for Chiles to crush Martinez by a 13 percent margin.

By 1994 as Florida was turning red and Chiles was being portrayed as old and past his prime, it looked as if Jeb Bush was on his way to becoming Governor. The polls showed Bush had a lead and was on his way to fulfill his family's dream. That is, until the final debate he and Chiles had just days before the election.

I remember covering it and thinking that Jeb was like a prize fighter, jabbing and jabbing at Chiles, who finally had enough of what he considered the pokes of "a young whipper snapper." Chiles walked from behind the podium and shook his finger at the young Bush as he taunted, "My mama told me, 'Sticks and stones will break my bones, but names will never hurt me.' But let me tell you one other thing about the old liberal. The old He-Coon walks just before the light of day."

I remember everyone in the press section at the debate looked around because now things were getting really interesting. I heard, "What the hell did Lawton say? And what the hell was he talking about?" But the phrase resonated with Floridians who got the meaning of it – sort it. Let's just say that they understood his warning.

Chiles would later explain it basically meant something akin to another interesting slogan: "Don't mess with the Lone Ranger." What made it worse was that he added the jab that Jeb had a "deer in head-lights look." I was there and knew that was true. Poor Jeb, raised to be King of the World, just didn't know how to respond, a sign of things to come in 2016.

It was like the moment in a prize fight where one fighter is against the ropes in every round and then before he plummets to mat, the fighter reaches back and throws a knockout punch.

It turned the entire election around.

On a personal note – and you can't make this stuff up, -- a few days after the speech (the Friday before the election) – I was scheduled for a vasectomy. Like most men, it wasn't an "event" I was particularly looking forward to participating in. I'm telling you this because there I was on the table with urologist, Bernie Hochberg, about to "cut my balls." The good doc looked at me and said, "Mike you've been covering the Gubernatorial race. Who did you think is going to win?"

NOW, HERE WAS MY PREDICAMENT: I HAD A DOCTOR WITH A SHARP knife who was about to cut my balls and the last thing I wanted was for him to be was unhappy with his frightened, yet uncommunicative communicator. So, I put the current event out of my mind and said, "Doc, who do you want to win?" I was relieved when he said, "I really like Lawton." As he grabbed his tools, I managed to say, "You're going to be a happy man on Tuesday."

You see, I really wanted him to go to his "happy place." And I don't know what I would have said if he told me he was a Jeb man.

Footnote - The night of the election, Chiles had his victory party in downtown Tampa complete with Stephen Stills of Crosby, Stills, Nash and Young, a Tampa native, crooning his heart out. He even introduced our re-elected governor who walked on stage to thunderous applause. Chiles stepped up to the podium and with a twinkle in his eye, donned a Davy Crockett-like Coonskin Cap and said, "Remember, the old He-Coon walks just before the light of day."

Maybe those words changed the world or at least put it on a new trajectory that would play out in the presidential race. His win combined with W.'s victory in Texas meant that instead of old Jeb, his less-inclined brother W. would become the 43rd President of the U.S.

History buffs will remember that Jeb, after losing to Chiles, ran again and defeated Lt. Governor Buddy McKay, who actually served as

Governor for 23, days because Chiles died while exercising at the Governor's mansion.

Personally, I always thought that Jeb Bush was an interesting politician who never seemed comfortable campaigning but was self-confident in his vision for the state and the country. As the son of the former President in a Republican-turning state, Bush had a short honeymoon period, but that ended quickly because of some of his views for Florida.

There was the Bush One Florida Plan which, in essence, was going to end affirmative action in Florida. It eventually brought 10,000 to 50,000 (depending on who was doing the estimate) people to the state capitol to protest on the same day that Jeb was going to give the State of the State speech, a year after being elected. The highlight of the protest was a speech given by Jessie Jackson who railed against the plan and Jeb as a leader. Jackson also attacked George W., who by now was running for President. Among Jackson's most stinging remarks included, "When you inherit a name, inherit legal protection, inherit wealth, inherit skin color, inherit your parents' friends for advantage, you just don't understand."

Jackson stirred the crowd with his speech and had what I thought was an interesting trait. He had prepared remarks which he read with great skill from a teleprompter, but then every couple of minutes, he would go rogue, take off his glasses and go for the big point. This meant just one thing: He was going to use rhymes to make it memorable. By the way, this became so obvious that every time he took off the glasses, I turned to Larry Perkins, my photographer for the assignment, and said, "Here it comes!" And like clockwork, we got another Jesse signature rhyme.

Back in the governor's mansion, I didn't agree with many of Jeb's policies or his vision for the state, yet I really respected him for the fact he was a hard worker, well-read and did what he thought was the correct path for the state and the country. Even if you disagree with someone, you can respect that they are doing what they think is right if they have honest conviction.

During the time he was governor, I asked Bush several contrary tough questions and I remember it coming to a head in his second term at a news conference. It was shortly after January 1, 2004, and after he told reporters about whatever it was he was pushing.

I interjected, "Governor, I have a question off-topic." Jeb looked at me and said, "Mike, you *always* have a question off-topic and drive me crazy." (Thank you, sir, that meant I was doing my job). He went on to say, "Mike, you are going to make a New Year's resolution to always ask questions on topic from now on." I looked at him and replied, "Governor!"

To his credit, Jeb smiled and said, "I didn't think so, but it was worth a try."

Charlie Crist was Florida's 44th Governor and currently a U.S. Congressman representing St. Petersburg, and a totally different personality than Jeb. Charlie loved being Governor, but hated the work involved in "being Governor."

As Tampa Bay Times Veteran Political Editor Adam Smith recounts *"In his long history as a politician, Charlie Crist excelled at two things: making news and running for other offices."* In that same Times Article *"The campaigning has always had more allure to him than the governing."* In that same Times article George LeMieux, Crist's former top political advisor who was appointed to an interim U.S. Senate post by the former governor added, *"The campaigning has always had more allure to him than the governing."* [1]

Crist, a good-looking, affable man who appeared to always have stepped out of a tanning booth, a Hollywood hair stylist salon and a Brooks Brothers convention, was one of the most likeable politicians you would ever want to meet.

I first met Charlie, who was an attorney for minor league baseball, when he ran for the State Senate in St. Petersburg in the mid 80's and lost a runoff.

Charlie then went to work for U.S. Senator Connie Mack, the grandson of the owner and manager of the Philadelphia Athletics.

By 1992 through redistricting and a shift in Florida Politics, Crist was able to take on longtime incumbent, State Senator Helen Gordon Davis, an icon in Florida Politics.

When Charlie was elected to the Senate he won as a conservative Republican. He was also a hunter.

That all came into play when I really got to know Charlie well after the Glazer family bought the Buccaneers in the mid '90's. The Glazers said there had to be a new stadium built with public money in order to keep the team in Tampa. The first place they turned for money was the state.

Throughout the '96 session of the legislature the Bucs tried to convince lawmakers to come up with the funding for the stadium. I spent a good portion of that session in Tallahassee covering the attempt to get the money and so did reporters for all the Tampa stations.

At the time, Charlie was dating a friend of mine, Cathy Unruh, the reporter for WTVT, the Fox station who was covering the Bucs stadium saga. At the time, Cathy was a liberal leaning Democrat, vegetarian which didn't exactly match with Charlie's philosophy.

Since we were all "stuck" in Tallahassee we would run into each other in the restaurants and bars and all I can remember is Cathy and Charlie arguing about their different philosophies while I sat there watching, drinking heavily.

Because the Bucs story was so dominant, I saw Cathy almost every day and she would recount her trials with Charlie and how she would break up and then get back together with him.

Cathy, a nice lady and an excellent reporter eventually broke up with Charlie and married the Vice President of an international circuit board firm, Jabil Products.

Charlie Crist, you have to understand, really likes people and loves running for office.

However, according to those in the Crist inner circle, and from my own anecdotal observations, while Charlie loved running for office and having the title, he never really enjoyed doing the work of the position he was elected to.

That meant Crist was a perennial candidate, but unlike the "gadflies" who often run and lose, Charlie would usually win the office he was running for.

Charlie, which by the way, is how he told everyone to refer to him no matter what office he held, spent two years as Education Commissioner. It was time to move on; and he ran for Attorney General on the same ticket Jeb Bush was running for reelection and he easily waltzed into that office.

Because there was really no other office to run for, Charlie actually served the entire 4-year term as Attorney General.

When Jeb Bush was term-limited in 2006, the door was open for Charlie to step in and run for Governor. He handily defeated Tampa Congressman Jim Davis, a truly nice man, but he had trouble matching the charisma of Charlie and was hurt by the fact he missed several votes in

Congress while on the campaign trail. A TV spot with an empty chair was particularly effective in highlighting Davis' lack of attendance in Congress.

Charlie easily won the election. On inauguration day the Governor is sworn in outside the Old Capitol Building, followed by a speech and then a parade from the Capitol to the Governor's mansion which is less than a mile away.

After the speech Charlie Climbed into a bright red Mustang Convertible, sat on the back and waved to people who were along the parade route. On this particular day it was a crisp, clear Florida January day, but cool enough to keep the crowds from being massive. There would be areas where supporters would be cheering as Charlie passed by, but there would be pockets where there was no one on the street.

Photographer Gene Yagle and I were waking alongside of Charlie's Mustang and during one of the lulls in the crowd Charlie turned to me and said, "Mike this is sort of a chilly day for an inaugural parade." As soon as he said it I could hear Gene laughing over my shoulder. Charlie looked at Gene and asked, "What's so funny?" To which Gene immediately replied, "You have just been elected Governor of the 4th largest state in the country (now it's the 3rd largest) and you have nothing better to do than shoot the shit with Mike Deeson about the weather."

Charlie thought about it for a sec and then smiled and said, "At this point, I've got nothin' better do!" He is always a charmer, but behind the scenes Charlie could be different and aides described, even difficult. He didn't want to delve into policy issues, didn't like being questioned and changed his position on issues quite often.

Although Charlie could have run for re-election, after 4 years he seemed bored with the job (not a big surprise). He decided to run for U.S. Senate, but couldn't get the Republican nomination, decided to run as an Independent and was soundly thumped.

That opened the door for the most unlikely Gubernatorial Candidate, Rick Scott. A multimillionaire, who many thought should have gone to jail. Before running for Governor, Scott was the CEO of the hospital chain Columbia/HCA which was involved in one of the largest Medicare Frauds in history. The company had to pay a $1.7 billion fine and during depositions Scott took the fifth 75 times instead of answering questions.

Still this shy, sort of goofy looking, terrible public speaker defeated Florida's Chief Financial Officer, Alex Sink, a bright competent woman who didn't connect with voters.

As I mentioned earlier, I got to know Alex extremely well when her husband Bill McBride was running against Jeb in his second term.

When she was CFO, we had a great encounter in the underground garage where the legislators and cabinet people park in Tallahassee. I was staking out the Speaker of the House, Ray Sansom, who was involved in a scandal and avoiding reporters. Alex's parking space was next to the speaker's and when she walked to her car about 8:30 pm, she saw photographer Paul Thorson and me sitting in plain sight in two ratty old card chairs we found in the garage.

When she saw me, Alex said in her thick North Carolina accent, Mike (which sounded like Maaaake) what are you doing here?" I said, "I'm waiting for the Speaker to come to his car so I can interview him."

Alex was perplexed and said, "He told you to meet him here?" "No Alex," I replied, "he doesn't want to talk and is avoiding me." After a second I could see the light bulb in her head go off and Alex joyfully smiled and said "Oh, I get it, a stakeout." I smiled and said, "Yes Alex, a stakeout."

I truly like Alex, who is smart, and honest, but somehow Scott was able to pull through and defeat her. I must admit I didn't have much of a relationship with Scott, but neither did any reporter. He would only answer two or three questions at every appearance and almost no matter what you would ask he would reply, "Jobs, Jobs, Jobs." That wasn't just with me, but with almost every reporter in the state. When I would say, "That doesn't answer the question I asked," his press people would say, "No more questions," and then he would try to walk away. I would usually follow him with whatever photographer I was working with. As we would run after him asking the question over and over, he would keep on walking and get into his car or go into the private meeting where we couldn't go.

Amazingly he won re-election defeating Charlie Crist, who had by now become a Democrat and tried to reclaim his old job. Then, when Scott was term-limited, he defeated 3-term Senator Bill Nelson in 2018 for a seat in the U.S. Senate. Of all the politicians I've covered in Florida, I still shake my head and wonder how this guy ever got elected.

CONFIDENTIAL RECORDS

THIS IS a story about how the state of Florida willingly sold me confidential records regarding abused children.

The records belonged to the state's child welfare system which was once initially called HRS or Health and Rehabilitative Services and changed to DCF, the Department of Children and Families. The agency was a mess in many ways, through no fault of its own. Whatever the name, it was under budgeted and the people there were overworked. As is the practice in many child welfare agencies throughout the country; severely underpaid caseworkers could not handle the large caseload leading to several children dying - yes, actually losing their lives - while their parents were under court-ordered supervision.

Due to the problems the agency faced, the flipside was that it often overreacted and removed children from homes where they should not have been taken. After an onslaught of fresh criticism, DCF would go the opposite direction again and they wouldn't remove children who needed to be removed. In other words, it was a mess.

As a journalist, one of the most frustrating parts of covering these stories was that the agency was lost in a paperwork nightmare and often couldn't find the necessary paper trail to justify what it did. Combine that fact with the fact that the agency had inadequate headquarters in Tampa, located in a former TB hospital named W.T. Edwards. It wasn't an appropriate building for a child welfare agency.

Finally, the state appropriated enough money for the Tampa regional office to move to a new building. Before leaving W.T. Edwards, the agency had an auction of old desks, file cabinets and items it didn't want to move to the brand-new building.

Our news director at the time, Lane Michaelsen, was a guy who always thought out-of-the-box. His philosophy was to do something different than all the other stations. Lane was aware of all the stories I did about HRS/DCF screw ups and he said to focus on the day of the auction, but not for obvious reasons.

"This agency is sloppy and unorganized. Do you think they will leave any confidential paperwork around the building before they leave?" Lane posed.

That question lurked in my mind when I arrived at the actual auction where there were several old desks that indeed had confidential paperwork lurking in them. My reporter instincts kicked into overdrive and I grabbed some of it. I hit the mother lode when I noticed that there was a room where they were going to auction off the contents, that included boxes and boxes stuffed with confidential paperwork that was never supposed to be made public. Quickly, I called the station and asked Lane how much I could spend bidding on the contents in the room and he said, "If you have to go over $200 then call me."

When the auctioneer got to the room of confidential papers, I was ready to bid...and made the winning bid. I still had to call Lane and tell him, "I didn't have a chance to call you, but I had to bid five!"

Lane's voice got louder and quite agitated as he ranted, "You just spent $500!"

And I said, "No, five bucks!" I was the only bidder and bought the room for a whopping five singles. That was the going rate for the life stories of children in peril.

The auction company put all the boxes on a flatbed cart and we took everything out to our station truck and drove over to the new headquarters the Child Welfare agency had moved into. I wanted to talk to the Tampa head of the agency and show that I had just bought boxes and boxes of the records that no one except agency officials were supposed to see. This was how St. Petersburg Times media critic Eric Deggans described it: *"And after weeks of reporting on problems with cases handled by the Department of Children and Families, WTSP reporter Mike Deeson gained national attention May 30 by buying a roomful of the agency's confidential records during an auction at a building that once housed some DCF offices.*

After buying the records -- and delivering boxes of them to Gov. Jeb Bush a day later -- Deeson made appearances on CNN and CBS Radio to outline his scoop, which came after news director Michaelsen suggested the reporter go to the auction and see if the agency left any files behind.

'In all my years . . . this is the biggest gold mine I've tapped into. . . .. It touches a nerve with everybody in the state,' said Deeson, who celebrated his 20th year at WTSP on June 2, 2002. 'It just points out that the whole system is a mess.'" [2]

This made major waves, so now suddenly Governor Jeb Bush had to get involved with that reporter who "drove him crazy" at times. His office now, obviously, knew I had the records and we arranged a transfer of the boxes because, obviously, we were going to give them back. I do have to say that Bush was great. He expressed the proper outrage, let us get a great photo op at a news conference, and then made sure that certain heads rolled at the agency because of what happened. To his credit, Bush did everything he could to make me look good while reprimanding his own agency.

At a Bay Area news conference, I even heard one of his aides say (just beore we turned over the records), "Governor, this is Deeson. He makes you crazy. Why are you doing this?" She meant why was he talking to the media about this sorry situation. Jeb replied, "It's a great scoop. He did a great job. I thought he deserved getting credit from me." It was very impressive to say the least.

Unfortunately, it wasn't the last time I would deal with the agency created to protect the kids.

TOO MUCH LOVE

I CALL this story "Too Much Love." It came to me when I got a call from a DCF caseworker who was actually prohibited by law from talking to the media. However, several caseworkers called and said something so egregious was going on that they needed public exposure to correct the wrong.

Rewind to shortly before Christmas in 2002. Jimmy and Eunice Goins, who lived about an hour and a half from Tampa in a town called Sebring, lost the ability to be foster parents to their niece, two-year-old Tisa Garcia.

The Goins had become foster parents after the little girl had been removed from her mother's custody. The natural mom was involved with drugs and would not put Tisa and her twin brother on sleep apnea monitors ordered by their pediatrician. The twin brother died, and the state moved in and took Tisa. They gave her to the mother's brother, Jimmy Goins, and his wife Eunice, who were named foster parents.

In cases where a child is removed from a parent, the state also appoints what's called a Guardian Ad Litem, who is charged with looking out for the best interest of the child, not the parents, foster parents or anyone else in the system. The Guardian Ad Litem assigned, was working his first case in the system. He seemed to have some sympathy for the mother and was concerned Tisa was bonding too much with Jimmy and Eunice Goins.

In an astonishing moment in court, this Guardian Ad Litem, over the protests of case workers, was able to convince Judge Frank Gomez that the Goins should be removed as foster parents because of one reason. "They are showing the child too much love," said the Guardian Ad Litem.

Gomez issued the order and the case workers went nuts and risked their jobs by calling me.

"Mike, we don't usually make calls like this one, but something must be done," they said.

My response was somewhere between stunned, shocked and angry that this would happen in court. But I went back to my reporter's questioning side when I wondered if there was indeed something wrong with this aunt and uncle. I also knew that child custody cases were rarely "clean."

Quite often, there was something about everyone involved that had everyone eventually shaking their collective heads.

By the time, I got the third call from a caseworker saying that aunt and uncle were "the salt of the earth," I decided to try to figure it out for myself and made the hour and a half drive to Sebring. I asked photographer John Barlow to tag along.

I found Eunice and Jimmy Goins to be just as the caseworkers described. They were great people who were trying to do the right thing for their niece.

As we talked through the tears about the judge's order to remove Tisa, there was a knock on the door. Two state workers who had to enforce the judge's order, couldn't hold back the tears. They were there to take this little girl to another foster home. Eunice got Tisa's things and we walked outside, everyone in tears including the Goins, the caseworkers and this poor, innocent two-year-old girl being torn from her only stable, loving family. John and I tried to keep it together.

As Tisa was placed in the car seat in the back of the caseworker's car, Jimmy was inconsolable. Before the caseworker could back out of the driveway, Tisa put her index finger up against the glass window, like

E.T. trying to touch Jimmy one more time. He put his finger against the window to say goodbye, as tears rolled down his face.

This story wasn't over.

Our story, and the photos, aired with a quote from Judge Gomez saying that this aunt and uncle "might be giving their niece too much love." All of a sudden, Gomez was inundated with irate emails and phone calls, but his order had been issued and he was not backing down.

We contacted Gov. Bush as did several high-powered attorneys who joined the fight. This was one, however, that Jeb wouldn't budge on. He refused to intervene and kept telling me that there MUST be more to the story, something we didn't know or a surprise. "No judge would remove a child from a home because she was receiving too much love," he said.

Now, let's go back to the man who put all this in motion, the Guardian Ad Litem who convinced Judge Gomez that Tisa needed to be removed. Remember that he was working his first case. That's why Charlie Nelson, the head of the Guardian Ad-litem agency in Hillsborough County, berated me for doing the story.

"You don't understand because you don't have all the information," he said. What he didn't understand was that his own DCF caseworkers were secretly supplying me (at the risk of being fired) the complete details of *exactly* what was going on.

Time passed and little Tisa's mother sunk deeper into her drug habit. Finally, instead of trying to reunite the girl with her mother, DCF was able to convince the judge there should be a TPR (termination of parental rights).

Once that happened, her status changed, and Tisa was returned to the Goins. She was out of the Goins care for MORE THAN A YEAR WHICH SHE SPENT WITH STRANGERS IN FOSTER CARE but thrilled to be back to that house with all the love.

Five years later, we actually played the story for the first time for Tisa during a follow-up story on the family. We covered them again to celebrate that she had been formally adopted by her aunt and uncle. Jimmy Goins said he felt "like the luckiest man in the world because now Tisa is my daughter."

Here's what we said on the air *"And while this may be a day for tears, these are tears of joy, not sadness, as the little girl wearing a pink dress is Tisa Garcia. From now on, she will officially be Tisa Marie Goins. She gets to call her aunt and uncle, Mom and Dad.*

Judge Jack Espinosa made Tisa 'Judge for a day' and had her help him sign the final adoption papers. The judge also made a family whole as Jimmy and Eunice and her brother Jimmy and extended family were all there to see this day they thought would never come."

This is the is the email we received after our final story:

"Dear Channel 10,
We would like to thank you guys for all you have done for us. There were times, we didn't think we could go on, but the encouragement from Mike Deeson and the great coverage gave us hope. The coverage and airtime got this story to the public and made them aware of situations that occur to children in foster care. This did become a happy ending for us, and especially Tisa, however I cannot help but to think of others lost in the system, it breaks my heart to think that others would actually have to go through what we have, but with the love of family and friends, anything is possible. To those of you out there, that maybe are dealing with a similar situation, keep your head up, stay strong and pray......God does make miracles happen!!
Once Again Thank You So Much!!
Love,
Eunice, Jimmie Jr., Jimmie III and Tisa Marie Goins"

WAR ZONES AND GENERAL NORMAN SCHWARZKOPF

SOME SAY you can't call yourself a complete journalist unless you've covered a war and a national political convention. I was more than happy to cover the Republican National Convention when it came to Tampa in 2012. War, well, that was another story, so to speak.

After successfully avoiding Vietnam in the 60's, the thought of going to the frontlines of any war and being shot at with a notepad in hand was not my idea of a good time.

My initial brush as a reporter with a military situation happened in the mid-90s when several thousand Cuban and Haitian Refugees were captured by the military as they tried to flee Cuba and Haiti on rickety rafts and boats. They were detained in tent cities at the U.S. base at Guantanamo Bay, Cuba. That resulted in an offer which came over the assignment desk. The Navy, in an assignment that few reporters or stations could refuse, dangled a trip where someone from the station could fly to the base and see firsthand how the United States was treating these refugees. Twice that summer, I made the trip to Cuba to cover what was happening. The conditions the refugees were living in were primitive to say the least.

"Deeson, you're going to Guantanamo," said my news director, and for a second it seemed like a scene out of that Tom Cruise/Jack Nicholson meeting, *A Few Good Men*.

But first, let's back up a moment and I'll tell you how I got ready to join the front lines by covering a terrible train crash in North Carolina. That disaster happened in the 90s when an Amtrak passenger train headed for Tampa derailed. I got a call from the station before I left for work telling me to go to the Amtrak Station in downtown Tampa to see if there were any family members waiting for their loved ones to arrive.

Before I got the call, I had at least three cups of coffee at home, drove down to the Amtrak Station, stopped at a Circle K on the way and got a large 20-ounce coffee. At the Amtrak station I didn't find any family members waiting and called the station to tell them it was a bust for me to continue waiting.

About 15 minutes later, I got a page to head to Albert Whitted Airport in St. Petersburg. The station, along with the St. Petersburg Times had hired a small airplane to take us to North Carolina to cover the story on the crash. I was going to meet photographer Fred Shearer at the airport. On the way over to St. Pete I stopped at another Circle K, got another 20-ounce black coffee and finished it by the time I got to the airport.

As I spotted the small airplane that was going to take us to North Carolina, I asked the pilot how long the flight would be and he said, "About three to three-and-a-half hours." Having flown on several small airplanes before, I knew there was no bathroom aboard and I had just consumed massive amounts of coffee.

I went into the bathroom at the airport before we left and tried to clear all the coffee out of my system.... but about three hours into the three-and-a-half-hour flight, my eyes were yellow, and my bladder was about to burst.

At that point, I was thinking about what Walter Cronkite told a young reporter when she asked if he had any advice for her career and Cronkite reportedly replied in his "And that's the way it is" voice of God by saying, "Yes dear, pee whenever you have the opportunity."

My opportunity was three hours ago so, I went up to the pilot and said, "You must have an emergency pee bottle, right?" To my chagrin he didn't, but he did have a bottle of orange juice he was thinking of drinking. I told him this would be a good time for him to get his vitamin C and he might think about chugging the OJ, which he did. I grabbed the bottle and went to the back of the plane where I used it to avoid disaster at 5,000 feet in the air.

I was feeling better after relieving myself, but my poor photographer Fred, was not feeling well as he was suffering a bit of a hangover from whatever he did the night before. Prior to landing, the pilot circled the train crash so Fred and the newspaper photographer could get aerials of the accident, but Fred told me every time he looked through the eye piece as the plane was bouncing around, he thought he was going to toss his cookies. I told Fred, not to worry. The real story was on the ground.

Once on the ground we rented a car, drove to the train wreck, and we were able to find some passengers and get a decent story before we had to jump back to the airplane so we would have the piece on the air for the 11 O'clock news that night.

However, on the way back to the airport, I made Fred stop at a Piggly Wiggly in North Carolina where I bought two-gallon jugs of water and promptly poured them out. When we got back to the airport the pilot saw my two empty jugs, he asked what they were and I said, "These are your emergency pee bottles. Don't leave home without them."

Fast forward to later that summer when I made my first trip to Guantanamo and realized the flight on another small plane was three and half hours. Although Havana is merely 90 miles from Miami, the county is 900 miles long and a flight from Ft. Lauderdale (our starting point) was relatively long.

After the experience in North Carolina and knowing how long the flight was for us, I did what I called "bladder maintenance" and only had one cup of coffee prior to the flight. In addition, I had two empty, one gallon water jugs or as I called them, "emergency pee bottles," to bring along on the flight.

In addition to our crew on that plane, there was a crew from the NBC station in Miami and the CBS station in Houston. When the female reporter from the Houston station saw my empty water bottles, she questioned me as to what the hell they were and I told her they were my "emergency pee bottles." That was it. She gave me unmitigated shit, however, she neglected to do "bladder maintenance" and about three bumpy hours into the three-and-a-half-hour flight, I recognized the familiar yellow look in her eyes. Then she crisply asked me, "When the hell does this plane land?" When I told her in about 30 minutes or so if we were lucky, she said, "If it is any more than that then we were all going to get extremely friendly on the flight."

Fortunately for her, the flight landed early, and she made it to the bathroom on the ground. However, on the flight home, the only thing she said to me as we boarded the airplane was "Got those emergency pee bottles?" I smiled with satisfaction.

"Yes, indeed," I said.

The bottles were not the only emergency we would face. While we were in Cuba, the tent cities the refugees were living in proved to be extremely primitive conditions. Several people were crammed into each tent and it was ungodly hot. The food they were serving looked like a mushy vegetable soup, however, compared to the conditions the refugees were living in before they tried to escape to the U.S., they seemed grateful for everything they were getting. It is always a matter of perspective.

In the meantime, the reporters stayed in military barracks which were spartan, but comfortable. Often when I'm out of town, I'll smoke a cigar, and the first night at GITMO --as Guantanamo is called -- I went to the back of the barrack to light one up. As I lit the match, my heart went still because I saw the largest rat I had ever seen in my life. It just stood in the back of the barracks staring at me and that cigar. I had been warned there was a species of banana rats known as Hutias that inhabited the island, but I didn't realize they were the size of fat, fat cats....and when it stared at me, it was terrifying.

The other spectacular part of one of the two trips I made to Guantanamo that summer was when the military flew us by helicopter to an aircraft carrier that was stationed off the coast of Venezuela.

We got the royal treatment on the carrier while we observed the planes taking off and landing. It was amazing to watch a jet airplane touchdown on a landing strip on a ship that is pitching up and down in the sea.

However, the most spectacular part of the aircraft carrier visit was at night. It was a warm summer night and photographer Dave Herring and I went up on the deck of the ship. We were in the middle of the Caribbean Sea and everything was pitch dark. We could hear the water run past the ship and the only light that we could see was from the glow on Dave's cigarette and my cigar. Bright stars filled the sky and it almost seemed like a Disney production, as the night appeared to get darker and darker and more stars popped out on the horizon. Intermittent shooting stars sparkled in the sky. It made me realize how vast the universe is and that we often get caught up in our own importance. The truth is we're just a speck.

It turns out my trips to Cuba were a prelude for even bigger action on an actual war front.

In August of 1990, Saddam Hussein decided to invade Kuwait and the military action launched in response was run by Central Command, which was stationed at MacDill Air Force base in Tampa. That meant several local troops, including the commander of the U.N. effort, General Norman Schwarzkopf were sent to the staging area for the war in Saudi Arabia. Meanwhile, the U.S. Military, after the press debacle it endured during Vietnam, made a conscious decision to play up the "local heroes" who would be fighting the crazy leader of Iraq, Saddam Hussein. To that end, they were extremely accessible to the local media.

MacDill Public Affairs made an offer (again, that couldn't be refused) to every media outlet in Tampa Bay including TV, radio and print. The offer: we would be flown to Saudi Arabia before the war started and interview the local troops.

There was no hesitation on my part and I quickly put in for the assignment. Quickly, I was accepted and the only one who wasn't 100 percent thrilled was my wife Laurie who was pregnant with our youngest child, Megan. "It won't be dangerous," I promised her. "We'll leave well before the war starts and be home safe and sound in Tampa before any shooting started." Laurie was actually great and very supportive, but told me, "If you get killed, I will kill you!"

Before taking off for Saudi Arabia, I was required to get a series of shots with needles that looked like they could harpoon an elephant. I never told Laurie about going through "gas gear" training at MacDill. The military told me that they weren't sure what measures Saddam would take and poison gas was an option that everyone feared. The idea was that we would have to assemble our gas gear in less than five minutes, which is something that all of the reporters learned how to do.

The other caveat was that we had to be ready to go on a moment's notice due to security reasons. That meant we waited and waited and then finally about three in the afternoon on a December day, my phone rang. "We need you to be at MacDill within the next two hours," I was told.

Racing home from the station, I grabbed my duffle bag that had been waiting and pre-packed for the trip and Laurie drove me to the Air Force Base. I kissed my pregnant wife goodbye and expected to be on a plane within a matter of minutes and then off to the Middle East.

Wrong! Once you're in the system, I learned, nothing in the military happens fast. Several reporters gathered at MacDill for a briefing about our flight to Saudi Arabia and then we waited...*and waited and waited.* Finally, about 10 p.m. that night, we boarded a C-141 transport plane that was our gateway to the Middle East.

If you've never been inside a military airplane, you must understand it is not built for creature comfort...in fact, it is not built for any kind of comfort. For starters, the seats come down from the wall and are made of material similar to a lawn chair with two fabrics crossing over each other for maximum discomfort. I knew we were in for an uncomfortable time when a grizzled old Sergeant stepped onto the plane, strung a red bandana through the material in the back and placed it in front of him like a bandit robbing a store. He knew how to fly on one of these birds: he used it to prop up his head as he quickly fell asleep before we took off.

The other thing about military planes is there are only two temperatures: Antarctica and jungle hot hell! I knew that before I boarded and had plenty of warm clothing on hand, but at unexplained intervals when the pilot would turn on the heat, you'd have to strip down to a T-shirt because it was so hot inside.

It was also so unbelievably noisy inside that you had to wear earplugs to keep from going deaf, but that also meant most conversation was limited to sign language or shouting. Basically, you are isolated on what turned out to be a long flight.

We flew five endless hours from MacDill in Tampa to McGuire Air Force Base in New Jersey. There we bunked on cots at McGuire for about five hours and then boarded another C-141 for a less than comfortable 12-hour flight to Torrejon Air Base in Madrid, Spain.

When we landed and taxied down the runway in Spain, we could look outside a small peep hole in the back. The sight was awesome, impressive and somewhat overwhelming at the same time.

The runway was packed with war planes of every size and shape, making one thing clear. The American War Machine was ready to go into action and our country wasn't kidding. I've never seen such a display of potential force and must admit there were mixed emotions ranging from pride in how powerful our country was as a force to fear. Also I was overwhelmed as I thought about the destructive power that we could wield.

It was December at Torrejon, bitter cold, and primitive when it came to conditions. We had a tasteless meal in a tent where we froze our butts off and then slept for a few hours on those hard cots. The wake-up call came too soon, and I was boarding our next C-141 for 12 more hours on a flight to Riyadh, Saudi Arabia.

When we landed, the display of America's military might was obvious again as the runway was littered with U.S. fighting planes of several varieties. We stepped off the C-141, but in stark contrast to Torrejon, where it was sub-zero, I walked into a world that was nearly 105 degrees. As I said Antarctica to Hell.

A military bus took us to our Sheraton Hotel in downtown Riyadh and check-in proved interesting. Instead of the usual "what's your credit card number," I was also asked to write in my religion. Suddenly, it occurred to me that writing "Jewish" on a form was probably not the best idea in an Arab country. I turned to Tim Collie, another Jewish reporter from the Tampa Tribune. He had travelled to Saudi Arabia before and knew the proverbial drill.

While the man behind the counter was waiting for me to hand over the completed hotel form, I took my pen and pointed to the religion line, nudged Collie and he looked at me and wiped his hand across it like you do when you are playing black jack and tell the dealer you do not want another card. I left the religious portion of the form blank and held my breath. He looked at it, nodded and gave me the key to my room. No questions asked.

Over the next several days, we toured many American Military stations in Riyadh where the troops from MacDill were stationed.

One of the most impressive facilities was a mobile hospital set up in the desert that had everything you needed to help cure any type of injury or disease our service members could potentially encounter while stationed in the Middle East. One of the earliest concerns was heat collapse. It was 115 degrees in the desert on a "cool day" and as we toured the area, there were rules. Everyone – from the media geeks to the four-star Generals, were "ordered" to grab a bottle of water in the barrels stationed throughout the entire area. You were instructed to drink it down.

Clearly, one of the most memorable days of the trip, was when we were going out to the desert to see the Patriot Missile Facility. It started when I came down to the lobby of the Sheraton where all my fellow journalists had gathered for the trip out to the desert to see how the missile defense system was supposed to work.

We had been in Saudi Arabia for a few days by then and I knew it would be one hell of a day. We had already been schlepping our camera gear and the gas gear provided to us in 115-degree temperatures. I made a tactical decision that morning that I wasn't going to carry the gas gear that day because it was the end of December and the real war wasn't supposed to begin until mid-January of 1991. It did seem strange that there was a date for the beginning of the war, but who was I to argue with the American Military?

My reporter friends saw me walk to the lobby without the gas gear and immediately questioned me about it.

"Look," I said, "the war isn't scheduled to start for at least three weeks from now and we have all this equipment to carry into the desert. It doesn't seem to make sense to schlep the gas gear in this heat."

My colleagues listened and looked at how unburdened I was for today's journey. "Mike, you are so smart," one said. It was like I was granting official permission for everyone to take their gas gear back up to their rooms.

Now that this was settled, we bussed out to the Patriot Missile site in the middle of the desert where we took on the dangerous task of sitting in a hot tent to listen to our intrepid Captain explain to us how the Patriot Missiles would shoot down any of Saddam Hussein's Scud Missiles. Almost on cue, he stopped speaking and over the loud-speakers and just like from the TV series *M.A.S.H.,* someone with the voice of grave authority announced "Incoming!" I heard: "Scud Missile alert! Scud Missile alert!" Since the Captain giving us our briefing didn't flinch, I didn't think much of it until a Sergeant ran into the tent and breathlessly exclaimed, "Captain! Captain, we are under a Scud Missile attack!" Yes, that was definitely confirmation.

At that point, the Captain looked at us and said, "You all sit tight." He ran out of the tent, which provoked a cold chill that raced up my spine.

Through the netting in the tent, I could see that the Patriot Missiles were moving into launch position and seconds later, the Sergeant was back in the tent in full gas gear screaming, "Gas Gear, everyone! Gas Gear, now!"

It was just two hours earlier that my friends were telling me how smart I was (and they were) for leaving the gear back in the hotel rooms. Slowly, I watched heads turn and look at me with utter distain. If I could read minds, I know many were thinking, "I'm going to die in the desert because this guy from Tampa told me to leave the stuff that would save my life behind.....*and for some reason I listened to him!*"

As I deflected their murderous glances and pondered my own demise, I watched the Captain race back into the tent. "There is a bus waiting for all of you. I need you to serpentine back to the bus instead of running in a straight line just in case...." *In case of what?* "There might be snipers nearby!" he answered almost in a panic!

Now, this was not my fault. If we all died of poison gas, then fine, I would take the blame for the mask incident. But it wasn't as if I asked them to leave any bulletproof vests in the hotel lobby. I was one hundred percent clean on that one!

In the end, we made it back to the bus (running a zigzag pattern) and were transported to a nearby "safe facility" deep in the desert where I was fully expecting that war would break out all around us. I had managed to avoid Vietnam, but now I was going to be in the middle of an actual war, get killed, die and never see my newborn baby while covering the Gulf War. And if any of that happened and I still had a shred of life left in me, my wife was certainly going to kill me.

Two of the longest hours of my life later, an all-important, all-clear was issued by the commanders and our group was transported back to the safety zone of the Sheraton in downtown Riyadh. We were told what reporters had heard in war zones for many years. "It was a huge mistake."

In this case, Israel had launched some kind of test missile and somehow had forgotten to tell the United States. However, we were close to starting the War three weeks early, because for a few hours no one was sure what happened.

Back at the Sheraton, I was finally able to breathe again, but my "fun day" of being a war reporter was far from over.

It wasn't long before the fireworks started again when Navy Lt. Commander John Jenro, the Public Information Officer assigned to babysit the Tampa Bay media sat all of us down for some "bad news." He explained that because of the Patriot Missile incident, we might not be able to interview General Norman Schwarzkopf. The good news, if you could call it that, was if we were able to talk to him, our time might be limited to one or two questions.

Leslie Spencer, the journalist on the trip from Channel 13 WTVT, which at that time was the CBS affiliate, became insistent. She told the rest of us that if we had limited questions, we had to talk to Schwarzkopf about "Operation Snowflake." That was a promotion by WTVT where viewers sent Christmas wishes to the troops in Saudi Arabia in snowflake-like cards created by the TV station.

Meanwhile, NBC affiliate reporter Linda Vester, a Fulbright

Scholar and fluent in Arabic, was a top-notch hard news reporter, and she was not buying it. Linda, was hell bent on getting out of the local affiliate and getting picked up by the national network. Linda eventually worked at NBC, MSNBC and had her own show on Fox and fully planned on covering the Gulf War like a network correspondent. This is the same Linda Vester, who in the Spring of 2018, accused NBC icon Tom Brokaw of sexual misconduct while she was at NBC. Meantime, when we were in Saudi Arabia in 1990, she didn't really give a you-know-what about snowflakes.

Competition amongst reporters is always a fun event that I liken to a sporting competition. This battle took place at the buffet dinner that night at the Sheraton where we ate what was also served at breakfast and lunch – hummus and pita. After that food fest, we somehow ended up in a common area of the hotel where Leslie told the assembled group that if we only had one or two questions for Schwarzkopf it would have to be about "Operation Snowflake" because that was the only reason we had been allowed to travel to Saudi Arabia.

"Are you out of your fucking mind?" That came from Linda Vester who mentioned that a war was about to break out and Schwarzkopf was the general in charge of it, plus he hailed from Tampa. In other words, she would focus on something real.

The snowflake side wouldn't listen to it. That's why the two women got louder and louder in their insistence that their position was right. I was settling in for an actual fistfight that might be the best action of the whole day when Jenro, a small and gentle man, decided to play referee. Just like in any prize fight or Rocky movie, he had to physically get between them and push the two women apart. "Take a deep breath everyone," Jenro insisted. "And go to your rooms."

It was like a ref telling the fighters to go to their prospective corners!

"We'll work this out in the morning." Jenro said.

The truth was it had been a long day and we were tired because part of the job was calling back reports to our stations. The time difference meant that we were up in the middle of the night to do "phoners" or telephone reports from the frontlines. We had spent the rest of the day shooting and worried about our lives.

The angst didn't end with the goodnights. A few minutes after I got back to my room, there was a knock on the door from Linda Vester who was there for one reason: Lobbying. She wanted to make sure I was on board to ask questions about the coming war. Linda, like most journalists wasn't shy about dropping "F-Bombs" and said something like: "Leslie is fucking nuts if she thinks we are here for "Operation Snowflake" and aren't going to ask Schwarzkopf about the war."

In the middle of her plea, my phone rang.

On the other end of the line was a woman who identified herself as an associate producer for *Nightline* in New York City. She told me that everyone in the U.S. was talking about the incident at the Patriot Missile range and they "had to have" my video for the ABC late night news show.

The only problem? There wasn't a satellite uplink in Riyadh. "What we want you to do, Mike, is rent a car, drive across the desert to Bahrain where there *is* an uplink and send the video back to us."

My response was simple. "Lady, are you crazy?" I said. "I'm a little Jewish kid in Arab Country where war is about to break out. And you want me to drive across the barren and dark desert in the middle of the night to get a tape to an uplink. You must be out of your fucking mind."

Now, I was swearing. Quite calmly, she replied, "Well, Ted (as in Ted Koppel) really wants that video."

"Well, Ted can get his ass on an airplane and come to Riyadh where I will personally put the tape into his hands. Then he can do whatever he wants with it."

Remember that we hadn't had a lot of sleep because of the time difference and the fact that we were doing those "phoners" with our stations in the wee hours.

"What kind of journalist do you call yourself?" the producer demanded. At which point, I lost it and said, "I am the kind of journalist who doesn't give a fuck about a stupid ass little associate producer who thinks she is hot shit! I don't give a fuck about *Nightline!* I don't give a fuck about the network where I don't intend to work, and I don't give a fuck about Ted Koppel! You can go fuck yourself and have a good night."

I slammed the phone down and Linda, who was crazy in love with the idea of working for a network, said, "Are you sure you want to do that?"

Yes, she even had a moment of lunacy where, as a woman alone in the middle of the night, she thought about making that trek across the desert to make points with ABC. A minute later, the phone rang again.

It was my assistant news director, Jon Halpern a great guy who died much too young of cancer. I always thought of him as the definition of a curly-haired, New York, hardened Jew. Jon had a wicked sense of humor. In fact, before he came to Tampa, he was a TV producer at WNBC in New York. At one time, he produced a newscast anchored by the legendary Tom Snyder after his network late night program, *The Tomorrow Show* was cancelled. My favorite story was when Halperin told me that Snyder, who was a stand- up guy, would come into the newsroom every afternoon, flair his nostrils and say, "Something smells like shit in here." According to Halperin he would then walk around the WNBC newsroom until he got to the scripts for the 6pm news, pick them up, sniff them and then say, "I found it...it's the show that smells like shit!"

But back to the war zone. Halperin quickly said, "ABC just called and said you were a little upset."

I replied, "You're damn right I'm upset. They want me to rent a car and drive it across the fucking desert in an Arab county where a fucking war is about to start, so they can upload a tape for *Nightline*."

"Well, fuck them," Halperin said. I told Jon that's exactly what I told them, and he wished me a "Good night."

The next morning was the day we were supposed to interview General Schwarzkopf. The deal was we were going to meet him at the Saudi equivalent of the Pentagon, which was close to our hotel. After a wake-up call that was the sound of the Islamic call to prayer over the city's loudspeakers, we had another hummus buffet breakfast (with dry meat and pita this time), and jumped on a bus to race to the big interview.

When we got to the "Saudi Pentagon" for the interview, we were ushered into the facility which was littered with guards in heavy moustaches who looked like they could be movie doubles for Saddam

Hussein. Each guard was holding a menacing looking Uzi in front of them and they had a look indicating that they would love to empty the weapon into anyone who crossed them the wrong way.

As we walked through the hallway, Leslie Spencer walked up to each guard and handed them the greetings the stations had received from viewers back home and said in a Glenda the Good Witch voice, "A snowflake from Tampa Bay."

All of us in the group admired her determination, but also had to hold back our laughter because it looked like, at any moment, one of the guards was about to fire his weapon and say in Arabic or broken English, "Here's what you can do with your fucking snowflake from Tampa Bay."

Our group was finally directed into a room where we were going to meet the head of the American War Effort, General Norman Schwarzkopf. The room had a long conference table where we all took our seats. I was on the right side of the table closest to the head of the table where Schwarzkopf would sit.

A Major came in, put the General's reading glasses down at the head of the table and started to leave when he noticed they were not at a perfect 90-degree angle to where Schwarzkopf was going to sit. The Major took immense pains to readjust the glasses at least ten times until they were at the perfect angle to please his boss and then he left. Protocol!

Schwarzkopf -- nicknamed The Bear -- burst into the room with a presence that was overwhelming and clearly dynamic. He shook everyone's hand and then sat down for the interview with the hometown Tampa Bay media.

He was gracious, friendly and more than happy to give us as much time as possible to answer our questions... that is until the WTVT photographer Tony Furlough said, "General, may I ask a question?"

"Of course," said Schwarzkopf. That's when Tony asked the question all of us should have asked: "Is the American public ready to see the sight of their servicemen coming home in body bags?"

At that moment, Schwarzkopf, who had been a Lieutenant in Vietnam, and had been accused of being involved in friendly fire deaths, lost it.

He started pounding on the table screaming as he beat up that furniture: "None (pound) of (pound) my(pound) (pound) men (pound) are (pound) coming (pound) home (pound) in (pound) body (pound) bags (pound)!!!!

I was sitting to his immediate right and every single time he pounded the table with his big bear-like closed fist, I backed up. Finally, he realized he sort of lost it. Schwarzkopf apologized to the camera and said, "I'm sorry, I hate the term 'body bags'. I have since Vietnam."

He acknowledged that there would likely be casualties in the conflict with Iraq, not realizing at that point how efficient the American effort would be when he added, "Our fallen heroes will come home in dignified coffins -- not body bags."

Just as quickly as he exploded in the fit of rage, he calmed down and became the charming General who was trying to woo the folks at home to make sure they backed our actions in the Middle East.

He continued to answer all our questions and even told Leslie Spencer he thought "Operation Snowflake was good for boosting the morale of the troops," and then as the interview came to an end, Schwarzkopf turned to our escort, Lt Cmdr. Jenro and said, "Lt. Commander, I have a favor to ask." You could see the blood drain from Jenro's face, because you don't turn down a four-star General who is your commander when he asks for a favor.

Jenro had no idea what was coming next. It was sort of like when Marlon Brando playing the Godfather asked for a favor and he knew it had to be fulfilled.

Schwarzkopf looked at Jenro and said, "The King of Saudi Arabia has given me a gift of a vase (he pronounced it *vaugh-essss*) that I would like you to take home to Mrs. Schwarzkopf. Would that be ok?"

"Of course, I would be delighted," Jenro stammered. From that moment on, he was a nervous wreck thinking he was going to break the treasured delicate gift from the King of Saudi Arabia before he could get it home to Mrs. Schwarzkopf. More on that later.

After surviving the Saudi Arabian guards who didn't shoot us because of the "snowflake cards" and the wrath of General Schwarzkopf, we ran into another major problem. For some reason, the

TV stations decided it would be wise to send one photographer to shoot the video for all the TV reporters and then we could do separate stand ups. To make matters worse, WTVT decided to send the oldest video camera with their photographer.

Following the Schwarzkopf interview, Tony's camera completely crashed, and we had to try to repair it by talking to WTVT engineers not only halfway around the world, but in a time zone more than 12 hours away.

It was almost comical seeing the video camera disassembled (and remember this was long before YouTube or the Internet were viable ways of seeing how to repair something). The engineers in Tampa would say things like, "Do you see the little screw that is toward the back end of the camera near the view finder. Take that off, then look for another screw that is inside the camera closer to the lens." Anyway, it was not a pretty picture, but somehow, we got the camera working again and all the footage of our big interview was fine.

After a stressful day, the entire Tampa Bay media group decided we had enough of the buffet and hummus at the Sheraton and wanted to venture out to a restaurant in downtown Riyadh. The man at the front desk gave us directions, but somehow, we got lost (again way before cell phones with a GPS to tell you how to get there). As we were walking in what seemed like endless circles in Riyadh, we came across a group of men wearing traditional headdress and robes.

I turned to reporter Linda Vester, who spoke fluent Arabic, and suggested she ask the men for directions, which she did. For some reason, this little interchange did not please them. They turned away from her and started talking to me.

I quickly figured out what was going on and said to Linda, "They don't want to talk to a woman, right?" She said, "Yes, they want to talk to the gentleman." Remember, we were all tired and irritated from the stressful day and now we were lost. I turned to Linda and said to tell them, "The gentleman doesn't understand what the fuck you are saying." She told them in a much gentler way, which was why they kept trying to communicate with only me.

Eventually, we gave up, continued to walk through downtown Riyadh and found what we thought was the restaurant.... or at least some eating establishment that was certainly tastier than the buffet at the Sheraton. It's a good thing that food digested before we got an offer later that night to go to town square to watch a thief's hands being chopped off. "We pass," I said, speaking for the group.

I was glad when the U.S. Military jet got us the hell out of Saudi Arabia. After a bumpy ride home, we landed back at Shaw Air Force Base in South Carolina, where we had to clear customs.

Customs was no big deal for the reporters, but when Jenro walked through with that priceless vase that General Schwarzkopf gave him to bring to the missus, a military watchdog working the customs desk was certain that Jenro was trying to smuggle this thing into the country because he didn't declare it. We were told that Jenro was going to be locked up in the Brig for his crime.

Jenro protested, telling the customs agent, "I'm not trying to smuggle anything. This is a vase General Schwarzkopf asked me to bring home and give to Mrs. Schwarzkopf." The Sergeant, who was in charge, said, "Ya, and I suppose the King of Saudi Arabia gave it to him." We all chipped in and said, "That's exactly right."

No one believed us and things began to heat up as talk continued of putting Jenro in the Brig. At that point, we asked how much the custom fees would cost. Each media outlet plunked down $50 each (which later we would expense) to keep our new friend out of trouble.

When the first Gulf War began on January 17,1991 with the bombing of Baghdad, I had just left the station with anticipation of the war starting that night. The deal was that nothing was happening, so I headed for home. That's when I heard Bernard Shaw and PeterArnett go live on CNN radio with news of the war breaking out. A beat passed and immediately I contacted the station, telling them that I was headed for main gate of MacDill Air Force Base. I suggested they send a live van to meet me, which the station did....and I spent the rest of the evening doing live shots trying to use my experiences in Saudi Arabia and the stories of the troops I met over there to localize the story.

The first Gulf War went amazingly well and General Schwarzkopf was a worldwide hero. The day he returned to MacDill was a big deal and big celebration. However, the Wing Commander of MacDill Air

Force base was pissed off that Schwarzkopf was getting all the adulation. He ordered all the F-16's at the base to leave with their crews, thus refusing to acknowledge Schwarzkopf's return.

Schwarzkopf and his support staff returned to MacDill at the end of April 1991 and it might have well been the middle of August. It was an ungodly hot (and I never complain about heat- I hate cold) and humid Florida day that we usually experience in the summertime. We were all assembled on the Tarmac at MacDill where the heat is reflected off the runway to make it seem as if we were standing in the middle of an oven.

Schwarzkopf's plane was more than 20 minutes late and the military people left at the base -the ones not ordered away by the commander of the 6th Air Wing -- were standing at Parade Rest on the tarmac. Unfortunately, the heat was getting to many of them. From the press platform, we watched legs buckle as they slowly collapsed onto the concrete tarmac. Medics were taking them away in droves, so there weren't bodies littered on the ground when Schwarzkopf landed.

Norman Schwarzkopf had become a real-life hero, especially here in Tampa Bay, and the community wanted to recognize him. The return to MacDill had limited public access, so the community wanted to stage a celebration, which it did at the Old Tampa Stadium where the Buccaneers played from 1976 to 1998. It was also the place ESPN's anchor Chris Berman named the "Big Sombrero" because of the way it looked. On a side note, while some people consider Berman somewhat bombastic, I found him to be a great guy.

I came to that conclusion when the Bucs were in a playoff game against the Washington Redskins. The Friday night before the game, everyone was doing stories at the stadium, because that was the big, if not the only, story in town. Both Berman and I were in the stands doing a stand up and we were pretty close to each other. We were careful not to talk at the same time or we would be heard on the other's tape.

Berman had started doing his on-camera piece first when he saw me and said, "You're local right? And have a 6 o'clock show?" I told him I did. He said, "My deadline is later. You go first and get your work done and I'll wait." From that moment on, I became a number one Chris Berman Fan.

The welcome home for Schwarzkopf and the troops at the stadium was complete with floats, Mickey Mouse, fireworks and about 28,000 people welcoming back the war heroes. Every station carried it live and I was part of the live broadcast.

I did some interviews with people coming into the stadium, talked to some of the troops and then headed to the press elevator to get to the press box where we would do our live show.

As I got on the elevator there were two other media people, Marissa Morris who was the 5 p.m. anchor on WFLA, the NBC affiliate. She was an extremely nice, pretty, and seemingly proper woman. The other person was part of the team of the WFLA Radio morning talk show, Tedd Webb. He always carried some kind of crazy fart machine with him and as we were riding up in the elevator, he kept hitting it and then looked embarrassed as Marissa gave him dirty looks.

I was close to tears by the time we got to the press box.

A DATE WITH DEATH - EXECUTIONS

FLORIDA REPORTERS PLAY a role when the state decides to conduct an execution. They're called to cover the event as part of the witness team to make sure the state carries it out correctly. While I tend to have a liberal view on most things, I am a supporter of the death penalty. I must admit I have no idea if executions act as a deterrent, but it certainly stops recidivism. In addition, every execution I have witnessed has been much less upsetting than the murder scene that was perpetrated by the condemned killer.

The first man I saw executed was Robert Dale Henderson. Here's how the New York Times detailed Henderson's killing spree: *"He was sentenced to death in 1982 for the slayings of three hitchhikers he had picked up near the end of a 19-day killing spree that started on Jan. 14 of that year in Ohio. Along the way he also killed people in South Carolina, Mississippi and Louisiana before ending the spree in Florida.*

The Florida hitchhikers, two men and a woman, were bound with adhesive tape and shot in the head. Mr. Henderson told the authorities he thought they were going to kill him.

Mr. Henderson, a high school dropout from Esther, Mo., said he first killed a woman in Ohio. A week later, he said, he killed his wife's parents and their 11-year-old son in their Ohio farmhouse.

He said his other victims included a 21-year-old model in Charleston, S.C.;
a nightclub owner in Baton Rouge, La.; a woman in Pascagoula, Miss., and a
store clerk and a retired doctor near Palatka, Fla." [3]

Henderson was executed in April of 1993, but when I first encountered Henderson he was not yet sentenced to death and was sent to
our area to stand trial for a murder that carried the death penalty. His
transfer from the Florida State Prison, where he was already serving a
life sentence for murder, to Hernando County, which was in our
viewing area, was one of the first stories I covered for WTSP in 1982.

It happened late in the afternoon and the station decided to fly in
our helicopter, which at the time was a Hughes 500 that was parked on
a landing deck behind the station. Although I had flown in a helicopter
before when I was in Norfolk, this was the longest flight I had ever
been in a helicopter, about 45 minutes, and the aircraft was much
larger than what I flew in Norfolk.

The configuration in the Hughes 500 was the pilot and the photographer sat in the front seat and the reporter sat in the back. The way
the helicopter was constructed, there was a transmission bar that ran
down the middle. When you put on the earphones (so you could talk
to the pilot as well as drown out the noise) your head would bounce off
the transmission bar.

As we were flying to Brooksville in Hernando County, my head was
bouncing against the transmission bar and I felt the backseat close in
on me. "A person could get very claustrophobic in here and freak out,"
I thought.

I was able to calm myself by telling that voice, "Mike, this is your
first week here. They don't know you yet. And if you freak in the
'copter then they will label you a nutcase and your career in Tampa will
be over."

Somehow, I kept it together and did a fairly simple story about the
arrest and the transfer of the serial killer. I thought that would be the
last time I ever dealt with Robert Dale Henderson, but I was wrong.
Some 11 years later when his execution date was drawing near, the
station was up on the list of media witnesses and because I had
covered his transfer to Hernando County, I was asked if I wanted to be
the one. I agreed, because one of the reasons I love this profession is

that it has given me the opportunity to see things firsthand that people only live vicariously through my eyes. I thought this would be a once-in-a-life time opportunity, but I was wrong about that.

Although I was interested in covering the execution, I had no idea what to expect. I knew it could be a life-altering experience. Two of my colleagues had been witnesses in the past and it shook them both. Doug Hoyte, called Dougie by most of his friends was one of the most lovable and carefree people I have ever known. He was a witness to the execution of Robert Sullivan in 1983 for the murder of an assistant manager of a Miami Howard Johnsons who was the father of five.

Sullivan, who was Catholic, got the support of the Pope who tried to convince then Florida Governor Bob Graham to spare Sullivan's life. Before he was executed, Sullivan said to his fellow inmates on death row shortly before he sat down in the electric chair know as Old Sparky, "In spite of what is about to happen to me, do not give up." He read a two-page statement concluding "I have no malice to none; God bless us all."

Dougie had done a death row interview with Sullivan shortly before the execution. He was shaken and told me he had nightmares for weeks. That was unusual for Doug, who was the most happy-go-lucky guy in the world. When Doug came back from the execution, he had the look in eyes as if he had seen a ghost. I remember him telling me, "Mikey, he looked right into my eyes before they dropped the hood over him. It was chilling." Doug said.

And Doug wasn't the only friend of mine shaken after witnessing an execution. John Wilson, our main anchor, told me a similar story and it surprised me. John had the look of a classic anchor with a booming baritone voice and always seemed in control. John was not just a reader; he was a real journalist and had covered all sorts of stories.

The event that shook John was the execution of serial Killer Ted Bundy. Bundy's reign of terror crossed the United States where he was involved in at least 38 murders, although some say it could be closer to 100. He was a well-educated, good looking, smooth talking man who was a psychopath.

Bundy was executed in Florida for the rape and murder of a 12-year-old girl, but he was also responsible for the rape and murder of two co-eds at the Chi Omega house at Florida State University.

When John came back from Bundy's execution, he had the same look on his face as Doug did after Sullivan's execution. He told me he had nightmares for weeks.

This gave me some concern as I was driving to Starke, north of Gainesville, where the death chamber was located, for Henderson's execution. I was thinking what it might be like in the witness chamber. I also thought about the story I did when I was in Norfolk. At the time Virginia was getting ready for its first execution after the U.S. Supreme Court lifted the ban.

After the Supreme Court ruling, I did a story about death row in Virginia and got a chance to sit in the Virginia Electric chair - which I hoped would be my only opportunity to have such an experience.

The State prison in Richmond gave us complete access to death row where there were six cells adjacent to the execution chamber. Before executions were halted while the Supreme Court decided if the act was a prohibited cruel and unusual punishment, Virginia would move the condemned men from cell six to cell one, next in line, as each execution occurred.

Cell One was the closest to the death chamber and we did a "point of view shot" where photographer Pat Dowd walked with the camera rolling as if he were a condemned inmate from the number one cell to the chair. He sat down in it. It was an extremely powerful piece of video!

After Pat sat down in the chair, I asked the warden who was conducting the tour if I could sit there and he said, "Of course." It was just a plane wooden chair that looked like the kind that teachers have in elementary school...and then the electrodes are hooked up from the side.

When I sat in the chair, I stared out into the same view the condemned man had of the witness room just seconds before he died. It was a view that has always stayed with me.

I was amazed how accommodating the Virginia Prison system was in terms of showing us everything about the death chamber, allowing us to video everything except the headgear with the sponge that helped conduct the volts of electricity through the condemned man's skull.

With the experiences of Doug and John and my encounter with the Virginia electric chair, I headed to the state Prison where the execution of Henderson would take place on April 23, 1993.

In those days, the executions were scheduled for seven a.m. which meant we had to be in Starke the night before. Starke was a town 25 miles north of Gainesville (where the University of Florida is located) but it could have been on another planet in contrast.

In order to get to Starke, we had to drive through a town called Waldo where the speed limit abruptly changes from 60 to 50 to 40 to 35 within the matter of seconds and the town makes a majority of its income from speeding tickets. Drivers going through Waldo can get pulled over going one mile over the limit. It was so bad at one time that AAA suggested motorists take a longer route instead of 301 South and avoid the town all together.

For me, going through Starke was a visible reminder that it was a whole new world we are entering. The facts are simple here: The further North you go in Florida, the more Southern it gets.

On the morning of the execution, we gathered across the street of the state prison at 5:30 in the morning. A van with a prison guard, who had a list of the witnesses, picked us up, checked our IDs and bussed us to the actual compound. Once inside "The Big House," we were ushered into a conference room where we had to leave all our metal objects including pens and belts behind. We were given a note pad provide by the department of corrections, a pencil, and then had a briefing by a spokesman who told us that we would be taken to the execution witness chamber approximately 30 minutes before the act would be done.

At 6:30 a.m., we were required to go through a metal detector. It was the only time in my life I have ever had my wedding ring off. It got stuck from years of wearing it, so I had to go into the bathroom and use a ton of soap to get it off. Luckily, it budged and then slid off. If not, I would be forced to turn around because no metal was allowed. Period. They changed that rule and I didn't have to deal with that at future executions.

The media entered a somber witness room where there were about six rows of chairs with around 10 chairs in each row about 25 feet from a glass window. There were other witnesses who sat silently, and we sat to join them. A curtain was drawn over the window, so we waited. At about 6:50 a.m., the curtain lifted to show the electric chair and suddenly the air even felt heavy. Within seconds, a door towards the back of the execution chamber opened and two guards escorted Henderson to his date with death.

The first thing I noticed was that Henderson's head was shaved and there was a blue cream squiggled across the top of his head. It looked like gel toothpaste and I knew it was there to conduct the electric current through him. The moment I saw the cream on Henderson's face, I thought to myself, "This is fuckin' serious!"

Unnerving. That's another word that came to mind.

I would not freak out.

I would not blink.

The guards sat Henderson down in the electric chair, strapped his arms to the side of the chair and lifted a pant leg to attach an electrode to one leg as they strapped the other leg to the chair.

Then the warden asked Henderson if he had any final words.

"No sir, I don't," Henderson replied.

Within a second, another guard took a chin strap, put it under Henderson's chin, pulled his head back and attached the head strap that had a black cloth that would cover his face.

He was seconds away from being put to death.

The warden was on the phone with an open line to the Governor's office for a last-minute reprieve, but there was none. He waited another second and then nodded his head to the executioner who flipped the switch.

I saw Henderson grab for the arms of the chair. His entire body seemed to lift up as 2,000 volts of electricity went through him.

After what seemed like several long minutes, the medical examiner put a stethoscope to Henderson's chest and then nodded, declaring him dead. A prison guard took the microphone and said, "The State of Florida has carried out its sentence of Robert Dale Henderson, please exit to the left."

I would witness several executions in my career and each time I heard those words, I felt as if I was at the end of a ride at Disney World. I even imagined another group being seated for a different execution, followed by a trip to the execution store for tee-shirts and giant cookies shaped like the electric chair. In my mind, I saw a sign that read: Thank you for visiting the Florida Death Chamber!

Of course, it didn't work that way. You came; you saw death; you went home.

Then you had to try to sleep through the nights, which wasn't easy.

The next execution witnessed occurred five years later, in March of 1998, when Gerald Eugene Stano, who confessed to killing 41 women in three states, was put to death in Florida via "Old Sparky." This execution was different for several reasons. First, I had done a death row interview with Stano about a year before he was scheduled to die.

Stano, who had received a stay of execution within 3 hours of being electrocuted, agreed to do the interview as long as we didn't talk about the case which was on appeal.

During the interview, we talked about what it was like dealing with his execution including his last meal, last shower and having his head shaved before getting the stay. Stano kept saying, "And they were going to execute an innocent man."

When we finished and started doing the cutaways (where you see the reporter over the shoulder of the interviewee), I said to Stano, "I won't use this sound because we can't talk about the case, but if you can answer one question, I promise I will do a story about you every week until you are cleared or put to death."

Stano, who looked like a nerdy guy instead of a serial killer, replied, "Sure, anything you want to know."

"If you're an innocent man, how were you able to give the police details of the murders that only the killer could know?" I asked. Stano looked at me hard before he said, "Mike that's a problem." "No shit, Jerry. That's a big fuckin' problem," I replied.

There was some controversy about the fact that Stano had confessed to the 41 murders. His attorney claimed that he was a serial confessor, which did not make him a serial murderer. In fact, the party line was he had been spoon-fed information about the murders from the lead detective in the case. However, the U.S. Supreme Court didn't buy that argument and refused to give him another reprieve from the electric chair.

In the end, Stano was put to death for the murder of a 17-year-old hitchhiker named Cathy Lee Sharf, who was stabbed to death in a remote area of Broward County near Ft. Lauderdale, Florida. There was extra anticipation for Stano's execution because the previous man put to death in Florida's electric chair, Pedro Medina, had a 12-inch flame leaping from his head in a malfunction of the device. Sickened witnesses said it appeared as if he was burned to death.

Unlike Henderson, who appeared resigned and almost calm as he was led to the death chamber, Stano had the fear of God written all over his face.

Frightened about the prospect of his impending death, he seemed to be in mortal fear that the chair would malfunction again and that his electrocution would be slow and extremely painful.

While Stano appeared to be filled with fear as he walked into the death chamber, it didn't affect his appetite hours earlier as he ordered a last meal of Delmonico steak, a baked potato with sour cream and bacon bits, French bread with butter and a tossed salad with blue cheese dressing. For dessert, he ordered a half gallon of mint chocolate ice cream and two liters of Dr. Pepper.

As he was led into the death chamber, he looked scared shitless. Stano peered through the glass window in the execution chamber to the witness room as he was strapped into the chair and said he had no final words. However, one of his attorneys released a statement after the execution where Stano contended he was innocent and didn't really commit the crimes. He just confessed – or so he said.

As the hood was dropped over Stano's face, the brother of one of the victims whispered loudly enough for everyone in the witness room to hear, "Die, you monster!"

As the electricity surged through his body, Stano gripped the side of the chair (and again appeared to almost be lifted out of it). The same witness kept loudly whispering, "Yes, yes, yes!"

At 7:15 a.m. – fifteen grisly minutes after the entire procedure began -- Stano was declared dead.

As usual, the prison guard took the microphone and said, "The state of Florida has carried out its sentence of Gerald Eugene Stano. Please exit to the left."

Once again, I had the feeling we would walk into the Disney-like souvenir room and be able to buy little figures of Stano in the electric chair or maybe a glass snow globe with him strapped to the chair. Maybe there would even be photos like they have of people screaming on a roller coaster, like Space Mountain. In this case, it would be our wide-open mouths as the electric current flowed.

I could go on. Journalists have a sick sense of humor.

By the time I witnessed my next execution, the State of Florida had switched to lethal injection and it was an entirely different procedure than the electric chair. While the electric chair, particularly "Old Sparky" clearly has a macabre dungeon-like death chamber feel to it, lethal injection seems almost antiseptic, like a hospital procedure. That's how I felt when I watched a man named Newton Slawson get that final shot.

Our worlds collided in April of 1989 when I had just finished a late dinner and received a call from the assignment desk about a gruesome murder scene not too far from downtown. There weren't any reporters nearby. As usual, I was game. A photog was set to meet me, and we would go live on the 11 p.m. newscast.

When I got to the scene, there were flashing lights, police cars and homicide detectives *everywhere*. Through the crime tape I could see trails of blood coming down the steps of a two-story home. One of the long-time homicide detectives I knew named Rick Childers came up to the edge of the crime tape and said, "Mike, this is the bloodiest murder scene I have ever encountered in my career. It is shocking and disgusting." That was an astounding statement from Childers who had seen his share of homicides and was one of the friendliest cops to reporters.

Childers -- Chili as everyone called him -- was an instantly likeable guy to everyone he met and was extremely popular with reporters and other cops. Sadly, Chili would eventually be murdered nine years later as he and his partner, who was also shot and killed, were transporting another killer, Hank Earl Carr to jail.

Slawson shot and killed the entire Wood family who lived next door to him. He was convicted of shooting a father, mother, three-year-old boy and four-year-old girl. If that was not vile enough, Slawson then took a knife and cut the belly of the 8 1/2-month pregnant Peggy Wood, yanking a now-dead fetus out of her body.

Wood could crawl to her mother's home, located behind her own, where she died in her arms. As she drew her last breath, she managed to say, "Newton did it."

The image of that bloody night 14 years earlier was imbedded in my mind as I sat in the execution witness room and the curtains opened. I saw Slawson strapped to a gurney in what looked like a hospital operating room. He had quit fighting any attempt to forestall his execution and appeared calm and relaxed on the gurney. In fact, he had asked for a valium and slept peacefully after having a final meal of fried scallops and a Coke. He visited with his own family members for a final time.

The only pain Slawson seemed to be suffering from the execution was when the procedure was delayed for 13 hours, thanks to Governor Jeb Bush granting a stay about an hour before Slawson was supposed to be put to death the night before. Slawson's attorneys tried to convince the Governor that Slawson was not mentally competent enough to be executed and Bush stopped the execution. This meant that Slawson could be evaluated one more time by a psychiatrist.

The real shocker was this actually irritated Slawson. I guess when a man's ready...he's ready.

That morning in the death chamber, Slawson seemed at peace with the world and ready to meet his Maker. He declined to make any final statement.

"No," Slawson responded when the warden asked if he had any final words. At that point, the lethal cocktail started seeping into his veins. I watched as Slawson's chest heaved a couple of times and then he stopped breathing. I couldn't help but think about the juxtaposition of the execution by the state and the execution Slawson carried out 14 years earlier.

Sorry, but it didn't seem as if the punishment fit the crime.

I was jolted back to reality when a doctor put a stethoscope to

Slawson's chest and nodded that he was, indeed, dead. The bailiff grabbed the microphone and said those familiar words, "The State of Florida has carried out its sentence against Newton Carlton Slawson. Please exit to the left." No, there weren't snacks or gift bags.

While some reporters have had a rough time being a witness at an execution, I walked away from each one without a problem. I always found it more upsetting to be at a murder scene with the yellow tape around the house of the victim or victims. It hurts to watch an unsuspecting relative drive up praying for the best and only to be told by the police their loved one had been murdered.

I can still hear the wails of pain from the family members as they pictured the heinous crimes that had befallen their loved ones. This was usually followed by sitting in a court of law for days or weeks as the State entered what mostly was horrendous evidence of that crime, which was also brutally described in the most graphic words to the jury.

I figured out that in a homicide, it's not only horrible for the victim, but also the survivor. The victim dies once. The survivors seem to die over and over again by reliving with what happened.

One of those unforgettable cases involved Danny Rolling, a mass murderer I covered. I wasn't a witness at his execution, but I did work the protests outside the prison where Rolling was put to death.

Rolling was the man who terrorized the University of Florida in August of 1990, eventually slaughtering 5 students. The killings panicked students and scared parents to the point where they pulled their children out of school before the semester started. The murders started when Rolling broke into the apartment of two co-eds and then raped them, stabbed them in their backs and then took the time to "pose them" in sexually provocative positions before he left.

A day later Rolling broke into another co-ed's apartment, waited for her to return and then raped her, brutally stabbed her and then decapitated the woman. Rolling placed the woman's head on the fireplace mantel and had it face the body to provide the most shocking scene.

The story crossed the Florida State lines and went national. Our news director at the time, Mel Martin, called me into his office to talk about it. Mel was one of my favorite news directors because he had once been an investigative reporter and was incredibly bright. An astronomy major in college, Mel was extremely well read, a complete computer geek who did Beta Testing for Apple and was even my age. Another plus. We spoke the same language, walked the same walk.

Mel and I used to have great philosophical discussions ranging from religion to the Kennedy assassination, but sometimes Mel would pause the conversation and say, "We will pick this up tomorrow." The next day, he would bring in a book from the "Mel Martin Lending Library" and tell me to "read it, so we can have an intelligent discussion later this week." Yes, he would expect me to go home that night, read an entire book, and report back to him the next day – his idea of fun. And it was fun, because we had very frank conversations with each other.

Case in point: There was a time I was in his office getting a script approved and he was on the phone berating a young reporter who truly did make a stupid mistake. When he hung up, I said, "Mel, you're being an asshole." "Deeson, you're an asshole," he shot back. I looked at him and said, "That may well be, but we are talking about you, not me." Kumbaya! I loved it.

Back on the beat, the Gainesville murders became the dominate story every news outlet was covering. One day, Mel called me into his office and said with a straight face, "Deeson, go to Gainesville and find out who is committing these killings." I laughed out loud. "Yeah, right,' I said. Mel was nodding. "Mike, it will be great for the station if you can solve this crime," he said, taking me seriously.

"Mel," I said, trying to shock him back to reality. "Every cop in the state is trying to find the murderer. Are you out of your fucking mind?"

Mel didn't mind the language. "But you're an investigative reporter and you won't have to turn dailies," he said. In journalism speak that meant I wouldn't have to do a story for each night's newscast. I would just have to "concentrate on finding the killer."

There was no way to convince Mel that he was indeed crazy, so I filled up my gas tank and drove to Gainesville, which is about two hours north of Tampa. Once I hit the city limits, I joined what seemed like half our staff "doing dailies." With all due respect to Mel, I actually did spend my time figuring out how I was going to "solve" the case.

Two days after arriving in Gainesville, two more students were murdered and all of a sudden, I was doing "dailies."

By now, the campus was in frenzy mode and precautions in the form of cancelling all classes were taken. The search for a suspect dominated every newscast while people double-checked the locks on their front doors.

Mel came up with the idea of doing an hour long special about the murders featuring UF president John Lombardi and stories about what was happening on campus. It was a great idea in theory, but it ran into major problems because Lombardi wanted to do the special from in front of the Student Union.

The Student Union location would have been fine, except Mel wanted the earlier evening newscasts, including the six o'clock news, to be across the street from the Alachua County State Attorney's Office (where Gainesville was located). In the park across the street, there was an impromptu memorial erected for the slain students and Mel thought that would be a great backdrop for our shows.

The Student Union, however, was about 15 minutes away from the State Attorney's Office and that meant after the six o'clock news we had to drive the live trucks to the Student Union and do new stories for the 7 p.m. special.

The problem was that we were all trying to edit our stories from the same tapes as we were driving to the Student Union. It was a cluster. There was no way we could get everything done on time despite all the live trucks parked next to each. In each one, an editor screamed, "Who has tape six?" Another would yell, "I need a soundbite from tape three." And the tapes were flying back and forth like a circus juggling act. The only thing we needed was the sabre dance music they used to play on *The Ed Sullivan Show* when there were jugglers.

Tracye Fox, our field producer, was near tears as we tried to get the show on the air. Although there was a lineup of what stories would run in what order, all of it was thrown out the window and the format of the show became whatever story was finished would be the next one to run.

Somehow, we got through the show, but the search for the killer took a nasty turn. The real law enforcement officers, not investigative reporters, thought they had broken the case by the end of the week when a University of Florida student with a history of mental problems named Ed Humphrey was arrested about 100 miles South of Gainesville. Ed had not only engaged in a fight, but also injured his poor grandmother. At the time of his arrest, he began babbling about Satan and the Gainesville murders. Police and prosecutors announced they had a break in the case and Humphrey quickly became the prime suspect.

Now that they had their suspect (maybe), the Gainesville Sheriff's Office paraded Humphrey in front of the media, insisting he was a vicious killer.

Humphrey, who was taking medication and looked disheveled, appeared to be the maniac who was responsible for all of the mutilations and killings.

The authority's case was bolstered by the fact that he lived in the same apartment complex as two of the victims.

Newspapers began to describe Humphrey as "a big, pudgy kid with unkempt hair, scars on his face and a glazed look in his eyes." At the same time, prosecutors and police were under intense pressure to find the killer and wouldn't give up the notion that this was their man. Another mark in this direction was the fact that the killings stopped after Humphries was arrested.

There was just one problem for prosecutors that was quite serious in nature. The DNA evidence collected at the crime scenes didn't match Humphries' genetic pool. However, Humphries wouldn't be cleared until the actual killer, Danny Rolling, was arrested and charged by a grand jury.

Rolling was a drifter who was arrested on burglary charges in Ocala, about 30 miles South of Gainesville. He not only had tools that matched the wounds of the murder victims, but lived in a tent in a wooded area near the apartment complexes where the students were slaughtered.

Eventually, police discovered recordings including self-composed songs where Rolling alluded to the murders. He was indicted in

November of 1991, more than a year after the five students were slain.

At times when he appeared in court, the unpredictable Rolling would break into song, an odd precursor to his execution. There was another unexpected twist. On the day Rolling's much anticipated murder trial was about to begin, four years after the killings, jurors were expected to be exposed to grizzly murder scene photos. Instead, Rolling shocked the courtroom by pleading guilty.

The mass murderer told Judge Stanley Morris, "There are some things you just can't run from... this being one of those."

The plea was such a shock that a Miami station completely missed it because it was having trouble getting the courtroom feed into its satellite truck. The Miami reporter was helping the photographer and engineer get the wires straightened out when Rolling entered the plea. It happens. The reporter wasn't in the courtroom and had no idea. The unexpected just happened.

As the crew was dealing with the technical problems with no feed inside the truck, all the other stations in the state were doing live cut ins saying Rolling had admitted his guilt and entered the guilty plea.

The reporter got a call from his station, which (worst case scenario) by now was watching the competitors announce the guilty plea. His boss asked when he was going to tell them what Rolling had done. The reporter said, "Don't fuck with me. I'm trying to get the feed into the truck so we can cover the trial." He had no idea it was over.

Although Rolling entered a guilty plea in 1994, it took *another 12 years* for the state to execute him.

The day of the execution, satellite trucks from TV stations around the state invaded the field across from the Florida State Prison in Raiford where Rolling would draw his last living breath.

Both pro and anti-execution groups gathered for the event as Rolling calmly ate a last meal of lobster tail, butterfly shrimp, a baked potato, strawberry cheesecake and sweet iced tea. He was another one who could push past the fate that waited him in a few hours in order to fill his stomach one last time. It turns out a fed serial killer is also a chatty one. Hours before he was put to death, Rolling confessed to three additional murders in Louisiana where he was also a suspect, but the state could never convict him of those crimes.

As the curtain opened in the execution chamber and Rolling was asked if he had any last words, he sang of angels and mountains. Witnesses say that as the chemicals poured into his veins, Rolling turned his head toward the mother of one of the victims and sang over and over, "None greater than Thee, Oh Lord. None greater than Thee." Within three minutes, the monster who terrorized the state in the early 90's was done. There would be no encore.

Although I wasn't in the execution chamber for that one, there was no doubt that when the doctor examined Rolling and nodded that he was indeed dead. The bailiff assigned to the death chamber grabbed the microphone and said, "The State of Florida has carried out its sentence against Danny Harold Rolling.... Please exit to the left."

And that was the case for every other execution where I was a witness.

DICK GRECO - THE TEFLON MAYOR!

DICK GRECO WAS PROBABLY the most entertaining politician I have ever covered. As Tampa's youngest mayor, he was elected in 1967 when he was a tender 34 years young. He then became Tampa's oldest mayor after taking the oath again in 1995 when he was 62 years old and much wiser. He served until he was 70.

The wild thing about Dick was his honesty. Most politicians who are accused of doing something questionable will try to tap dance around the issue. Dick would just smile wide and say, "Yep, I did it!" Combine that truth gene with the fact that he loved to tell disparaging stories about himself and you have a unique individual.

Another of Dick's politician-like traits was that he was somewhat of a ladies' man or, as some might say, a womanizer, who almost always took the politically incorrect approach of squeezing and hugging female reporters and then telling them how cute they looked. #MeToo would have had a field day with the guy. Meanwhile, he would approach male reporters, grab their arm and say, "Looks like you've been working out."

Each time he would say that to me, which was every single time I saw him, I would look at him and say, "Mayor, you know the only

workout I've been doing is lifting a cocktail glass of Bombay Gin."
"Keep it up," the Mayor replied. "It's obviously working."

Mayor Greco loved telling stories about his wild days. I remember when he was re-elected in 1995, he told me about a lunch he had with a reporter for the Tampa Tribune. Greco explained that the reporter said to him, "I don't know how to say this, Mr. Mayor, but I heard during your first term that you were...sort of...." At this point, the reporter began to struggle to find the words. "I heard you were somewhat," she began again, forcing out, "Promiscuous."

The Mayor was loving it and told me, "I pushed back from the table, threw my napkin on the plate and told her, 'That is a damn lie!" Then Greco said, "I looked at her and said, 'I was not even a little bit promiscuous. If she is good looking and wore a skirt, I screwed her!'" (Can you even imagine!)

The Mayor then added, "And when that was happening, your editor was with me."

It turns out that the editor of the Tampa Tribune wasn't the one with Greco, but instead it was worse. It was Stewart Bryan, the son of the majority stockholder of Media General, the corporation that owned the Tribune and several other newspapers and TV stations across the country. Bryan had been sent to Tampa to work at the Tribune and learn the family business from the bottom up. He became pals with Mayor Greco, which proved interesting, given the particulars that I just described.

About a week after the encounter with the Tribune reporter, Mayor Greco said, "I got a call from Stewart saying, 'My reporter called me and said that you and I were whoring around Tampa.'" Greco told me that he replied, "Well, Stewart, it's true. So, go ahead and print it." Not-so-strangely, it never made it into the paper.

Meanwhile, Greco's city attorney for both his first and second time in office was a man named Jimmy Palermo. He was also the Mayor's cousin, which meant he had some not-so-public responsibilities. Basically, he told me that his main job the first time around was to "get Dick out of Tampa's world renown strip clubs before the police raided them and there was a photo op."

Naked local women aside, no matter what he did, our Dick couldn't wait to tell you about his latest adventure or misadventure. A prime example was on a trip to Atlanta. A contingent from Tampa, including reporters from the TV stations and newspapers went to the city to see how Atlanta had handled the Olympics, because Tampa was making a bid. Our guy Greco had another yarn to tell me. As Dick got off the private plane that flew the Tampa politicians to Atlanta, I was already at the airport waiting when he ran up and said, "Mike you won't believe what happened Saturday night." Not Monopoly!

Greco explained that the Mayor from Tampa's sister city, Oviedo, Asturias, Spain, was visiting Tampa to see Gasparilla, a Mardi Gras type of event held each year. It's complete with floats and "crews" comprised of some of Tampa's elite society who dress up as pirates and stage a parade down Bayshore Boulevard, a place lined with million-dollar homes.

The event started in 1904 and for years all the crews that participated in the parade were white and anything but inclusive. That changed drastically in 1991 when the Super Bowl came back to Tampa and Gasparilla was supposed be part of the big weekend.

The NFL learned of the elite all-white nature of the parade and pressured "Ye Mystic Krewe," which ran the parade, to become more inclusive. The Krewe took offense and called off the parade. An alternate weak sister parade called Bamboleo replaced Gasparilla.

By the next year, the Krewe allowed African Americans, women and all sort of groups to participate and throw beads to the slightly and sometime overtly inebriated crowds including women who flipped up their tops and flashed their breasts for plastic beads.

Tampa's Finest not only marched in the parade but had a tendency to imbibe. By the end of the parade route, let's just say that they were usually feeling very little pain.

A prime example occurred in 1988 when I just turned 40. At the time, we were living in a three-story townhouse on Bayshore right on the parade route. My wife Laurie and I always had a Gasparilla party. That year, I remember standing on Bayshore with some of my friends when Bill Branch, the head of "Ye Mystic Krewe" spied me.

Bill, dressed up in the traditional Gasparilla pirate gear, was not three sheets to the wind...he was four or five and screamed at the top of his lungs, "Mike, Mike, Mike! I bet if you saw me looking like this last week you wouldn't have let me stick my finger up your ass!" "No, Dr. Branch, the urologist, I certainly would not have," I said. He thought it was hysterical and quite frankly so did I. Clearly it was before HIPPA went into effect.

That was what Greco was talking about when he told me about the visit from sister city mayor to see Gasparilla. Greco said it was a wild day capped off by a visit to Bern's Steakhouse.

Bern's is the most famous restaurant in the city. Every president or dignitary that makes a pitstop in Tampa made a reservation. For one thing, the booze collection was a lure. They have a wine list bigger than the New York City telephone directory.

Following dinner, as is the tradition at Bern's, the Mayor's group went on a tour of the wine cellar which has more than 500,000 bottles in all price ranges including an 852 Gruand Larose going for a whopping $10,000.

Back in Atlanta, it was Tampa native Greco who was telling me about the tour of the wine cellar. "I have done that tour more times than I can count," he said, "So I thought I'd have some fun."

The wine cellar is dark and damp. Dick's wife Linda, a pediatrician, was very ticklish, so he thought he would pinch her on the butt to see if she could hold it together in front of all the dignitaries.

Dick said when he pinched his wife, she didn't jump like he thought she would, "So I pinched her harder," Dick told me. "And she still didn't jump." Then Greco says, "I pinched her as hard as I could and still no reaction until I saw in the dim light that Linda was in the front of group with the mayor from the sister city."

Greco says, "Now I realize that instead of pinching Linda, I was pinching the butt of the wife of the Mayor of the sister city."

Did he cause an international incident? Dick thought he did. He also didn't know what to do about it at the time, as caressing the butt of a visiting dignitary isn't the way to say, "Welcome to Tampa."

After the tour of the wine cellar, the group went up to Bern's world-famous desert room where Greco explained, "I had to say something, so I told the visiting mayor what I had done, and his wife started to laugh hysterically." "I've never seen her laugh like that before," said the visiting mayor. To which Greco replied, "Maybe you should pinch her in the butt more often."

The stories don't end there. Mayor Dick also liked to "kidnap" reporters for a ride around town to hear about his latest plans. I never did it if I was on deadline, because his promise of "let me kidnap you for 15 minutes," always turned into an hour and a half, however, it was also fun to be with Dick. On one of my favorite rides, he wanted to show me his plans for revitalizing downtown. We stepped into Dick's big Lincoln Continental, which was equipped with police lights and sirens. Other mayors had police drivers to shuttle them around, but not Dick. He had a pretty tricked-out ride.

That day, Dick was in the driver's seat, city attorney and cousin, Jimmy Palermo, rode shotgun in the passenger seat and I was in the back.

We drove past a development of downtown shops and bars called Channelside, past the Florida Aquarium and then to an industrial type area between those areas and Ybor City, Tampa's Latin Quarter.

Dick told me the plan was to bring the Seminole Indian gambling operation to the industrial spot. This was long before the Seminoles built the Hard Rock Hotel and Casino, about six miles northeast of town and became the fourth largest casino in the world.

I said to Dick, "But I thought the way state law read, that for the Seminoles to be able to run a gambling operation, it had to be on some kind of sacred Indian burial ground."

Without missing a beat Dick said, "Ya that's true, but all we have to do is just bury a couple of fuckin' bones and – *bingo* -- it's a sacred burial ground."

At that, moment Jimmy turned into the city lawyer and I thought he was going to shit as he turned to me. He whispered loudly, was moving his hands back and forth in a signal that clearly said no as he and kept whispering, "Off the record! Off the Record!" Since it never happened, and I think statute of limitations has passed, I don't think I'm breaking Dick's confidence. And the general rule is, you can't say off the record after telling someone something.

In the end, the deal never worked out because the city couldn't buy enough land in the area to accommodate the Seminoles.

It was always the Greco way. When he was working to bring a new art museum to downtown, he would always tell me, "I don't know a Picasso from a paint by numbers painting, but I know to be a great city, you have to have a great art museum." Dick was able to hire world famous architect Rafael Vinoli to design a world class, unique museum. The Vinoli design was eventually killed by his successor Pam Iorio, because she thought it was too expensive. Many in the art community never forgave her for that.

When the Buccaneers were threating to leave unless they got a taxpayer funded new stadium, Greco kept saying, "It is a crazy damn thing to own a football team because it is a bad return on the investment, but we've got to try to keep them in Tampa or it will be a black eye for the city."

That was one-time Greco was wrong. The Buccaneers turned out to be a great investment for the Glazer family. They purchased the team for $192 million in 1995, and today the franchise is worth $2.2 billion and expected grow, as the NFL is a non-stoppable money-making machine.

When it came to politics, Greco knew his stuff. I learned about Greco's political acumen the night of the vote on a half-cent tax to fund the stadium. I was covering the group pushing for the tax and as Greco walked into the room, he whispered in my ear, "This thing is going to go down in flames." The issue was extremely controversial, and many were against funding a stadium for billionaires like the Glazers.

About 15 minutes after the results started coming, Greco walked up to me again and said, "I was wrong." It wasn't only going to pass, but also by a pretty good margin. I asked him how he knew, and Dick said, "It's holding its own in the county and it will win in the city by a healthy margin."

Although vote totals were coming in, the totals didn't say where they were from and I asked Greco how he knew the votes were from the county and not the city. This is when I learned how this lifelong Tampa resident and consummate politician knew the area.

Dick smiled and said, "Look, Herb Berkowitz who is running for judge and another candidate, who was Hispanic, were getting creamed by the votes that have been counted." Dick said. "The people in the county don't like or vote for your people, meaning Jewish, or my people, meaning Latin. So, all the votes were from the county. He mentioned that he didn't believe there would be enough votes from the city to help those two judges. He was right. However, years later, Herb (a truly fine man) was finally appointed to the bench.

As for Dick, well, he continued to charm everyone, including Cuban President Fidel Castro. Dick and a group from Tampa went on a secret trip to Cuba, figuring at some time the embargo would be lifted and Cuba would be a prime trade and tourist partner for Tampa. Dick, who was fluent in Spanish, spent five hours trading stories with Castro and he says they became fast friends in that five-hour meeting. When he came home, I did an interview with Dick at his Harbor Island home. It was getting to the end of his time in office, so we talked in detail about the Cuba trip.

In the middle of the interview, Dick jumped up and said, "You smoke a cigar every once in a while, right?" I said yes and he went off to retrieve a box of Cuban cigars he had in the kitchen. Dick took out two Cohiba cigars and said, "I've never smoked one of these in my life." That was interesting since Tampa used to be known as "Cigar City." Dick handed the choice cigars to me and said, "From Fidel, to me, to you." I thought about not smoking them and keeping them as a souvenir for about half a second, but within two days I smoked two of Fidel's finest. It was my own secret trip to Cuba.

IN GOD WE TRUST: A CON MAN'S DREAM

I'M OFTEN ASKED if I get scared that someone is going to attack me while doing an investigative story. I always say no, because it rarely happens and while I don't consider myself a mean and macho person, I get emboldened with a photographer holding a camera behind me. Sometimes, however the "bad guy" loses it and actually gets physical, as was the case in a story called "In God We Trust."

This was one of my favorite stories because when I found out what was happening, I got really angry and knew I had to expose what was going on.

"In God We Trust" was a charity that made its money from selling specialty license plates. Florida has what seems like 10,000 specialty plates (actually it's only 120) including state schools and sports teams. Non-profit groups can sell the specialty plates and use the extra $25 people pay for the plates for the charity.

The premise of this particular group was that it would use the money it collected to help the widows, widowers and children of fallen firefighters and police. On the surface, it sounded like a great thing and the plates sold extremely well; despite some opposition by civil liberty groups who thought it violated the separation of church and state for Florida to be selling a plate with the phrase: In God We Trust.

With the help of an Orlando legislator, who worked the bill extremely hard, the legislature approved the plates and they quickly became a hit. They were so popular, in fact, the charity had collected $466,000 from the sale of the tags.

Krista Colquhoun, whose husband Alan was a firefighter, experienced a tragic loss when he was killed. Alan's truck flipped as he was going to a fire and he died. It wasn't long before she contacted me.

Krista knew a friend of mine who suggested that she reach out after receiving a foreclosure notice on her home. Turns out, she had approached the charity for help, but essentially was told, "Go pound sand."

I remember Krista saying, "And then to contact an organization when you're desperate... when you're pretty much at the end of your rope ....and they tell you no, too...I don't know how I haven't had a nervous breakdown."

That's when I started looking through the financials of the charity. It didn't take long to discover through both public and state records and IRS forms (which all charities must fill out) that despite collecting almost half a million dollars, the "In God We Trust" charity had paid out less than $10,000. To make matters worse, I found that Darrell Nunnelley, the founder and president of the charity, was paying himself, plus making contributions to the legislator who shepherded the bill through the Florida House and the Senate. In fact, he shelled out more money to that end vs. the victims who were supposed to receive the money.

I met with Krista and had her read the E-mails she had received on camera. Yes, she was denied the money. And I was determined to do anything I could to expose this injustice.

My first move was to call Darrell Nunnelley and inform him that I was doing a story about his "charity" and wanted to interview him. "Not interested," he stated. I used my standard line. "You don't have to talk to me on camera, but I will ask you on camera, 'Where is the money?'"

Let's just say that he less-than-politely declined and then hung up on me. I made a plan to visit him at his office or home, both located in Windermere, a suburb of Orlando known for multi-million-dollar homes. Tiger Woods and Shaquille O'Neal call the place home. My first concern was if I couldn't get Nunnelley at his office, it would be tough to knock on his front door, because many homes in Windermere are in a gated community where access is restricted to residents or their guests.

One of the first places I tried to track Nunnelley down, was the address listed with the state for the charity, but as I said in the story, "The people who run In God We Trust must also trust UPS, because the headquarters for the charity was a UPS Post Office box." When we tried to track him down at his real estate firm, the office was closed because he filed what's called an "intent for bankruptcy." Our only other alternative was to go to his house.

In Florida, which has the broadest and best public records act in the country, all real estate transactions are public record, so we could easily find his home. When we got there, it was sort of a good news/bad news situation.

The address on the property appraisers' website showed Nunnelley lived in a huge mansion on a lake with a 15-foot gate around it. The gate to the driveway, however, was open. There weren't any "No Trespassing" signs, so we parked down the block and walked onto his huge brick paved driveway with camera and microphone ready to confront him.

At the front door, we knocked several times, rang the bell and screamed his name, but there was no answer.

Since the gate was open, I figured he had gone somewhere. Photographer Paul Thorson and I would just wait for as long as it took for him to drive back in so we could confront him.

It was one of those typical hot and humid Florida summer days, but we had to just sweat it out and stand there. Let me say, I hate stakeouts. I've been on way too many where you don't get anything that day and have to do it over and over again until you find the person in question. In other words, it's a major pain the ass. The flipside is that the 10 to 15 seconds you get of video confronting "the bad guy" can make the story. It's like liquid gold and the viewers love it.

In my mind, it's not an ambush if I tell you I'm coming. And I had told Nunnelley over and over again that I would get him on camera.

As an aside, I have to credit a former assistant news director, Chris Ford, who was extremely intelligent, intense and drove everyone crazy, but had some ideas that were right on point. Chris started out at our station as an intern and several years later, he made it back as second in command in the newsroom. While he intimidated lots of people, that wasn't the case with me. Basically, I had worked in the business longer than almost any colleague or boss and I wasn't frightened by anyone at the station.

Chris' philosophy was, "If you don't get the bad guy, you don't have a story." When Chris first started pushing that, I wasn't sure I agreed with him, but I must tell you in 99 percent of my stories I have the bad guy on camera and that was particularly true in all my Emmy winning pieces.

Back to Nunnelley. We were determined to get him on camera and waited in that fancy driveway. Finally, Paul screamed, "The door is starting to open!" We rushed to it, expecting Darrell Nunnelley, but instead a drop-dead gorgeous woman in a string bikini waltzed out. I assumed it was his wife, so I called out, "Stephanie?"

"No, I'm not Stephanie," she said. "You must be looking for Darrell. A lot of people are looking for him. We just brought this house from him."

I started to explain why we were looking for Darrell, but I was having a tough time concentrating. She was a good-looking woman, but that was only part of it. My eyes were focused down, way down, to her lower legs where her pet pig stood. It had burst through the doors and started snorting and sniffing in my direction. It wasn't long before the pig made a beeline for me and started to do a smell test. The whole thing was...rather bizarre.

Anyhow, when I told the woman our story, she explained that she gave swimming lessons in their Olympic sized pool in the back of the house, but her next student wouldn't arrive for about 10 minutes. The woman in the bikini said she would help us because "He screwed us over in the sale of the house, so I'm delighted to help you, and I know where he lives."

Although she didn't have his exact address, she called a friend who lived down the block from him. The friend then drove over to Nunnelley's house and called us back with the correct address. I thanked the woman in the Bikini, said Goodbye to the pig and headed off to Nunnelley's house.

When we got to Nunnelley's home, I was relieved to find there was no gate around the rather large house, so we parked the car, got the camera and went up to the door (it was like déjà vu all over again) knocked, rang the bell and shouted for Darrell, but nothing.

This location was better than the previous, because we could see the driveway and the front door from the comfort of the air-conditioned car. Paul and I waited and fortunately, Nunnelley walked out to talk to the pool man who had come to clean his pool.

I walked up and tried to shake his hand saying "Heeeeeey Darrell, Mike Deeson, 10 News Investigators. How you are doing?" "Great," was his reply adding, "Turn that off and we'll talk. We've already had this conversation." I told Nunnelley, "But I want to know where the money went."

At that point Nunnelley was getting irritated and said, "I will disclose that when that goes off (meaning the camera). He told me make an appointment, you're trespassing on property right now."

I was persistent and again said, "But I want to know what happened to the money Darrell!"

Once again, he said getting angrier, "I'm going to ask you to turn it off."

With that, Darrell rushed the camera, grabbed it by the lens and tried to throw it to the driveway to break it. I replied, "Get your hands off the camera or you will go to jail, my friend." That's what I always say when someone touches our camera and usually people back off, but not this time as Nunnelley said, "You know what, I'm going to go to jail anyway."

I immediately tried to pull Nunnelley's hand off the camera, and within seconds the three of us (Nunnelley, Paul and I) were wrestling and fell to the ground. We rolled halfway across his lawn before Paul was finally able to pull the camera free and we headed back to the truck to see what kind of video we had.

Now I must be honest, the moment Nunnelley grabbed the camera and started wrestling with us, all I could think is this going to turn a really good story into an Emmy winner, which it turned out to be. The video, however, had to capture the encounter. Because we were rolling around on the ground, I wasn't sure if the camera was damaged and was afraid nothing would show up.

Back in the truck, Paul turned the camera on and started playing the video, which captured a good portion of the encounter until it went off in the middle of the wrestling match. I turned to Paul and said, "That was really great, but the damn video is out of focus!" Paul looked at me and said, "That's because you don't have your glasses on!" He was right. In the wrestling match, somehow my glasses flew off and now I had to go back onto Nunnelley's property and retrieve them.

When I went back, he came out once again and said, "I thought I told you to get off my property." I explained I was looking for my glasses and he left me alone. When I did find the glasses, I saw how far we had gone from the driveway and it was a good 15 to 20 feet... and then I concluded the wrestling match which seemed like forever, must have been at least a few minutes to get that far.

Once we looked at the video, I immediately called the Windermere Police Department to file battery charges. At the same time Paul called the station, where I believe, the first question the folks at the station asked was "Is the camera damaged?" Then they asked if we were all right.

As I said, Windermere is a quiet, rich community where being attacked was the last thing on my mind. I've been in situations before where I was concerned and uncomfortable about my safety, but this was not one of them.

An assault and battery must have been big news in Windermere, because they sent out five squad cars that might have been everyone at police headquarters at the time. I half expected "Barney Fife" to roll up and take the one bullet in his pocket and load it into his gun.

We showed the police officers our video and the police agreed it was a battery, so they went to talk to Nunnelley. Although they didn't arrest him on the spot, they said they would turn the information over to the state attorney's office and he would be charged, which he eventually was. Because it was his first offense, he didn't score jail time, but had to do community service, pay the station for the $900 dollars damage he did to our camera and I was insistent that he write a letter of apology, which he did.

In fact, a few months after that apology letter he called me and said he was sorry it escalated as it did, however, he is still facing much stiffer criminal penalties from the State of Florida and the IRS, which have not been resolved as of now.

The state stepped in and froze the funds that were still available through the charity and found another group to take over, which started handing out money to those in need. All in all, a satisfying conclusion as well as an Emmy winner!

OSHA - A WORKPLACE ATTACK AND A BLACK EYE

ALTHOUGH WE WERE ATTACKED when doing the "In God We Trust" license plate story, as I said, it rarely happened. Once however, I did get a black eye doing a story, but unfortunately, I couldn't use the attack in the story, which was extremely disappointing.

The attack happened when I was doing a story about the Tampa Office of The Occupational Safety and Health Administration (OSHA). The OSHA office was a mess, with several people not showing up on time or leaving early, shirking their responsibility and giving some companies breaks when they should have been fined.

There was a whistleblower in the office who reported the activity to the Inspector General of OSHA and to me. I was contacted shortly before the Inspector General finished investigating the allegations and had written a report detailing what had happened. Somehow someone in OSHA had worked a deal where the report would go only to someone in an OSHA managerial position and then the "problem children" in the office would be disciplined or fired.

My source was outraged that the public wasn't finding out what was really happening in the office and he somehow got a copy of the I.G. report and leaked it to me. Because it was an official document, I could mention all the allegations without fear of losing a libel suit.

(Notice I didn't say without fear of being sued, because anyone can file a suit, which is something I've learned over the years.)

The truth is, that anyone who does investigative reporting as long as I have, has put stories on the air where you get a little sick feeling for a moment after it airs and a voice in your stomach says, "Yes I could defend that story if I have to, but I hope I don't have to." A longtime investigative reporter who doesn't admit to that is either lying or does not regularly do accusatory investigative stories.

I have been fortunate, never to be called on the carpet for any of those stories where I get that "sick feeling after it airs," but EVERY single law suit I've been involved in were for frivolous reasons that the plaintiff had no chance of winning.

Having said that, it is still a major pain in the ass to be sued, because you have to go through hours of explanations and depositions with managers, lawyers and corporate folks and it can be extremely irritating.

Anyhow, back to the OSHA story. I had all the info for the story from the report that had been leaked to me, but I needed to get video of the "slackers" mentioned in the IG report to go along with the story.

On that particular story, I was working with photographer Mike Venable who always seemed "combat ready" and reminded me of the character Animal in the Muppets. Venable was a tough little guy who blared heavy metal music (not my style) on the car radio and always seemed "ready to rumble."

We went to the public garage adjacent to the OSHA offices and took pictures of everyone who pulled into the OSHA assigned spaces. The plan was to go to my source after we got the video and he would help us match the pictures to the report. At this time, OSHA was aware we were working on the story and we were not the least bit surreptitious about getting the video. It was a public garage; we had the right to be there, so we didn't hide and just took our video.

Most of the people pulling into the OSHA spots either totally ignored us or gave us an irritating look that seemed to be saying something like "Die, you gravy sucking pig!" It's a look I've seen several times before.

Everything changed however, when one guy pulled into an OSHA designated spot and aggressively got out his car saying, "You better not be taking pictures of ME!" I replied, "This is a public spot, we have every right to take your picture and that is what we are doing."

The man started walking quicker and quicker toward us, screaming at this point, "I'm warning you, turn that camera off, you better not be taking pictures of me!" As he got closer, the almost-out of control government worker took his brief case and flung it toward the camera lens in order to try and break it.

At that point, the newsroom mantra was "The camera must be protected at all costs" (the mantra didn't include "who cares about the reporter or photographer", but I thought that was implied). That's why I stepped in front of the swinging brief case to protect the camera and I was hit directly in the eye.

Although the blow hurt, I was thrilled thinking this is going to make great video for our story. Viewers, and those who give out awards love it when the reporter is the victim of a physical confrontation with "the bad guy."

The assailant ran off and I started to go after him, but since he was driving a government car and we had video, I knew I would be able to track him down, which we did. Unfortunately, the guy who hit me with the brief case didn't work for OSHA, but instead was an undercover "Narc" who worked for the DEA. Had he mentioned that instead of going ballistic when we were taking his picture, we would have turned off the camera and not used the video. The man however, didn't want to tell us where he worked, because he had been disciplined in the past by the DEA for parking in the OSHA spots, which were closer to the elevator than the DEA spots, and he was concerned he would be disciplined again.

Once I figure out who the man was, I called the U.S. Attorney, Bob "Mad Dog" Merkle. I told Merkle about the incident and said I would let the matter drop if the DEA agent called and apologized. Merkle said he would contact the DEA agent, but wasn't sure if the man would issue an apology.

A day later Merkle called me and said the DEA agent was adamant that he would not apologize and I said, "I have an assault and battery on tape and if I don't hear from him by the close of business today, tomorrow morning at 9 a.m. I going to the Tampa PD to file a criminal complaint, which will negatively affect his career and might even cost him his job."

Merkle got the message loud and clear and said to expect to hear from the agent by the end of the day. Around 4:55, I did get a call and an apology, but it was not the most heartfelt apology I've ever received, but I did let the matter drop. I didn't mind the black eye; I was just pissed the agent didn't work for OSHA and I couldn't use the video in the story. Which turned out well, but not as exciting as it would have with a briefcase to my face.

THE DUMP OF THE CENTURY

THE NUMBER one question people ask me is how do I get my stories? I'd like to think it's because I'm incredibly good looking and smart, however I am committed to the truth and the honest answer is that 99 percent of the stories come to investigative reporters via tips. That was the case in a major story that went national and changed the way prisoners were treated at the Hillsborough County Jail. We called it "The Dump of the Century."

It began when we got a call on a Monday morning in February of 2008 from a man who said he was a quadriplegic. He made quite a claim—that he was dumped out of his wheelchair as he was being booked into the Hillsborough Jail. Then he said the magic words: he could prove it.

I told the news managers and producers this could be a huge story if it was true, but at that point I just had a phone call and the man's words to go on.

Photographer Adam Vance and I drove to the man's house and Brian Sterner explained on camera that he was arrested about two weeks earlier for fleeing and eluding a law enforcement officer. It involved a traffic violation from the previous October.

Even though Sterner was a quadriplegic, he had some movement in his hands and could drive a car with special attachments on his steering wheel. According to Sterner, when he was brought into the jail in a wheelchair, the booking deputy didn't believe he was a quadriplegic because he could drive.

He told us the deputy, Charlette Marshall-Jones, told him to stand up and get out of the wheelchair. Sterner says when he told her he was not able to do that, she dumped him on the floor.

I told Sterner if this was true, his story would become national news, but was probably going to be his word against hers. That's when Sterner dropped the bombshell that made my investigative reporter juices run with excitement. He said, "The entire incident is on tape." Sterner explained that everything in the Hillsborough jail was recorded on several cameras from various angles and he was positive the incident was caught on tape.

This revelation was like when Alexander Butterfield, who was an aide to President Richard Nixon before becoming the head of the Federal Aviation Administrator, told the world that Nixon taped everything that went on in the Oval office while he was in office, in order to preserve everything for history.

While this disclosure didn't approach the far-reaching impact of the Nixon tapes, the fact that the Hillsborough Sheriff's Office taped everything in the jail was something nobody in the media was aware of, and it changed how arrests were covered in Tampa Bay forever.

After we interviewed Sterner, I called the Sheriff's Office around noon and made a public records request for a copy of the tape and any incident report that was filed as a result of the Sterner arrest. I told them I needed it that day.

The Public Information Officer I talked to, J.D. Callaway, said he would call the jail and get back to me. Within minutes Callaway, a former newspaper reporter, who in my opinion, seemed to hate the media after he left journalism, called me back. That was a surprise, because I felt he rarely did anything quickly to be helpful and I thought he was a general pain in the butt to deal with. It was a true disappointment that someone who was an excellent "cops and courts" reporter when he worked for the *Tampa Tribune* appeared to have such distain for his former colleagues when he left the business.

Almost everyone I knew who had to deal with Callaway felt the same way.

Anyhow, on this particular day Callaway told me the guy who makes the copies of the tapes at the jail gets off the clock at 3 pm and if he could make a copy beforehand, we could have it.

Photographer Adam Vance and I drove to the jail at 2 o'clock to wait to get a copy of the tape while I called the station, reiterating this could be a huge story. I explained I would need extra time on air, but only if the tape proved what Sterner said was true.

The time waiting outside the jail seemed to drag by and I was concerned, because I had told the producers to leave a three-minute hole in the six o'clock news (which is huge for a daily story), for my segment. Keep in mind the average "news hole" in each half-hour newscast is only 11 to 13 minutes because of weather, sports and commercials. So, I was asking for 25 percent of the "news hole that night, however at that moment I wasn't sure if we had a story or not.

Finally, around 3 o'clock, I had Adam go into the jail to see if the copy had been made of what I knew would be TV gold, while I listened to the video we shot earlier with Sterner, and sketched out the story I planned to do if the video supported it.

Shortly after 3, Adam walked out of the jail with a DVD. We were really excited, but still had no idea what we would see. We popped the disc into my computer and saw Sterner being wheeled into the booking area, just as he said, but then he sat there for a minute or two having a discussion with a booking deputy, who we later learned was Marshall-Jones. Then just as Sterner said, she walked behind the wheelchair and dumped him on the ground.

"Holy Fuck!" we both screamed as we watched in amazement. Not only were we appalled at how the deputies could be so cruel and callous to someone in a wheelchair, but also, we both realized the implications this story and tape would have.

"This is going to be huge!" I stopped the DVD, replayed it and was stunned to see it again. There was Sterner dumped from the wheel-chair, crumpled onto the floor and no one helped him. In fact, one deputy, who we learned later was a supervisor, Corporal Steven Dickey, walked past the camera, smiled and "appeared to think it was funny."

That phrase is extremely important because it plays into the lawsuit Dickey filed against me because of this story. More on that later.

I asked Adam if they said anything in the jail when they gave him the tape and whether they had an incident report, which is usually generated if something unusual happens at the facility. Adam replied, "The guy who made the copy was just interested in getting off the job on time. He handed me the DVD and said there was no incident report."

I immediately called the station, said we had a grand slam homerun and asked them to give me as much time as possible in the six, and to plan on my doing something more in the 11, but first I had to contact the Sheriff's Office.

I called Callaway and thanked him for getting me the DVD, but also said I had to show it to him. Callaway must have taken a "nice pill" that day because he said, "Sure. How quickly can you get to the Sheriff's Operation Center?"

It was about a 10 to 15-minute drive from the Orient Road Jail to the Sheriff Operation Center in Ybor city and I told Callaway I would be there quickly. It was already 3:40 and I needed to have the story for the six o'clock news.

When we went into the Operation Center, I had my computer with me and I played the DVD for Callaway. The look on his face was priceless, but to his credit he did not scream, "Holy Fuck!". In a candid moment after the incident, Callaway admitted he was thinking something like that. All Callaway said was, "This has just come to light today, so the review is very active." He then reiterated there was no incident report because the Major who ran the jail said that as far as he was concerned, the jail didn't have a problem with, or cause a problem for, any inmate.

By now it was after 4 p.m. and we raced back to the station and hit the newsroom fairly close to 5 p.m. I immediately recorded an audio track and Adam edited like a madman to get the long piece done in time to lead the 6 p.m. news.

Our executive producer, Carolyn Dolcimascolo, came over to the editing bay and suggested shots as we ran the wheelchair dumping several times at regular speed and in slow motion to match my audio track. We included some of Sterner's interview where he said not only was it degrading to be dumped from his wheelchair, but also, that he hit the concrete floor so hard he broke two ribs. And of course, we played Callaway's reaction to the tape of the dumping.

I had to slap on some make-up (just enough so it didn't look like I needed a shave) because I was doing a "set piece" where the anchor introduces the reporter, then I introduce the story and come back at the end to chat with the anchors about what we've just seen.

As soon as I got off the set and into the newsroom, the phones started ringing off the hook. Viewers were outraged, and I was told by my friends at the competing stations, managers in other TV newsrooms and at the two major newspapers went crazy trying to get what they could regarding the story.

The *St Petersburg* (Now Tampa Bay) *Times* wrote:

"Hillsborough sheriff's spokesman J.D. Callaway said the agency is looking into what happened to Brian D. Sterner, 32, during his Jan. 29 booking at the Orient Road Jail.

Footage aired on WTSP-Ch. 10 Monday night showed a uniformed officer unseating Sterner from his chair, then searching him as he lay on the floor where he had fallen. Callaway said he could not provide the booking video to the Times on Monday. He offered no explanation for the actions of the officer. 'That will all come to light in the coming days,' he said." [4]

It was really a great scoop, and because we were the only ones with the video, we really did have a grand slam homerun. As I recall, some outlets used a still picture of our video and had to credit the station. CNN heard about the story in between our 6 and 11 and I did a live talkback with the video for them.

CNN wasn't the only network that was interested. One of my good friends, Don Wood, who works for NBC, told me after our story aired, his marching orders were to get Sterner and Attorney John Trevena, another friend of mine whom Sterner hired, on the Today Show. Don was successful and the next day, Sterner and Trevena were flown to New York to talk with Meredith Viera.

Meantime, for the 11p.m. I wanted to try to get some of the deputies who were involved, but that seemed like an impossible task. It was after hours, no one at the jail would talk to me. While Florida had probably the most liberal public records law in the nation, the addresses and phone numbers of law enforcement personnel are exempt from disclosure.

While I was going over the video of the wheelchair dumping for the 11 p.m. piece, I got a call from a woman who was irate about my story that aired at 6. From the moment I picked up the phone and said, "10 News, Mike Deeson," the caller started screaming at me.

To be honest, it didn't faze me because of the stories I do; it is not uncommon for someone who is a target of one of my stories or is a relative or friend of the target to call me or e-mail me to say what a complete asshole I am.

So, the caller kept haranguing me about the six o'clock story saying I didn't know what I was talking about regarding the wheelchair dumping, and that the supervisor, Corporal Steve Dickey, was not laughing at the fact that Sterner was dumped from the wheelchair. The woman angrily told me I needed to make a retraction at 11pm. I asked her how she knew all of this and she told me, "I am Steve Dickey's wife."

Thrilled at this revelation, I asked if I could talk to her husband, but she refused and then told me that if I didn't make a retraction, they would sue me, which they did. Getting sued is a pain in the ass even if you are right.

In the Dickey lawsuit, he didn't have a leg to stand on, because he was initially suspended by the Sheriff's Office for his involvement (the Union was able to get that overturned). In addition, Dickey was considered what's called a "semi-public figure" and that makes the standard of proof in a libel case much higher.

That stems from a case called Sullivan vs. the *N.Y. Times* where the court ruled that to libel a public person, a reporter has to have had reckless disregard for the truth with malice toward the subject.

Although Dickey claimed I disparaged him by implying he was laughing at Sterner, the judge granted a summary judgment, meaning he believed there was no way a jury would convict, and it would be a waste of court time to go forward.

The lynchpin in the argument in front of the judge at the summary judgment hearing was my videotaped deposition. During the depo,

Dickey's attorneys kept hammering away for almost two hours about how their client was not laughing at Sterner and that I had misinterpreted what had happened.

At the end of the deposition, one of Dickey's attorneys asked a question he didn't know the answer to, which is a major mistake in the legal field. He said to me, "Knowing what you know now, would you have written the story any differently in regard to Corporal Dickey?"

I looked at him and said to his surprise, "Absolutely not!" The shocked attorney said, "What in the world do you mean?" I replied, "I said in the story, *the Sheriff will have to live with the fact that one of his deputies dumped a quadriplegic out of a wheelchair and another appeared to think it was funny.*"

I added, "At the time, it *appeared* as if Dickey thought it was funny, it will appear five years from now as if he thought it was funny and it will appear the same way 25 years from now!" Then I admitted, "I have no idea if Dickey *actually* thought it was funny or not, but that is what it *appeared* to look like on the tape the day I first saw it and that's how it will appear in perpetuity."

Dickey's lawyer was clearly unprepared for that answer and said, "I have no more questions."

When we went to the summary judgment hearing, after our attorney, George Gabel, a silver-haired senior partner in one of the largest law firms in the state, Holland and Knight, went through the standard for public figures, he played the last section of my video deposition regarding whether I would have done anything differently, and then we rested our case.

Within a day, Judge William Levin dismissed the lawsuit and issued a summary judgment.

Meantime, back to the night of the wheelchair dumping story. As I was putting the 11 p.m. piece together, our 6 p.m. story had hit the wire and the internet, and I was getting calls from the network, and around the country. My hunch had been right—our Sterner wheelchair dumping segment became a national story.

The next day, the Sheriff's Office had a news conference at the operations center in Ybor City. All the media from Tampa was there, and I must admit there was great satisfaction in knowing I had scooped everyone.

At the time of the incident, Hillsborough Sheriff David Gee was out of town at a conference and I thought he'd made a huge mistake in not flying back to Tampa to deal with the situation.

Instead, the Sheriff had Chief Deputy Joe Docobo, a character out of Central Casting, do the news conference. Docobo was a strait-laced, chiseled-faced, humorless man whom I'd never seen smile in all the years I have covered the Sheriff's Office. Docobo said that he watched the video for the first-time last night and found himself "in disgust" and "appalled at every level."

Docobo also announced that the two corporals and sergeant involved were on administrative leave with pay, and that the jail supervisor on duty did not have knowledge of the incident.

Eventually the Sheriff released a statement that gained national attention. CNN described it as follows:

"The Hillsborough County, Florida, sheriff on Wednesday offered a personal apology to a disabled man who was dumped onto the floor from his wheelchair while in deputies' custody.

"I am personally embarrassed and shocked by the horrific treatment Mr. Sterner received," Sheriff David Gee says in a statement on the department's website."

The statement went on to say,

"A video now making the rounds on television networks and various websites shows a deputy tipping Brian Sterner, 32, out of a wheelchair at the county's booking center in Tampa on January 29.

"I cannot and will not even try to offer an explanation for what is seen on the video, other than to say that once it was brought to my attention, I immediately initiated an internal investigation," Gee said.

"'This deputy ... she looked at me, she didn't believe that I was a quadriplegic, I guess, and she walked behind me with those handles on the back of that hospital-grade wheelchair and she just dumped it straight forward,' Sterner told Tampa television station WTSP." [5]

Eventually the Sheriff returned to Tampa and had a meeting with Sterner and his attorney, John Trevena, about the story which had now gone viral.

Here's what appeared in the *St. Pete Times*:

"Gee said he apologized to Sterner face-to-face during their first meeting Friday night. 'To say this is unacceptable is an understatement,' Gee said during the news conference. 'I will not attempt to explain why this deputy dumped this man from his wheelchair. There can be no rational explanation. I don't think I will ever understand the reasoning for such actions.' Until late Friday, sheriff's officials had been unable to speak with Sterner of Riverview, because he spent much of the week in New York making appearances on national television shows like Today. News of Sterner's treatment first broke on Monday night during a WTSP-Ch. 10 newscast." [6]

When Sterner finally met with the Sheriff, he arrived at the Sheriff's Operations Center in Ybor City just after 5 pm Friday in an airport limousine. He struggled to get out as reporters swarmed the passenger's side. His legs shook uncontrollably as he made his way into his wheelchair. As he made his way up a handicap ramp, he stopped the chair in front of the center and looked up at the ceiling. Internal affairs Sgt. Danny Tewmey opened the front doors to allow Sterner inside.Besides offering words of contrition to Sterner, Gee publicly asked the forgiveness of citizens for the incident, which he said has "brought disgrace on this office and every employee here."

But the allegations didn't stop with Sterner. After the news of the video recordings at the jail surfaced, attorneys for others who claimed they had been abused at the jail started making public records requests for tapes showing the infractions and then would hold news conferences to show the alleged abuse.

By now, the Sheriff's Office tried to close ranks and told reporters that what looked like excessive force, was actually justified, and that attorneys were trying to piggyback on the Sterner case looking for a big payday.

The public outcry was so huge, however, that Sheriff David Gee had to take some kind of action.

The *Tampa Tribune* explained:

"With accusations of inmate abuse surfacing on a regular basis, Hillsborough Sheriff David Gee has announced the creation of an independent review commission to study the policies, practices and procedure in the Orient Road and the Falkenburg Road Jail... Sterner's treatment on Jan 29th by Deputy Charlette

Marshall-Jones resulted in her arrest on a felony charge of adult abuse and her resignation after 22 years with the agency. The video of the then-inmate's treatment made its way around the globe prompting outcries from the public and an apology from Gee." [7]

Because of the public outcry over the dumping, the Sheriff appointed a commission to study how inmates, and particularly those who have disabilities, are treated in the jail. Some of the findings were used in other parts of the country to ensure that those who are arrested and booked into jail are dealt with in a humane manner.

And while Sheriff Gee initially thanked us for bringing the issue to light, he took a "dump" of his own on me. As is the case in so many stories, when you peel back the onion, more and more people come forward and more dirt rises to the surface. That was exactly what happened in the next several weeks.

Gee finally had enough of our negative stories and put out a news release which he sent to all the TV stations and newspapers saying he was cutting off all relations with our station because he said I had a vendetta toward him. All the newspapers and other TV stations covered it, which in some ways was irritating, but also a badge of pride that I had rattled the Sheriff and the Command Staff at the Agency.

According to the Sheriff I had been turned down for a job as a Public Information Officer, which was a bald face lie, and he said that's why I was doing the negative stories. The reason I did the negative stories is because of the myriad of problems that I uncovered in the Sherriff's Office. It is important to note that it is called the Sheriff's Office, because it is a political position and the Sheriff is an elected official. Clearly Gee didn't like the heat.

Here's how the Tampa Tribune described the incident:

"This time, the Hillsborough County Sheriff's Office says, TV reporter Mike Deeson went too far. The agency Wednesday announced it will no longer send media notifications about news conferences and other newsworthy events to Deeson's station, WTSP, Channel 10. The decision came after an incident this afternoon in which the WTSP reporter "verbally berated a civilian employee of the Sheriff's Office in what we believe to be an unethical, abusive and threatening incident of unprofessional conduct," according to a news release from the Sheriff's Office.

Ken Tonning, WTSP president and general manager, stands by his reporter and denies any wrongdoing. 'He got passionate, but was he disrespectful? He denies it,' Tonning said. 'We're very concerned over this and will not back off.' At the end of a Deeson story on a Wednesday evening newscast, a station anchor said Deeson had reported several stories critical of the Sheriff's Office and that the station stood by their reporter but would talk to the Sheriff's Office about the agency's concerns.

Tension between the Sheriff's Office and Deeson came to a head Wednesday when the agency held a news conference to respond to an attorney's allegations of police misconduct. Channel 10 was not invited to the news conference because of Deeson's 'pattern of abusive conduct toward the Sheriff's Office and its employees, coupled with Channel 10's disregard for previous complaints about Mr. Deeson's conduct,' according to the statement." [8]

When I challenged him to provide my application for the job, he couldn't. I reminded the Sheriff one of my colleagues, Bill McGinty, was the one whom applied for the PIO job. Gee relented and did an hour interview on camera with me to talk about the problems I uncovered.

And two days later the office rescinded the ban as described in the St Pete Times:

TAMPA — "After meeting with top executives from WTSP-Ch. 10, the Hillsborough County Sheriff's Office Thursday rescinded a ban on providing news releases and notifications of news conferences to the CBS affiliate.

Two days ago, sheriff's officials announced they were suspending contact with WTSP. Sheriff's officials accused reporter Mike Deeson of verbally berating a civilian employee and having a vendetta against the agency because he was turned down for a job there in 2004.

Both sides said they have resolved their issues for now after a summit at the Sheriff's Office. The meeting included Hillsborough County Sheriff David Gee, Chief Deputy Jose Docobo and Deputy Larry McKinnon. From WTSP were general manager Ken Tonning and news director Darren Richards."

But neither WTSP nor the Sheriff's Office would say what will change, despite the fact that officials in Gee's office have accused Deeson of serious journalistic misconduct.

'We felt that the meeting was very productive ... (allowing us) to express our concerns and to have a voice,' said McKinnon, one of the sheriff's public infor-

mation officers. 'We felt confident that they were sincere when they said they would review our concerns.'

Richards said Deeson would keep offering incisive stories — he has a regular report on government waste called 'What's That Costing You?' — though Richards declined to say how WTSP would address Gee's concerns." [9]

Bottom line had the tape of the incident not existed, I believe the Sheriff's Office would have said Sterner was lying and the incident never happened. Which why I firmly believe every police officer in the country must wear a working body cam. It sometimes protects the police officer and shows he or she did the right thing, but in some instances where law enforcement goes too far and beyond the pale as it did with Sterner, it is there for the whole world to see and I believe will cut down on police abuse of an innocent person.

SEXTING CAN CAUSE MEMORY LOSS

WITHOUT A DOUBT, my favorite soundbite of my more than 50 years in the business came from Hillsborough Property Appraiser Rob Turner, a clean cut, straight-laced, yuppy dressing guy who had a job he could have kept forever. The property appraiser in Florida is an elected constitutional officer who reports to no one but the voters.

It's a six-figure job that rarely draws a serious challenger, which means the job is basically for life, and in addition to the huge six-figure salary, there is a six-figure tax payer funded pension if the official stays in office for more than 20 years, which is normal, unless the official steps on his or her dick....and that is exactly what happened with Turner.

Turner was elected to office after the previous property appraiser got caught in a series of scandals including violating election laws, drinking on the job and allegations of sexual harassment. Turner seemed like an Eagle scout compared to Ron Alderman.

As the *St Pete Times* explained in an article after Alderman was arrested on domestic violence charges in 2005, his time in office was an investigative reporter's dream and a public embarrassment.

"First elected Hillsborough property appraiser in 1988, Alderman survived two stormy terms in office. After being re-elected without opposition in 1992, he

was upset by political newcomer Rob Turner in 1996. By then, Alderman had jokingly begun to refer to himself as 'the most investigated man in Florida.'" [10]

In his first term, Alderman ran afoul of election laws, was accused of keeping his cronies on the payroll and got caught on WFLA-Ch. 8 videotape barhopping during business hours. (That great investigation came from one of my competitors, Steve Andrews, at Channel 8, who happens to be the father of Fox sportscaster Erin Andrews.)

As an aside, because we were both longtime Tampa Bay investigative reporters with moustaches, viewers often confused us for each other. The day after a Sunday football game, for example, I'd often talk to someone giving me a tip who would finish the call by saying, "You must be extremely proud of your daughter, I saw her reports during the football game yesterday." When that first started, I used to correct callers and point out they were confusing me with Steve Andrews at Channel 8, but as I told Andrews, I finally stopped correcting them, and when they said, "You must be very proud of your daughter," I'd respond, "Yes, I *am* very proud of my daughter." Which I was, but I never mentioned being proud of her for *other* things than being a sideline reporter on NFL football, because that wasn't my daughter's job. Andrews told me he also talked to confused viewers who asked him about the songs he had written. (*I* am the investigative reporter who writes music and *his* daughter is the sports reporter.)

In his second term, Alderman rented campaign office space from purported organized crime figure Joe Digerlando, was investigated by the Florida Department of Law Enforcement and the state Department of Revenue and was faulted for using inequitable assessment methods that benefited his associates.

Alderman was cleared of criminal allegations, but his office continued to generate controversy. His top lieutenant, Deputy Appraiser Donald Beach, quit when confronted with a history of ethics violations and allegations of sexual harassment. His community affairs director, Maida Cronin, got suspended when she was found to have faked both her high school diploma and college attendance on a job application.

So, Turner easily defeated Alderman, and from all appearances ran a smooth operation that could have kept him in office until he retired.

Respected by his peers, he was elected president of the International Association of Assessing Officers, an organization that offers training for people in jobs like Turner's. Despite the rumors Turner wasn't in the office 40-hours a week, news stories regarding that never surfaced.

The news story that exploded in his face, however, came from a scorned lover, Carolyn Filippone, who also happened to work for him in the property appraiser's office.

Filippone acknowledged in an EEOC suit that she filed against Turner, that the two once had "an adult relationship" in 2006, which she alleged Turner, though married, tried to "rekindle" four years later.

Among the allegations in the EEOC suit were that Turner not only sent suggestive text messages to Filippone, that his wife discovered, but also sent her several pornographic pictures.

In the suit, Filippone also charged that Turner tried to transfer her to a satellite property appraiser office as punishment. Turner later said he felt compelled to fire Filippone because she filed a false EEOC suit against him.

The day Filippone was fired, word spread through the property appraiser's office and I got a tip that Bill Varian, a top-notch reporter at the *St. Pete Times*, was going to break the story the next morning.

The tip came in about 3:30 p.m. and I pieced together enough information to do a story for the 6 o'clock news that night, before Varian's story broke in the *Times* the next morning. In all fairness, Varian had all the details of the tawdry event and I only had a partial picture for my story at 6, but I had only been able to work on it for two-and-half hours before we hit air.

The next day, however, I sat down with Turner, whom I always got along with, for what turned out to be an extremely uncomfortable interview for him.

We talked about all the allegations Filippone had made in her EEOC complaint. Then I got to the question about her contention that, among other sexual items he sent her, Filippone said he had texted her a picture of his penis.

I remember looking Turner in the eyes as I sat across from his desk with the camera rolling. "Rob, she said you texted her a picture of your penis, what do you have to say about that?" I expected a flat-out denial, an indignant *"That is the biggest fucking bullshit lie I have ever heard!"* or anything else other than Turner's response: "I don't recall sending her a picture of my penis."

"I don't recall sending her a picture of my penis!" I could hardly catch my breath. I wanted to say, "Are you fucking kidding me?" That means not only did he take a picture of his penis, but he admitted he conceivably *could* have sent the picture. There is no other soundbite that could ever top that, although one did come close from a woman who lived in a mobile home in rural Polk County which was in our viewing area.

As background, every time I have covered a story where someone's home was destroyed or damaged by a tornado, the victim invariably mentions the horrendous noise before everything "went to hell" and that "It sounded just like a freight train!"

On this occasion in Polk County, a woman in a mobile home escaped serious injury when a freight train backed through a berm and tore her mobile home apart.

When I interviewed her about this tragic incident, I almost lost it when she said it was horrible and then added, "The noise was horrific, it scared me to death! It sounded just like a tornado!"

I once swore I would retire if anyone ever said something like that on camera, until Rob Turner's "I don't recall sending her a picture of my penis." The "It sounded just like a tornado!" was my all-time favorite, but the "I don't recall sending her a picture of my penis" soundbite certainly topped that.

Meanwhile, Turner stubbornly refused to resign and drew primary opposition from State Senator Ronda Storms, a polarizing political figure that I happened to get along with famously.

Ronda, a County Commissioner before being elected to the State Senate, was known for her ultra-conservative views, including having the county adopt a policy "that Hillsborough County government abstain from acknowledging, promoting or participating in gay pride recognition and events;" ending the county's funding for planned parenthood because it taught teens about safe sex; and causing a stir in the black community when predominately African American Florida A and M wanted to establish a law school in Tampa and Ronda noted,

"We can get them through law school, but we can't get them to pass the bar."

In addition, Ronda had a tart tongue, publicly blasting county employees who failed to live up to her expectations. The prime example was when an assistant county attorney, whom most in the know were aware she was having an affair with a high-profile county executive, came before the board to explain some issue the county attorney's office had a position on.

Ronda looked at the woman and said something like, "Have that large-breasted tart step away from the podium and have someone else come here and explain the county attorney's position."

There was another side to Ronda, though, that most people never saw because of her position on so many issues.

She had, like they say in Boston, a wicked sense of humor. A liberal weekly publication featured a letter to the editor filled with "F' bombs regarding Ronda's conservative views; the former English teacher responded by saying she was completely offended by the letter. Ronda never mentioned the content which eviscerated her, however, she instead focused on the improper grammar the letter writer used with his "F" bombs, explaining he used the word "fuck" in the adjective form when it should have been used in the adverbial form and so on.

Even though I disagreed with Ronda on her social stances, I admired her for being so comfortable in her skin. She was born with a cleft lip, and we had this exchange when I was about to interview her following a luncheon where she was the keynote speaker.

She said, "A plastic surgeon came up to me after my speech and said, 'I can fix your face.'" After catching her breath from the indelicate comment, Ronda went on. "I said, 'And what is wrong with my face?'" She said the doctor stuttered and stammered and said, "You know, your...uh ...er... hare-lip." And that's when she said, "When I was a child, I was teased over and over about my hare-lip and it made me who I am today."

She added, "While I clearly have the money to do something to change my appearance, there's no way in hell I would do that. I am fine, and as a matter of fact, *thankful* for the way I look."

But the most spectacular part of Ronda's public persona that many didn't know about, was her total commitment to the welfare of children in the state of Florida.

Ronda sometimes called to tell me about a problem involving children that needed public attention and it would turn out to be a great story. Whenever I interviewed her about such issues, I would kid her and say, "Ronda, be very careful." She'd say something like, "What do you mean?" And I'd tell her, "You're starting to sound like a liberal." She'd wrinkle her nose and say, "Mike, cut that out."

There was a great life lesson I learned from Ronda: politicians are not black and white or good or bad, but shades of grey. And some that I may disagree with on certain issues have good points on others.

Meantime, Ronda, who was morally offended by Turner's indiscretions, opted out of a safe Senate Seat to run against him. She crushed him in the primary, but in a county-wide run, her ultra conservative views didn't play well, and she lost to another former State Representative, Bob Henriquez.

Bob, a bright, personable guy who went to Princeton, came back to Tampa to become the head football coach for Tampa Catholic, where he went to high school. He told me after winning the election that he thought of using the flex time in his new office to keep his head coaching job, but added "The thought of you catching me on camera in my coaching shorts with a whistle around my neck was enough of a nightmare to shelve that idea."

Finally, we had someone in the Appraiser's office who was aware of the power of having the right image. Though seeing Henriquez in his gym shorts would never cause a stir like Turner's famous sext, but it sure would have made for great video and a story that would have raised eyebrows regarding his commitment to the six-figure job he was elected to. Whether it was fear of me catching him in gym shorts or his commitment to the job, all I can say it was a good call for a good man!

TAMPA BAY: THE BARE FACTS

WHILE PORN BROUGHT Tim Marcum down, it brought me another Emmy for an investigative piece I did about pornography in Tampa Bay. The city had the reputation for years as the nude dancing mecca of the country with numerous strip joints, including the world-famous *Mons Venus*.

The word in Tampa for any convention that came to town was that people had two goals besides attending meetings and conferences: The first is have a steak at the world-famous Bern's Steakhouse—which claims to have the world's largest wine cellar with 600,000 bottles and the restaurant says the wine list is bigger than the New York phonebook. As I explained before, President, whoever is in office, almost always eats at Bern's when they stay overnight in town. The second on the list for many convention attendees is to go to Mons Venus, the most risqué nude nightclub in Tampa and perhaps in the country. I never heard of any President making that part of his Tampa experience!

The owner of the Mons, Joe Redner, is a fascinating man who knows First Amendment law better than most attorneys.

As Tamara Lush of the Associated Press explained just before the Republican National Convention came to town in 2012:

"Redner started the club 30 years ago. Back then, according to him, his main pursuits were "drinking, philandering and snorting cocaine."

He knew nothing about business or politics. But over the decades, he stopped drinking and doing drugs, became a vegan, a businessman and a progressive politician.

At one point, the Tampa Bay Times *reported that he was worth $18 million. He has a deep box of yellowing newspaper clippings from around the world, chronicling his outspoken, and some would say outrageous, views.*

'The clubs in Tampa wouldn't have notoriety if it wasn't for Joe,' said Don Kleinhans, the co-owner of 2001 Odyssey, a strip club across the street from Mons Venus that's notable for its large, silver spaceship where patrons can obtain expensive, and more personal, lap dances. 'He just has strong beliefs in his rights and his freedoms.'

Redner says his biggest accomplishment has been in the battles he's waged against local, state and federal governments — some successful, others not. After opening his first strip club — Redner prefers the term 'adult entertainment club' — he was arrested 36 times on obscenity charges by officials. He claimed that it was his First Amendment right to operate the club.

In 2000, Redner vehemently opposed the so-called 'six-foot rule,' a city ordinance preventing adult entertainers from coming within six feet of their clients. The rule is still on the books, but isn't enforced." [12]

During the battle between the nude clubs and the city over the six-foot rule, the police raided the clubs on a regular basis and arrested strippers, sometimes even the customers. After the police made another of their nightly raids, we often ran a story the next day about the arrests and Redner was more than accommodating.

While the photographer I worked with that day tried to tastefully shoot video of the dancers on the stripper pole, I went into the office to talk to the owner and listen to him cite Supreme Court opinions that what his "dancers" were doing was protected First Amendment speech.

I found him fascinating, especially since he was one of the few people I ever encountered who had been rehabilitated in prison and came out a new man who had shed his drug-using ways.

The Mons has a stable of regular dancers who actually paid Redner to be able to dance there, as they made their income from the tips they got from "lap dances," which some have called a step away from prostitution. Because of its reputation and the fact that it's totally nude dancers could pull in several hundred dollars a night, top strippers from around the country came to dance at the Mons.

As *Deadspin journalist* Sean Manning wrote prior to the 2012 Republican Convention:

"Inside is just as unassuming: an octagonal stage surrounded by chairs, padded booths along the mirrored walls, a cocktail table or two. There are no cocktails, however—Tampa law prohibits alcohol in full-nude clubs. Instead, waitresses take orders for bottled water, soda, and Red Bull. There's no DJ—the girls play their own songs on a jukebox. There are no private "What are they doing in those rooms." Celebrities don't get any special treatment at the Mons.

'Shaq O'Neal wouldn't come in 'cause I wouldn't let him in free with his entourage,' Redner says. 'I figure he makes enough money, let him spend some of it.'

What makes the Mons such a popular workplace is its laissez-faire approach toward its principal product. A girl can work every night a week or just one. There is no schedule. And provided she retains her looks, she can come back to work no matter how many months or years she's been away, no advance notice necessary: just walk in, hit the dressing room, and hop onstage. The only rules are a three-hour shift minimum; no leaving and coming back; no drugs on the premises; and no customers touching between the dancers' legs." [13]

One of the times we went to Mons I was working with video photographer Mike Dixon who had a wicked sense of humor and an ability to shoot nice video, but Mike rarely pushed himself to work too hard.

As an example, he and I worked together on a story I did featuring a car dealership about to be indicted by the U.S. Attorney's office. When we got on location, Mike asked, "How many shots do you need? Two, three, four?" I looked at him and said, "Mike the only video we have is the interview with two senior citizens who were victims of the car dealership, some paperwork, a shot of the U.S. Attorney's Office and the dealership." Mike continued, "Five, six, seven—will that cover the story?" Exasperated I said, "Mike, it's a two and half minute piece! You know what video we have; you tell *me* how many shots we need."

The point is that Mike NEVER overshot on a story. On this particular day he shot the naked dancers while I talked for about 20 minutes to Joe Redner in his office. I walked back into the strip club which was very dark, and I didn't see Mike. I ran out into the parking lot and he wasn't in the station truck, so I went back into Mons and asked the manager, "Did you see the photographer that I came in with?" She pointed to the stage where the dancer was in her third set, which meant she was stark-ass naked and there was Mike sitting with his camera almost in her crotch. He'd been shooting from the time we walked into the strip club.

I walked up to him as I saw the camera capturing the dancer in her complete naked glory and said, "Mike, we can't use that video." He turned to me and said, "Trust me, it will be put to very good use!"

Meanwhile, as I mentioned earlier, strip clubs and the six-foot rule violations were often in the local news. Bob Buckhorn, who was a city councilman at the time and later became Mayor, admitted that he was overzealous in pushing the city to enforce that ordinance. Each time we did another story on it, however, instead of using file video of naked dancers we went back to the strip clubs for new footage, much of which we had to blur to hide certain anatomical parts.

One day when we were assigned another six-foot rule story, I suggested to photographer Mike Dixon that instead of the Mons, we go to Thee Dollhouse, which was more upscale. It featured a buffet lunch and liquor as well because the dancers were not completely nude and wore skimpy thong bottoms and pasties

When we got to Thee Dollhouse I went in and asked the man who appeared to be the manager if we could shoot inside. He explained he wasn't in charge, but that the manager would be there shortly, and I could wait for him at the bar.

In addition to the buffet and the practically naked dancers, Thee Dollhouse had a wall of TVs adjacent to the bar playing mostly sports channels. On one of the monitors I noticed an infomercial for a golf method encompassing the "Single Plane Method" developed by a golfer named Moe Norman, who most agree was the purest ball striker in all of golf.

In occurred to me after I stood in front of the TV with the infomercial playing (with the sound down) that I was staring at *it* instead of at the mostly naked women on stage, because I was more interested in improving my golf game than I was in watching them. It was one of those moments where I realized I was getting old.

The important point, though, was that Tampa Bay was filled with strip clubs and women willing to parade around in a state of undress, and many were more than willing to be part of an ever-growing adult film industry in Tampa Bay. And with some of the top talent in the adult stripping industry coming to Tampa on a regular basis, it was only natural for the porn industry to take advantage of that talent.

Although rumors persisted for years that porn was big in Tampa, it was tough to get those involved to agree to talk to a reporter. As the industry continued to grow and thrive in the area, I kept trying to pierce the wall that was determined to keep reporters out.

I contacted a guy named Paul Allen who, at one time, published a sports magazine in the area that morphed into an adult magazine called "NightMoves," which sponsors the third largest adult industry awards in the country. I explained what I was trying to do, and he agreed to help, however everyone he contacted or put me in contact with was worried I would do a "hatchet job" on their business.

It took more than six months of face-to-face meetings, telephone calls and assurances from not only Allen, but also Joe Redner, to convince potential interviewees that I would treat the industry fairly and not be judgmental. A number of producers, distributors and actors finally agreed to talk to us. Now I had to convince the station that this was a worthwhile story that our viewers would be highly interested in and that I could pull it off tastefully.

"When people ask me in a grocery store what I do for a living, I tell them I have sex and I get paid for it. I'm Caylee O'Toole. I live in Tampa."

"I love showing up in front of the camera," is what Shelly Berlin, a Tampa adult film actress, told us adding, "I love sex and I get paid to do it!"

That's how our story began and all those involved in the industry were extremely candid about what they did.

As Paul Allen, who runs the annual NightMoves Awards Show in Tampa explained, "There's a whole lot of sex movies that are shot right here in Tampa. It's a 10-billion-dollar industry and people don't understand that General Motors, who owns DirecTV makes more money in the porno film industry than Larry Flynt." Allen added that Tampa is a hot spot for the porn industry.

Adult producer Christopher Blue told us, "I love shooting outdoors, that's part of the ambiance of Florida."

Ironically those in the industry believed the moral crackdown on nude dancing was helping the porn movie business.

Producer/Actor Mack Cannon explained that ever since the city council and the Mayor put pressure on the strip clubs, the girls were making a lot less money. "So, we've got girls beating down our doors to do videos now."

The enforcement and raids at the nude dancing clubs finally ended, but the industry continued to thrive. Producer John Fantasy said, "We probably get 50 calls a week from girls or couples that want to be in movies." Christopher Blue agreed saying, "I have had people from Tampa, Lakeland, Punta Gorda, Bradenton, all over the Florida area. It is one of the few parts of the entertainment business in the world where somebody off the street can get into show business."

At the time we did the story, the industry was so popular, 711,000,000 hard-core movies were rented a year, and that didn't include the moves that were *sold*.

The reason so many producers want to get into the industry has a lot less to do with sex, and a lot more to do with money. Mack Cannon explained, "People aren't producing these things for the fun of it. People are making money and a lot of it."

A Florida porno distribution company turned into a nonstop factory as it duplicated, packed and shipped out tapes all day long. Each year the adult industry releases 10,000 new videos; the demand is huge.

While some may protest porn on moral grounds, with increasing technology that allows hard-core material to come right into the home, expect more in the future rather than less.

Since the story initially ran, technology and the internet have made it even easier to produce and distribute porn. That galled the ultra-conservative Sheriff Grady Judd in Polk County, adjacent to Hillsborough County where Tampa is located. Judd, who was once asked why his deputies shot a suspect 63 times answered, "Because we ran out of bullets," had undercover deputies obtain online pornography from a housewife and her husband who were legally producing it in their own home. Judd convinced a politically like-minded judge that it was obscene, and they were arrested in their home. To avoid a lengthy court battle, the couple plead guilty to a lesser charge, agreed not to do any more porno in Polk County and moved somewhere else. Wise move!

Meanwhile, one of the challenges of doing that story was to get video that showed adult films being shot in Tampa Bay without it being so salacious the we couldn't put it on TV. When I mentioned the problem to adult movie industry insiders Mack Cannon and his wife Shelly Berlin, they invited me to their home to screen which videos we could use.

The couple, which had high paying jobs before getting into porn, lived in an upscale neighborhood in Tampa that actually wasn't far from my house. They said they both were making much more money making porn films than when they had regular jobs, and they added they were having a lot more fun.

When I got to their house, I ended up on a couch adjacent to the one they were sitting on. They put in the first video saying, "This might have a scene or two you could use."

As soon as the tape started playing (this was before DVD's dominated the industry) I saw a close-up of Shelly having oral sex with another actor. It didn't faze them in the least that I was watching this; it was like they were showing me their home vacation movies.

It was more than a little unusual for me, however, and uncomfortable as well—not that I'm opposed to watching an adult movie, but it was a bit weird to be sitting next to the woman performing the sexual act on the screen. I didn't know where to look—at her, the video, the ceiling or what?

They finally decided the blowjob scene wouldn't work for my story, so they put in another tape showing Mack, Shelley and some other woman doing all sorts of sexual acts, and again we all decided it wasn't appropriate either. We kept going through additional porno tapes until we found a couple of outdoor scenes with downtown Tampa in the background that we could fuzz out enough to get on TV.

The story worked out really well and actually won two Emmys, one for me and the other for video photographer Gene Yagle, one of the most talented photographers in Florida and probably the country. Although I've been fortunate to win several Emmys, they pale in comparison to how many Gene has won.

The night we won for "Porn in Tampa Bay," the ceremony was in South Florida, as it was most of the time. That year, however, in 2001 it was at the Miccosukee Indian Reservation and Casino, one of the weirdest places for the awards. They were usually at big hotel and resorts, such as the Fountain Blue or Eden Rock in Miami, or big-time resorts in Ft. Lauderdale or Orlando.

They were always black-tie affairs and, like the Network Emmys, they played a clip of the piece after the envelope was opened and they announced the winner. You then give a short thank-you speech and the music starts playing if you talk too long.

On this particular night, Gene's category for photography had come up and he won, but my reporting category was much later in the ceremony. The winners were announced by various TV personalities in our chapter, which covers Florida, Puerto Rico, Louisiana and a couple of other states.

Anyhow, the woman who was one of the two people announcing my category stepped to the microphone before revealing the winners and said, "We are all blessed. We should all thank God and say a silent prayer of thanks for being here."

Then she continued. And although she worked in New Orleans as a reporter or anchor, it was clear she did not like debauchery of any sort when she opened the envelope and exclaimed in disgust, "Oh no! Here it is again, 'Porn in Tampa Bay!'"

As I ran up on stage, she handed me the Emmy with a look of revulsion and I'm sure if she had such powers, instead of handing me my Emmy, she would have turned me into salt like Lot's wife. I don't think she was any too pleased when, in my acceptance speech, I mentioned that reporting on the story was actually a labor of love.

TAKING DOWN AN ICON

THE MOST REVERED coach in the Arena Football league was Tim Marcum. Marcum was the league's winningest coach who had captured seven titles, but he was also a collector of emails that freely use the "N" word; his computer was full of racist jokes and pictures; and there was evidence of his viewing and sharing hours of extreme pornographic images.

Among a small sample of some of the e-mails was an image of Air Force One during the Obama administration years with the word "Watermelon One" superimposed on it; a takeoff on Nicorette Gum that used the "N" word instead of "Nicorette;" a spoof of *Sesame Street* called *Ghetto Sesame Street* and finally, one missive comparing Michelle Obama to a chimpanzee.

We broke the story and used Marcum's own words from video depositions that were taken in a lawsuit between Marcum and the former owner of the team. We had obtained the video from a confidential source, but we needed to hear Marcum explain his actions to us, and we were intent on getting Marcum on camera. The team was getting prepared for the 2011 season at the *St. Pete Times* Forum, now Amalie Arena, where both the Tampa Bay Storm and the NHL Tampa Bay Lightning played. Both teams were owned by former hedge fund manager Jeff Vinik, who made a bazillion dollars in Boston and wanted to own a hockey team. Vinik bought the Lightning, moved to the Tampa area and became a major developer of downtown Tampa.

In our effort to get Marcum on camera, an offer he declined, photographer Tim Burquest and I waited and waited and waited for Marcum to show up for practice.

Finally, he drove up and walked into the building. Tim and I chased after him and I started firing questions. Marcum moved faster and faster until he got into the Forum and headed for the elevator. Fortunately, the elevator didn't come right away. I kept interrogating him and when the elevator finally arrived, Marcum got in and pushed the button. I jammed my foot in the threshold making the elevator door open and shut as I continued asking questions and he kept denying he did anything wrong. Finally, I had all I needed and let the door slam.

The story caused a furor through the sports community, not only because Marcum was such a successful coach, but also because he was more than friendly with some of the people reporting on the team.

Popular radio personality, the late Steve Dumig on WDAE, blasted our coverage of this Tampa Bay icon, so I called the show and got into a heated debate with him. Over and over Dumig defended Marcum and said it wasn't a story. "The Big Dog," as he was called, asked me if I had ever watched pornography and I told him, "Absolutely! And I think most of my friends have. However," I added, I NEVER use the "N" word or pass along jokes using that word."

Nonetheless, Dumig kept harping on what a terrible person and reporter I was for exposing his friend, and I told him he was way off base.

Happily, *St. Pete Times* Reporter/Columnist Tom Jones agreed with me as he wrote in his column: ***Most Indefensible***

"Tampa Bay Storm coach Tim Marcum is taking heat after it was learned that his work computer contained pornographic material and e-mails that contained the "N-word" and other racist remarks. The story was first broken by Ch. 10's Mike Deeson after he dug up a deposition Marcum gave as part of a lawsuit against the Storm's former owner.

What's almost as disturbing is those who defend Marcum by blaming Deeson for uncovering the story. It wasn't Deeson who forwarded the e-mails and, based on his past, Marcum has proved he doesn't need anyone's help to get in trouble. And, yes, this is a story. The coach of a local professional football team and a known public figure

allegedly forwarding racist e-mails? That most certainly is news. And this isn't about free speech. No one is suggesting Marcum be sent to jail." [11]

Still, for many of Marcum's supporters, excelling on the field over-rode his problems off the field. His fans wanted to overlook the bad behavior, which also included two drunken driving arrests and convic-tions and an arrest on insurance fraud.

The Monday after I broke the story about Marcum, Jeff Vinik held a news conference about his pride and joy, the Tampa Bay Lighting, to announce a new logo for the hockey team.

When I arrived at the news conference, Lightning PR head Bill Wickett saw me and immediately knew why I was there, as did every other reporter in the building. Wickett's main goal that day was to promote the announcement of the new logo for the Lightning and he certainly didn't want me being "the turd in the punchbowl," which he knew I had no problem doing.

Wickett came up to me after talking to his boss and said, "If you avoid asking about Marcum during the news conference, Vinik will give you a one-on-one interview afterwards."

I knew it was a gamble to go along, because they could just end the news conference and Vinik could bolt, edging me out of the interview. I felt confident I would be fine, however, because I said to Wickett, "If I agree and Vinik screws me I will hunt him down and label him a liar."

Wickett was a decent guy and he promised that wouldn't happen. And Vinik, who had been straight forward and upfront since the day he arrived in Tampa Bay, didn't seem to be the kind of guy to blow off a reporter.

My instincts were right. Vinik began his news conference about the Lightning, saying he wanted to build a world class organization on and off the ice with first class values. He kept his word and talked to me one-on-one afterwards.

I asked Vinik if he felt sending out hardcore pornography and racist e-mails were reflective of the goals for his organization. Vinik said the organization was doing an investigation to see what happened.

As soon as the story had hit though, Marcum claimed he didn't do anything wrong. And while the values Vinik said he wanted for his organization certainly didn't fit racist e-mails and hardcore pornography, the new owner of the team wasn't ready to part ways with the most successful coach in Arena League history.

Vinik turned me over to Chief Operating Officer, Todd Leiweke, who handled most of the day-to-day operations of the hockey team. Leiweke explained Marcum was on paid suspension. He said the team encouraged him to leave the building and take a time out. And during that time, the owners would determine if the Storm coach would survive this storm.

Four days later Marcum was out as head coach. As he faced reporters he said after 15 years, he would step down. And with that, the winningest coach in Arena Football League history ended his association with the team.

CEO Tod Leiwike, who was also at the news conference, chimed in to say that what Marcum did on the field was very impressive, however the off-the-field actions were what led to the coach's downfall.

While the organization said Marcum would do one-on-one interviews after the news conference, we wanted to sit down and give him the opportunity to complain about the stories that exposed what he had done. The coach declined.

He *did* have a special goodbye, however, as he left the news conference. He told reporters it has been great and he appreciated everyone. Then Marcum pointed at me and said, "Especially you."

INTERVIEWING THE GREATS

A HUGE BENEFIT of being journalist is that I've been able to meet some famous and interesting people and that included my childhood hero Chicago Cubs Icon, Ernie Banks. Actually, I interviewed him twice.

Here is the story about my two "Ernie Encounters." First, I will never forget how wonderful Ernie Banks was to me. The Hall of Fame baseball player, known as "Mr. Cub," was the number one hero of all the people I grew up with, and no doubt that was true of most people my age who lived in Chicago in the 1960s.

The first time I interviewed Ernie was more than 50 years ago (I am an old fart). I was a young radio reporter at the time, still in college but working for station KTGR in Columbia, Mo.

The Cubs were making a run for the pennant (until the Mets spoiled that). Anyhow, I walked up to him before the game and asked if I could do an interview. He said, "Old Ern is pretty tired these days," I thought he was going to turn me down, but then he added, "Would you mind if we did the interview in the Cubs dugout so Old Ern can sit down?" Growing up a Cubs fan I couldn't believe I got to sit there in the dugout with Ernie Banks, where he treated me like a long-lost friend.

After the interview, he asked who else I had talked to. As I told him which players I'd already interviewed, he asked why I hadn't talked to "Fergie," meaning Ferguson Jenkins who was inducted into the baseball Hall of Fame in 1991. I explained that Fergie was scheduled to pitch the next day and looked too busy throwing balls in the Cubs bullpen to talk to me. Ernie said, "Come on," and took me up to Jenkins. He introduced me, remembering my name which gave me a thrill, and said Fergie should talk to me. As Ernie walked away, he turned to me and said, "If you have any problems getting interviews with anyone 'Old Ern' will be sitting in the corner of the dugout, so come see me," I could hardly believe it.

Years later after he retired, Banks participated in a charity homerun derby in Norfolk. By then, in 1979, I was doing TV news. Our sports department didn't have anyone to cover the event, so I volunteered. I told Ernie about our first encounter years earlier and what a great impression he'd made on this young reporter. The Hall of Fame baseball player smiled. "That makes me happy. I always tried to treat people the way I would like to be treated and I'm glad it made an impression on you." *WHAT A CLASS ACT!* They don't make them like that anymore. Ernie, I hope you're resting in the heavenly dugout getting ready to play two.

That day that I first interviewed Banks at Wrigley Field, the Cubs were playing the San Francisco Giants. Little did I know that years later I would be covering the Giants' potential move to Tampa Bay, but on that day, back in 1969, I talked to many of the big stars on the team.

One of my most memorable experiences: trying to get an interview with the biggest of the big stars, Hall of Famer Willie Mays.

I had talked to several players on the Giants team as they took batting practice and worked out in the infield and outfield before the game. I was about to approach Mays, but before I could ask him for an interview, a reporter from *Jet* magazine beat me to it. At the time, *Jet* was the premier African American magazine. Their reporter walked up to Willie Mays who, though in the winter of his career, was still one of the biggest stars in baseball. The reporter (whose name I can't remember) introduced himself and said, "Hi, Willie. I'm here for our interview." I was shocked to hear Mays answer in a high squeaky voice, speaking in the third person. "Willie's not giving interviews today."

The *Jet* magazine reporter protested, saying, "Willie, you're the cover story for next week. We talked about doing this interview today!" Mays looked at him again and repeated, "Didn't you hear me, Willie is not giving interviews today!" And then he walked away.

Clearly, I wasn't going to approach him, even though Mays had a reputation for being pretty affable, but he certainly wasn't on *that* day. I asked the guy from *Jet* what he was going to do. "I'm going to call my editor and tell him I'm spending another night in Chicago." I nodded. "What if Willie isn't giving interviews tomorrow?" The reporter said he hoped Mays would be in a better mood the next day, and if not, *Jet* would have to do a different cover story. It was a good lesson for a young journalist, 21 at the time: Even the stories you plan in advance don't always work out the way you hope.

I was lucky enough to be in on one of the great Tampa Bay sports stories of all time: Phil Esposito, the Hockey Hall of Famer, may have pulled off his most impressive plays of his life when he convinced a group of Japanese backers to finance a $50 million bid for a hockey team and convinced the National Hockey League to grant an expansion franchise to Tampa Bay. Phil became the general manager and president of the franchise, which really had no place to play.

The team ended up playing its first regular season game in October of 1992 in the 11-thousand-seat Expo Hall at the Florida State Fair grounds. It was hardly a National Hockey League venue, but the Tampa Bay Lightning shocked the Chicago Black Hawks with a 7-3 win.

From the tiny Expo hall, the Lightning moved the next year to the Florida Suncoast Dome (which eventually became Tropicana Field where the Tampa Bay Rays—first known as the Devil Rays—played) and started drawing crowds of 25-thousand people in a city which many predicted would never be a bastion of Hockey—that is until the Lightning came to town.

The team realized that it had to have a stadium more suited for Hockey and eventually, in partnership with the Tampa Sports Authority, built the arena originally named the "Ice Palace," now known as Amelie Arena in downtown Tampa.

The building was completed in time for the 1996 season, but before it officially opened, there was a huge celebration and dedication. All the dignitaries from Tampa arrived for the ceremony on a steamy, summer Tampa day. To protect people from the summer sun, the organizers of the event erected a huge tent, which did its job as a sun protector, but also acted like a sauna holding in the humidity.

There was an ice sculpture of the Lightning logo that melted faster than the wicked witch after being doused with water. Meanwhile, the speeches seemed to go on forever.

After the event finally concluded, close to the noon newscast, I went up to Phil to do an interview and said, "Phil, this must be one of the proudest moments of your life, to not only bring a team here to Tampa Bay, but to see the dedication of this spectacular arena for hockey in Tampa." Phil looked at me and said, "Mike, you want to know what I really think?" Of course, I said, "Yes, I do." Phil said, "I think it is awfully fuckin' hot and this ceremony went on too goddamn long!" Suddenly, a panicked look crossed his face. "We're not live, are we?"

I laughed. "Good time to ask, Phil!" and then I revealed we weren't live and that our interview was all on tape.

Fast forward to 2012, the 20th anniversary of the Lightning in Tampa Bay, and Phil was on our noon newscast to talk about the team and how big a success it had become for Tampa Bay, including winning the Stanley Cup in 2004.

After the noon newscast, our producers wanted something with Phil for the six o'clock news and though I was working on an investigative story, I was the only one in the newsroom at that moment who knew anything about sports or hockey, so I conducted the interview.

I reminded Phil about his colorful language at the dedication ceremony and his concern that he had dropped an "F-Bomb" on live TV, and he let out a huge laugh.

Phil, who despite his fame, was one of the most down-to-earth athletes or persons of any stature for that matter that I ever met said, "Yeah, that sure sounds like me." By this time, he was the "color announcer" on the Lightning broadcast team and had done several network hockey games. He noted, "Whenever we do a live broadcast, the producer or someone always says, 'Phil, remember we are on live

TV or live radio, so, just remember, whatever you say goes out for the entire world to hear.'"

Being in the local television business, I rubbed elbows with people from all walks of life. One memorable celebrity I got to meet was Cybil Shepherd, a former model and Hollywood star, winning critical acclaim in the *Last Picture Show* and *Taxi Driver* and dominating the TV airwaves in the mid-80's with Bruce Willis in the popular show, *Moonlighting*, and following that, the *Cybil* show.

I met her in the late 70's when she was between movies, touring the country doing local theater with "A Shot in the Dark." At the time, I was doing "The Mike and Lynn Show" a noon newscast/talk show that our general manager at WAVY TV, the NBC affiliate in Norfolk, created as a local midday version of the "Today Show." I was "Mike" obviously and "Lynn" was Lynn Fischer, who, in her bio, describes herself as a model/actress—an apt description.

Cybil had ended up in Norfolk at the "Tidewater Dinner Theater of the Stars" which brought in some well-known actors and they always came to appear on our show.

The day she first came to the station to be on " The Mike and Lynn Show", we also had some kindergarten kids there. Whenever we had little ones on the show, at the end of the interview, I'd shake the boys' hands and ask the little girls to give me a kiss on the cheek, which they always did.

When Cybil sat down for the interview, she was hilarious and candid. It was a great interview and the time flew by. As we were wrapping up, Cybil, who had been there for the kids' segment beforehand, looked at me and said, "Aren't you going to ask me for a kiss like you did the other little girls?" I said, "Absolutely!" and expected quick little peck on the cheek, but that was not to be. Cybil jumped out of her chair, grabbed me around the neck and planted a big on-the-lips kiss that almost made my chair tip over! It was a great TV moment, and she laughed and laughed.

Her play ran in the area for a couple of weeks, and because she was such a great guest the first time, we had her back, and again she was wonderful— a charming, funny, beautiful woman. As the interview was wrapping up, we thanked her and Cybil looked at me and said, "You know what time it is!" Once again, she jumped of her chair and laid another big smooch right on my lips. *Bruce Willis eat your heart out!* Not a shy bone in her body, and at least in the two times I met her, no Hollywood ego—just as down to earth as she could be. I will always have warm thoughts about her and as Jimmy Carter said, I will always "lust in my heart" for Cybil Shepherd.

We had other notable guests on "The Mike and Lynn Show" and the most amazing was Roy Rodgers, King of the Cowboys. During all the times we did the show, the guests would come, do the interview and then leave without much fanfare, but not Roy Rodgers.

The day he arrived at the station—of course, we'd been promoting his appearance for weeks—a crowd of more than 350 people gathered outside and even spilled into the lobby. This man was a superstar. When Roy finally came in, he was mobbed by the crowd, signed some autographs and then we took him to the "Green Room" (I don't know where that term comes from, but clearly one was once green and every TV studio and theater stage worth its salt has one) where our guests hung out and relaxed before they came into the studio. When we got to the Green Room, Roy turned to me. "Was there a little boy downstairs in the lobby in a wheelchair?" I told him that I thought there was but wasn't quite sure. He asked me to go and check, which I did.

It turned out he was right, and Roy said, "I've got to go downstairs and talk to him." I reminded him he'd be mobbed again. "I don't care," he said. "If a little boy came here in a wheelchair to meet Roy Rodgers, he's going to meet Roy Rodgers." It was really touching how he interacted with that boy.

When we got into the studio and started the interview, we knew ahead of time that Roy was booked for a 13-minute segment. We kept talking, however, and we asked if he could stay through another segment and then another. Before we knew it, he was there for the entire show, a full hour answering question after question, including why he stuffed his horse Trigger after Trigger died. He was as nice in person as the character he portrayed on TV, white hat and all.

Roy had come to the area because he was going to make an appearance on the Christian Broadcasting Network with its founder, Pat Robertson. CBN was in Virginia Beach, a city adjacent to Norfolk.

Many of the guests we had on "The Mike and Lynn Show" came our way courtesy of CBN. Which meant we had more than one opportunity to interview CBN Founder Pat Robertson.

CBN was the first Christian Broadcast Network in the country. CBN started on a small UHF station that launched into a massive powerful network, now seen by almost 96 percent of the country.

Pat, an ultra-conservative, anti-feminist and anti-gay media mogul, is known for making outrageous statements like, "Gay people wear a ring to cut people when they shake hands and then infect straight people with AIDS." He also said that he wore a magic necklace to repel gay people, that women needed to be totally subservient to men, that abortion was a lesbian plot, and so on. He was extremely smart, however, with a law degree from Yale, and also extremely well-connected in political circles, as his father served for more than 30 years in the U.S. House and U.S. Senate.

The most memorable interview I did with Pat was after CBN furloughed several people who were angry about being laid off. Not only did he address the issue head on, he also wanted to take live calls on the air during our program. I was in awe. Quite frankly, I didn't buy anything he said, but I couldn't believe how he looked right into the camera, smiled and convinced people that it was in their best interest to move on to something else. By the end of most of the calls, people were actually thanking Pat for leading them to something better.

Even back in the 70's Pat made rumblings about running for President and for liberals and progressive thinkers like me, that was frightening. His vision of America was not only ultra-right-wing conservative, but also a country that would be a Christian Nation. And with his political connections and his ability to manipulate the TV camera, I worried he could actually convince a nation to vote for him. As we have learned with the election of Donald Trump, someone who knows how to manipulate the TV camera can be a powerful and almost unstoppable force in politics.

Another ultra-conservative guest we had on the show was also a real-life hero who had undergone unbelievable torture as a prisoner of the Viet Cong: Jeremiah Denton. Denton was a Navy commander whose plane was shot down in July of 1965. He was routinely beaten and tortured for eight years, spending four of those years in solitary confinement, where he tried to communicate with other prisoners by tapping out signals on the cell floor and wall.

His treatment as a POW was unthinkable, and as he described in his book, *When Hell Was in Session*, he endured many incidents like this one:

"A special rig was devised for me in my cell. I was placed in a sitting position on a pallet, with my hands tightly cuffed behind my back and my feet flat against the wall. Shackles were put on my ankles, with open ends down, and an iron bar was pushed through the eyelets of the shackles. The iron bar was tied to the pallet and the shackles in such a way that when the rope was drawn over the pulley arrangement, the bar would cut into the back of my legs, gradually turning them into a swollen, bloody mess. The pulley was used daily to increase the pressure, and the iron bar began to eat through the Achilles tendons on the backs of my ankles. For five more days and nights I remained in the rig." [14]

Denton endured torture like this over and over and then in 1966, was forced to participate in a televised news conference where he was questioned by the North Vietnamese about his feelings regarding the war. Denton replied, "I don't know what is happening, but whatever the position of my government is, I support it fully. Whatever the position of my government, I believe in it, yes, sir. I am a member of that government and it is my job to support it, and I will as long as I live. I believe in it, yes, sir."

More importantly, however, while Denton appeared in the televised news conference, he used Morse code to blink out the letters "T-O-R-T-U-R-E."

As Denton explained when he appeared both on our show and when he spoke to the *Los Angeles Times:*

"The blinding floodlights made me blink and suddenly I realized that they were playing right into my hands," he wrote. "I looked directly into the camera and blinked my eyes once, slowly, then three more times, slowly. A dash and three more dashes. A quick blink, slow blink, quick blink...." [15]

While his impromptu blinks silently told the world that prisoners were being tortured, he was unabashed in the interview, which was later broadcast around the world, in his denial of American wrongdoing.

Following that interview, Denton was tortured even more brutally than in the past. As he told us, one of the ways he was able to endure the horrible treatment in Vietnam was to replay in his mind the images of the America he loved, knew and left to fight for. But when he returned home in 1973, he found a much different country than the one he'd first left and imagined through his time as a POW. What he shared with us was similar to the thoughts captured in that same *Los Angeles Times* article about Denton:

"After he arrived back in the U.S., Denton signed on for a different kind of war -- a never-ending battle against what he believed were immoral and godless forces destroying America from within. When he was recuperating in a naval hospital, he viewed films of Woodstock, the 1969 rock festival, and vomited at the sight of 'hippies fornicating publicly, high on drugs.'" [15]

Denton wrote in a 2009 epilogue to his book:

"To me it was a nightmare...this nation, firmly founded as One Nation Under God, was in the process of becoming a pagan nation with a shocking degeneration of national integrity." [14]

In an interview on the WorldNetDaily website (WND) Denton said, *"I saw the appearance of X-rated movies, adult magazines, massage parlors, the proliferation of drugs, promiscuity, premarital sex and unwed mothers. That scenario was coupled with the tumultuous postwar Vietnam political events, starting with Congress forfeiting our military victory, thus betraying our victorious American and allied service men and women, who had won the war at a great cost of blood and sacrifice."* [16]

That was the tone of much of our interview with this true American Hero, who fought for the country he loved and wanted to somehow take it back to the way America was before the drastic changes it underwent while he was in captivity.

He was a fascinating person to interview, but the sadness he felt about America was palpable. It clearly shook him to his core. I truly admired what he had endured and I appreciated and respected his love for America, but as someone who went to college in the '60's and thought the war in Vietnam was wrong, I vehemently disagreed with his desire to turn back the clock and make the country what it was before he left. Talking to Denton brought out great sadness in me, not only for the pain and torture he suffered through, but also by the fact that he couldn't accept the more progressive country to which he had returned. Quite honestly, at the time I didn't know, and today still don't know, what made me sadder.

Denton, by the way, eventually moved to Alabama, was elected to the United States Senate where he pushed a conservative agenda for his one term, and was then defeated by Democrat Richard Shelby who later became a Republican.

Denton eventually died in 2014 in a hospice in the Norfolk area.

On a much lighter note, our interview with Colonel Harland Sanders, the founder of Kentucky Fried Chicken, was one of the funniest we ever did. "The Colonel," as he was known, (who really wasn't a Colonel, he got the title from a Kentucky Governor) was able to build his chicken empire by driving through the South, going into restaurants and begging them to let him prepare his "finger-licking," pressure-cooked chicken for the staff. If they liked it, he would convince the restaurant owner to use his secret recipe of 11 herbs and spices for a percentage of the business.

The Colonel, who always wore a white suit, had white hair, a white goatee and a black string tie, told us that though he failed in business several times, he was convinced he would always succeed, because money was not his main motivation. It was all about making people love his chicken.

He also explained that he never smoked, rarely drank alcohol—save for an occasional glass of wine—never played cards and didn't like people who did, but he didn't have a problem with cussing. He admitted in colorful terms he often used the Lord's name in vain, but always felt bad about it and said he was sorry. He couldn't help himself, however, when he saw an incompetent person, and the word "idiot" just flew out of his mouth.

By the time Colonel Sanders came to our show he was close to 90 years old and had sold the company— which at that point was owned by Pepsi. He told us , "I didn't give a Damn (and offered if he weren't on TV it might have been stronger using the Lord's name in vain again) about what people thought."

Although the Colonel still loved his original recipe for Kentucky Fried Chicken, the company was also doing very well with what it called "Extra Crispy" KFC. I'd heard that the Colonel, who at the time was doing public relations for Pepsi and KFC, didn't like the "Extra Crispy" too much and planned to ask him about it. In fact, right before the commercial break ended as we were about to introduce the Colonel, he leaned over, tugged on my pants and whispered, "Be sure you ask me about the KFC Extra Crispy."

After getting through some of the background on the Colonel, who had been close to bankruptcy several times, the history of KFC and the success of the company, I asked the question he was waiting for saying, "Colonel, I have heard you are not fond of the new Extra Crispy version."

His eyes lit up, he sat up straight and with a twinkle in his eye, said, "Not fond, not fond.

It's a damn fried grease ball with no taste and no resemblance to my Kentucky Fried Chicken!"

I said, "Colonel aren't you getting paid by Pepsi to promote KFC, including their Extra Crispy chicken?" And once again, he straightened up and bellowed, "I don't give a *damn* what they want, it tastes like a fried grease ball and I wouldn't eat it on a bet!" He then added, "The new gravy the company has come up with is really good, if you want to use it as a paste for wallpaper."

The Colonel, whose father died when he was five years old, explained that because he'd had so many failures and was able to bounce back, he wasn't afraid to tell the truth or speak his mind about anything. He was totally charming and expressed several other opinions about the restaurant business and fast food and didn't pull punches throughout the entire interview—a true delight.

About a year into our run of "The Mike and Lynn Show" at WAVY, our general manager, Ed Frecht, decided it would be a great idea for us to interview movie stars who were promoting their latest flick.

Since the advent of easy-access via satellite, such interviews are currently conducted with the movie star sitting in a studio, usually in Los Angeles, wearing an earpiece and doing interview-after-interview with TV personalities they can't see, but only hear. In this way, they promote their movie, book or whatever they're trying to sell to multiple media outlets.

Back in the '70's, however, that technology wasn't inexpensively available, so movie studios flew local TV personalities to a location where they did the interviews on 16-millimeter film, which is what we used back then for news stories.

The movie studios paid for everything and I remember saying to our station General Manger, Ed Frecht that it didn't seem "journalistically" right allowing the studios to pay. He was insistent telling me, "We don't have the budget, but we want the stars, so don't worry about it." I shrugged my shoulders and said, "Ok, you're the boss," and did what I was told (I was much younger then).

The best "Movie Junkets" were for films produced by 20th Century Fox, because the studio did everything top-notch, from flying journalists first class to putting them up in the fanciest hotels wherever they went and even providing a photographer who shot the interview.

When I flew to Los Angeles, I would usually interview the stars for three movies in a whirlwind, three-day trip, and I rarely paid much attention to what movies I would be seeing or what stars I would be talking to until I got on the long plane trip to L.A.

On one trip, I remember getting on the plane sitting in first class, sipping a Bloody Mary and looking at *Time* magazine before we took off. I noticed the cover had something about an unknown movie, *Star Wars*. I thought to myself, "*Star Wars, Star Wars, where the hell have I heard that?*" I reached into my briefcase, took out my press packet and saw that one of the movies I was going to see and do interviews for was indeed *Star Wars*.

The next day we watched *Stars Wars* at the Academy Theater in Los Angeles and then we were driven to the 20th Century Fox studios for the interviews. Mark Hamill (Luke Skywalker) was extremely friendly and excited to be in this movie. Harrison Ford (Hans Solo) was pleasant, yet it was clear not only to me, but to the others who interviewed him, that he didn't really want to be there and wasn't into the publicity "thing," however it was part of his contract. Then there was Carrie Fisher (Princess Leia).

Fisher was hysterical and great fun, but I was highly distracted during the interview because the zipper on the black pantsuit she was wearing was moving down throughout the entire interview as we talked, and I must confess I kept staring at her underwear.

There was no way to stop the interview and tell her to zip up her pants because we shot everything on film, we were on a tight schedule and they counted you down, giving you exactly five minutes with each star.

After shooting the interview they moved the camera behind the star to get a "two-shot" over the shoulder of the star (in this case Carrie Fisher) and then me on camera. While we were doing the two shots, I explained that I might have been distracted because of the zipper. She thought that was the funniest thing in the world and said we should have talked about it. I was feeling pretty good thinking; "*Princess Leia thinks I'm extremely funny.*" However, years later when I read an excerpt from her autobiography, I learned she was high on cocaine and pills through most of that era, so it was the drugs, not me, that she found so charming.

Larry King was another one of my favorite interviews. It happened during the Florida Republican Party Presidential convention in 2000 in Orlando. Every GOP candidate came to Orlando vying for the nomination and it attracted media from all over the Country, including King, who was doing a nightly interview show on CNN.

King was a huge personality and we wanted to do a story with him, so we contacted his media people in order to set it up. We were told he was extremely busy, and it might not happen, but we got a call one afternoon during the convention saying we could talk to him for 10 minutes and that was it. Photographer Gene Yagle and I went over to the hotel where King was staying, knocked on the door and we were ushered into his suite.

King was sitting on a couch with a white shirt, beige pants and his trademark suspenders, but he didn't have any shoes or socks on, just bare feet.

As Gene was setting up, King, in his iconic gravelly voice, looked at both of us and said, "Fellas (that's what he called us) my feet are killing me. I'll make a deal with you two. If you promise not to shoot my feet so I don't have to put on my shoes and socks, you can have a much time as you want!" Since we rarely shot anyone's feet, that was an easy deal to make.

The interview was going great as King, the consummate storyteller, had an unending amount of fascinating tales. However, 10 minutes into the interview one of his "handlers' came in and pointed to her watch indicating our time was up.

King saw that out the corner of his eye and turned to his staffer saying, again in the gravelly voice, "I made a deal! They're not shooting my feet and they get all the time they need." The staffer seemed irritated, but he was the boss and turned back and said once again, "Fellas take all the time you want!" Just a great guy that helped do a wonderful profile of him.

HANGING WITH THE KLAN

ONE OF THE most unique experiences I had in Norfolk is when the Ku Klux Klan decided it was going to try to recruit like-minded members of the Navy, who shared their beliefs. With all the Naval bases in the area, the Klan was convinced it could drum up some interest and announced it would hold a rally in October of 1979.

I contacted a "Klan PR advance man" who was posting me on the upcoming activities, including the fact that Imperial Wizard or Grand Dragon—I think the terms were interchangeable—Bill Wilkinson was going to be in town for the event. He also explained they were going to have a clandestine cross burning the night before the rally, and that all the Klan sympathizers were extremely excited about this.

Clearly, I was apprehensive about going out with the Klan for several reasons, not the least of which was because I was Jewish. After African Americans, the Klan had Jews and Catholics, in that order, on their hate list. Still, I asked the Klan PR guy if there was any chance I could go along with a photographer to the cross burning. He said he wasn't sure, but would get back to me. He fell off the radar for a couple of weeks then the Wednesday before the Friday night rally, the PR guy called and said, "We're going to have the cross-burning tomorrow night and you're invited along with your photographer."

We were told to be on Atlantic Avenue in Virginia Beach at a particular intersection and they would find us at 7:30.

We got to our rendezvous point by 7:00 that night and waited....and waited...7:30, 7:45, 8:00, 8:15. I remember telling photographer Pat Dowd, "They're not showing, they were just fucking with us." Those words had just come out of my mouth when a caravan of crazies drove up and the guy in the lead car shouted, "Get your camera and jump in!"

The thought of getting into a car full of Klan members clad in their goofy outfits, all riled up about burning a cross freaked me out and I said, "We have a ton of equipment, how about we get in line and follow you guys?" Happily, the guy in the front car said, "Suit yourself," and off we went.

The caravan continued down Atlantic Avenue and more and more cars joined the procession, and then we headed to a parking lot adjacent to a woodsy area.

The cars stopped, and everybody in the Klan contingent jumped out and put on their KKK sheets and hoods and ran into the woods. Pat and I followed along (with no sheets or hoods) and then everyone converged in front of a huge wooden cross that looked as if it were made with two huge tree trunks.

At that point Wilkinson, the Imperial Wizard, stepped forward and started going on about how the black man, the Jew and Catholics were all inferior to the fine Klan members who were gathered together.

That's when my internal paranoia kicked in. *They know I'm Jewish, I'm with the media, they're going to beat the shit out of me or worse.* I got a grip and thought, *No, that's not going to happen, and everything will be alright*, until a bunch of the goofballs took cans of gasoline, doused the wooden cross and then lit it...in the middle of the fucking woods!

Now I figured we were all going to be burned to death in a raging inferno and the headline would be: "Jewish Reporter Found Dead Attending KKK Cross Burning."

Obviously, that didn't happen, and my thoughts returned to reality. It was after 9:30 and I had to get back to the TV station and get the story on the air for the 11 o'clock news.

Luckily the rally ended as quickly as it started, we got our butts out of there, headed back to the station and the pictures of that cross burning in the woods were spectacular. When we added the sound of Wilkinson proclaiming the white man's supremacy, it was unbelievable. I thought it couldn't get any better than that, but I had no idea what was going to happen the next night at the recruiting rally.

The next evening was a spectacular fall night with a giant full moon lighting up the Atlantic Ocean and Atlantic Avenue in Virginia Beach. The temperature was in the 70's and hate and protest were in the air.

Whenever the Klan stages a rally in a city, there is always an anti-Klan demonstration to shout down the hate.

On this particular Friday night, the anti-Klan demonstrators were on the west side of Atlantic Avenue, the Virginia Beach Police Department in full riot gear was positioned in the center of the street and the Klan supporters were on the east side.

There were shouts back and forth between the two sides when Imperial Wizard, Bill Wilkinson came forward wearing full Klan regalia. Wilkinson stepped onto a platform and started to speak his hate message into a megaphone.

As he started to talk about the dominance of the white man, about 20 protestors from the Committee Against Racism broke through the line of about 100 police officers and one of them "cold-cocked" Wilkinson with a swift punch to the jaw. It was spectacular as he collapsed like a house of cards, and the next thing we knew there was a full-blown riot.

While the *Norfolk Virginian Pilot*, the local paper, described the skirmish as lasting just a few seconds, that was far from the truth.

Before Wilkinson was hit in the jaw, photographer Pat Dowd and I stood about 10 feet in front of him. Pat was shooting on the first video camera the station had recently bought to replace our film cameras. It was an RCA TK-76, which was the camera body that recorded on a heavy recorder attached by a 10 to 15-foot umbilical-like cable.

I had the recorder on my shoulder as Pat was shooting and the next thing I remember after Wilkinson was down on the ground, was that we were somehow behind him shooting our footage, standing above the crowd.

People were punching, kicking and screaming. A Virginia Beach police officer was about to hit what he thought was a kicking protestor who was on the ground, when the man yelled from the bottom of the pile, "Don't hit, I'm under cover."

Then a K-9 officer tried to break up the melee with his German Shepard, but somehow the dog slipped loose from his collar and the K-9 officer ended up trying to break up the fight with the leash, but no dog attached. He then started running down the boardwalk to retrieve his dog, while Klan members and protestors were screaming, kicking and punching each other.

The police finally separated both sides and the protestors started setting fire to some of their own protest signs, while each side shouted at each other. It was a spectacular sight with the full moon, the burning signs, the riot gear-dressed police and the two sides shouting at each other.

It was a made for TV story...and I know it lasted more than 20 seconds, because, over my protest, the Virginia State Police was given permission by the station to view our video. They looked at it multiple times and the melee actually went on for several minutes.

As I watched the video, it occurred to me that we had been shooting the story in the middle of a riot and could have been clobbered by the Klan members, the protestors, or the police. At the time the adrenaline was flowing, and the potential danger of our situation never entered my mind. It's amazing how brave you can be with a camera in front of you when everything is collapsing around you in chaos. When I looked at the video over and over from the safety of an edit booth at the TV station, however, it hit me that this was indeed very scary stuff.

TRAGEDIES IN SPACE

When NASA started the space shuttle program in 1981 all of the Tampa TV stations—and for that matter almost *all* the stations in the state—sent crews to the Kennedy Space Center, which is about 130 miles east of Tampa.

Watching a shuttle lift off is not only thrilling to see but is also a total sensory experience. The press viewing area is three-and-a-half miles from the launch pad. Like a scene out of a science fiction movie, there's a big countdown clock on site, along with massive loudspeakers, and mission control gives updates to holds in the countdown, as well as when the shuttle will lift off.

Excitement builds as the mission control announcer gets to "T minus ten seconds, nine, eight, seven, six, five, main engine ignition start, three, two, one, liftoff!" The same announcement is given before every mission that explores planet earth and space beyond.

By the time the countdown gets to "T minus five," spectators can see the bright yellow fuel fumes, which on night launches turns night into day. Whenever I was there, I felt my heart beating like a snare drum with anticipation and excitement.

The visual delight of watching a shuttle lift off its giant launch pad always amazed me, but except for the cheering crowd and the NASA mission control updates, an eerie silence initially pervaded the scene. That's because we were three-and-a-half miles away and sound travels much slower than light. The silence never lasted for long, though. All of a sudden, the ground rumbled, the huge mirrors on our satellite truck began shaking and the sound built to a crescendo that was so deafening, you felt it deep inside your chest.

The shuttles were something I never got tired of seeing and covering, especially the launches. Although not as visually dramatic, I also liked covering their return, because it was an awesome technological achievement. The astronauts had to perfectly position the shuttle, burn off extra fuel and then fire the thrusters that sent the craft back to the landing area, sometimes in Florida, sometimes in California. Although the returning shuttle can be flown like an airplane, it has virtually no power and becomes a glider as the astronaut in charge lines it up for touchdown.

At the landing area, you hear a large sonic boom and see the shuttle overhead as it creases the atmosphere and then is guided down onto the runway. A giant parachute deploys and then brings the craft to a halt. What a thrill to see the shuttle land and the parachute instantly fan out! It was something we covered on a regular basis, but I never once felt blasé about seeing it.

Newsrooms, however, often have short attention spans and tire too quickly of stories. The shuttle launches and landings were a prime example of that. Although I thought these space missions still held the public interest, by 1986, after 24 successful launches, those in charge shouted me down and said they'd become as commonplace as airplanes taking off and landing each day at Tampa International Airport. So, we stopped going over to Cape Canaveral where the Kennedy Space Center was located to cover the launches.

While the news managers believed there was no interest, I often pointed out the fact that on days when there was a launch, most of the newsroom and people from other departments in the station went out to our private Sky 10 helicopter pad in the back of the building, and looked toward Cape Canaveral.

On clear days you could see the white smoke from the shuttle climbing through the atmosphere on its way to space. You could feel the excitement from those on the helicopter pad, but those in charge either couldn't feel it or didn't see what was going on in front of their own faces.

January 28th, 1986 was one of those unusually cold winter days in Florida. The air was crisp, the sky was absolutely clear, and NASA was about to launch STS-51, the 10th flight of the Space Shuttle Challenger. Since this was the first shuttle flight that had a civilian school teacher, many other stations and the national networks covered the launch. But for some reason, our management, in a decision I am sure they regret to this day, decided not to send a crew to the Kennedy Space Center and instead decided to take a network feed of the liftoff which those in charge of our station decided had become all too routine. Not a good call.

At the time I was anchoring our noon newscast and because I always helped write the broadcast, I waited as long as possible to finish up before going outside to watch the launch at 11:38 with a group of my colleagues.

As the Challenger lifted off, within 45 seconds there were "oohs" and "aahs" from our helicopter pad as we viewed the thick white smoke and watched the shuttle climb into the atmosphere on its way to outer space. Then to our horror, at 73 seconds into the flight, when mission control said, "Challenger go with throttle up," and the commander, Dick Scobee said, "Roger, go with throttle up," the shuttle exploded. 130 miles away in Tampa we could see the smoke-filled split that looked like horns on a medieval monster.

Our noon producer, Barbara McCleod, stood next to me on the helicopter pad. "Mike, does it always do that?" I gulped and replied, "Barb, no! There's some kind of a problem, we better get inside and be on the news set as soon as possible. I'll adlib into the network video and we'll show what we have and say what we know."

It was a good plan, but totally useless. In 1986 we were still an ABC affiliate, and by the time I got inside, onto the set and put my microphone on and earpiece in so I could hear the control room, Peter Jennings was on the air with a special report that ran throughout the entire noon newscast.

By 12:30 when I was able to leave the anchor desk although we never hit the air, because our entire show had been preempted by the network, the station had already sent several crews to the Kennedy Space Center. I was assigned a story in a nearby county with a science instructor who had applied to be the first teacher in space.

It was about a 45-minute drive to her school and she had to leave by 2 p.m., so we had to hustle to get there.

I remember seeing remnants of the contrails of the exploded shuttle in the sky as we left the station and it gave me a sick feeling. It was a precursor of the horror that went through the entire country after 9-11, as everyone focused on a terrible event and the loss of the seven astronauts: Commander Dick Scobee, Michael J. Smith, Ellison Onizuka, Judy Resnik, Ronald McNair, Gregory Jarvis and of course, the first teacher in space, Christa McAuliffe.

As we rushed to the school in order to arrive before the teacher had to leave, we worried we wouldn't be able to find the location or make the deadline. This was before the days of GPS and cell phones. We used huge map books available for each county that were hard to navigate.

I was the one looking at the map, and photographer Bert Moreno was driving. Somehow, we missed the street we were supposed to turn on and I realized we'd gone about 15 minutes north of our turn off. Now we were panicking that the teacher would leave before we could get our interview, but we made it to the school by 1:55. The woman, whose name I can't remember, was finishing up an interview with another TV station and she agreed to stay past her deadline to do our interview. She, like most of America, was shaken. I don't remember much about our conversation except that she said if she had to do it all over again, she would still apply to be the first teacher in space.

For the next several days we did story after story about the Challenger. We did profiles about the astronauts, reports about the broken "O" ring seals that couldn't handle the unusually cold conditions at launch, and we speculated on the future of the space program.

It took 32 months before NASA decided it was safe to go back into space and on September 29, 1988, when Discovery was launched, every TV station in the state and many from around the country covered the event. From then until the shuttle program ended, we and most Florida TV stations, reported on the launches.

While the space program was now part of our newscast again, most newsrooms, including ours, decided the return from space and the shuttle landings had become too routine and the coverage dwindled, if not entirely stopped.

That all changed on February 3rd, 2003. I vividly remember that day. It was a Saturday, with Tampa preparing to begin its huge Gasparilla Parade, part of the Gasparilla Pirate Festival that's been held in our fine city almost every year since 1904.

I was at the station around 8:30 in the morning in order to view some taped interviews I'd done for an investigation, planning to go to the parade later on. Back in those days we shot on videotape which could only be viewed on huge playback machines at the TV station. These days we shoot on small SD cards that can be inserted and viewed on practically any computer.

As I watched the tape in one monitor in the edit booth, I had the other monitor tuned to the CBS Saturday morning news. (By this time, we had switched from being an ABC affiliate to CBS.)

Sometime after 9 a.m., Russ Mitchell announced there had been a problem with the Space Shuttle Columbia's return to the Kennedy Space Center, and the non-stop programming commenced as experts tried to explain what was happening until the eventual conclusion. The shuttle had disintegrated when a piece of foam broke away from the fuel tank, struck the craft's wing and allowed super-heated gases to act like a blowtorch. All seven astronauts—Rick Husband, William McCool, Michael Anderson, Kalpana Chawla, David Brown, Laurel Clark and Ilan Ramon—instantly died.

I was stunned when I heard the news, and that tragedy brought back a rush of memories from the Challenger disaster.

I stepped outside the editing booth to go to the canteen and get a cup of black coffee to try to process what had just happened and I noticed our news director, Lane Michelsen, in his office, also working on a Saturday. I stuck my head in. "Lane did you hear what happened with the Columbia?" And then I saw he was transfixed by the special report on CBS as well. Lane shook his head. "This is horrible!"

I told him that while the families of the astronauts were at the Kennedy Space Center, the plan was to fly them back to Houston where most lived and where they trained, and all the news was going to come out of the Johnson Space Center in Houston. "We need to go to Houston," I told Lane and immediately he responded, "Find a photog and book a flight." In those days before budgets got tight, we travelled a lot.

I called our Chief Photographer, Gene Yagle, (I think I woke him), told him about the Columbia disaster and asked if he wanted to go to Houston. Gene, whom I loved working with— we'd traveled together to cover several stories—said yes.

Next, I had to book flights and hotels with the goal of getting to Houston and the CBS station KHOU in time to broadcast live from their newsroom for our six o'clock newscast.

I was able to find a flight that got us into Houston sometime after 4 p.m. Tampa time, which meant by the time we got our luggage and rented a car, it was going to be a mad dash to get to our affiliate station on time.

I called KHOU when we landed in Houston and said I would make it there in time for the 6 o'clock news in Tampa. Then I called our station and asked them to put together some video from the network that I could use to cover what I would be saying from the KHOU newsroom, which we flew into about 10 minutes before our broadcast.

They knew we were coming and had everything ready for us. There's no doubt we got some help from KHOU anchor Lisa Foranda, who was a good friend and was, at one time, the weekend anchor at our station.

I barely had time to put on the microphone, stick in my earpiece and dab a little bit of makeup on my face when I heard, "Mike Deeson joins us live from Houston with the latest on this tragedy." Somehow, we pulled it off and after we nailed it, there was a rush of satisfaction.

The next week we did several reports from the Johnson Space Center where most of the NASA employees seemed to be walking around like zombies.

Three days later, President George W. Bush came to the Johnson Space Center to eulogize the seven astronauts. Among his remarks he said, "Each of them knew that great endeavors are inseparable from great risks. And each of them accepted those risks willingly, even joyfully, in the cause of discovery."

That point about the astronaut's courage and sacrifice was driven home to me seven years later at my Dad's 85th birthday party in Chicago. We held the celebration at a restaurant called Lovell's, owned by the son of astronaut Jim Lovell. He was the commander of the ill-fated Apollo 13 which had a critical failure in 1970 on its way to the moon, had to abort those plans and almost didn't make it back safely. You may recall Tom Hanks portrayed him in the movie, *Apollo 13*.

Captain Lovell sometimes visited his son's restaurant and mingled with the guests. On that night in 2010, he came up to the private room where we had the party, and when he learned I was an investigative reporter from Florida, he spent several minutes bending my ear, urging me to do a story about NASA. Lovell exclaimed, "They're too damn conservative and too damn timid at NASA!" He went on, "Space flight is dangerous—I'm living proof of that—but you have to take chances to advance science and mankind, and you need to do that story."

Had I been able to travel back to Chicago and do an interview with Lovell, I might have followed through on his request, but budgets were tight, we didn't travel much, and as I mentioned, newsrooms lost interest quickly. The Columbia disaster occurred only seven years before and the Challenger catastrophe had happened 24 years prior to my meeting Lovell. It would have been the proverbial feather in my cap to interview one of the most courageous astronauts of our time. Still, I was well aware that my news managers wouldn't be interested in an story about NASA and the perils faced by astronauts, particularly because we had to spend money and travel to get it. So, that part of the "danger of space" story from a remarkable source remained a private one between Lovell and me, until now.

THE BUCS STOP HERE

FROM AUGUST 25TH, 1994 until September 3rd, 1996 almost 50 percent of the stories I did for WTSP involved our football team: the Tampa Bay Buccaneers.

Although anything about the Bucs would seemingly fall into the sports category, it became a major news item on August 25th, 1994, when the original owner of the Bucs, Hugh Culverhouse, died.

From that moment until the city voted to build a new stadium, the Buccaneers were often the lead story on TV and the above-the-fold front page story in the local newspapers.

Initially, there was concern about to whom the team would be sold; would the new owners move the team; would the Bucs get a new stadium and, if so, who would pay for it?

The team was eventually bought by the Glazer family, headed up by billionaire Malcolm Glazer and his sons, Joel and Bryan, who were made vice presidents of the team.

Glazer, who initially said the area needed a new stadium in order for the Bucs to stay in Tampa Bay, promised to put up some of his own money for it, but never did. The Bucs, however, were able to get a new stadium by threatening to move to another city.

So, there were plenty of stories to do, because not only the Bucs, but several other NFL teams and their cities were in turmoil regarding relocation. As a news reporter, I represented my station at every NFL meeting to check out whether teams were going to move from city to city. The Houston Oilers, for example, announced in 1995 they were moving to Nashville; the City of Cleveland was looking for a team to replace the Browns (who had moved to Baltimore to become the Ravens) and the Bucs were threatening to go *anywhere* and particularly to Cleveland, if they didn't get a new stadium.

At each NFL get-together, rumors and stories flew around and we went to every one of them to report on what was happening with the Bucs. There was drama at each meeting. For example; at the yearly NFL meeting in Palm Beach at classic, ritzy old hotel The Breakers, I joined reporters from around the country who, whenever we saw the owners of the teams going into meetings, would yell questions to them about moving or staying in their respective cities, but after-hours there was a "news truce." The networks that carried NFL football programming hosted parties on different nights for the owners, football execs and the media, and questions were off limits.

On the first night at the FOX Party I spoke to Linda Glazer, the wife of Malcolm and mother of Joel and Bryan, who were running the team. In an extremely human moment, she said, "I'm sorry, I know you said something to me, but I wasn't paying close attention because I was looking at my boys over your shoulder, and I was thinking how proud I am of them."

This was a woman who was just being a mom, despite the fact her husband was a billionaire and despised by many people in the Tampa Bay area because he was trying to get the community to build him a football stadium so he could make more money. (And quite frankly a certain percentage of people disliked him because he was Jewish. Several times I heard him described as a "rich billionaire greedy Jew" from people who didn't realize I was Jewish.) Instead of revealing my religious background, I just marked it down in my brain that this or that so-called "icon' of Tampa society was a bigoted son of a bitch!

My favorite party during those NFL meetings was the ABC bash with Lynn Swann and Al Michaels, the *Monday Night Football* team at the time. A ton of ABC execs and fabulous food.

ABC put out a buffet spread of all sorts of edibles, but the highlight was the unlimited supply of lobster tails.

The smart guys passed everything up and ignored Lynn Swann, Al Michaels and the salad and veggies and went straight for the lobster.

That night when I had eaten my fill, I saw the chief photographer from the ABC affiliate in Tampa, Eric Moore, go for his 12th trip back to the lobster chafing dish. I told him that forevermore his name would be "Lobster Boy, "which is what I call him to this day.

The reason these parties have relevance is because they show the huge amount of money that NFL football brings in, and the fact that the NFL and the networks spare no expense to entertain anyone associated with the game.

The NFL got set on its ear once again when the owner of the Cleveland Browns, Art Modell, announced in the middle of the 1995 season that he was moving his team to Baltimore at the end of the season to become the Baltimore Ravens.

That sparked a huge fight from the city of Cleveland and resulted in their hosting another December 1995 "semi-official" meeting of cities concerned about losing their teams as well as cities hoping to get an NFL team to relocate to their area

Tampa Bay sent a group there because of the continuing fear that if the Bucs didn't get a new stadium, they would move to Cleveland and the area would lose its franchise.

The anger in Cleveland was palpable as many of the urinals had pictures of Art Modell, the owner of the Browns, on the drain guard with the inscription, "Piss on Art Modell," and signs all around town had Modell's picture with the words, "Muck Fodell!" on them.

Although the Mayor of Cleveland, Michael White, continually tried to assure reporters from Tampa Bay that his city was not after the Bucs, the future of our team became more ominous after the NFL cut a deal with Cleveland, promising it would get a team by 1999 through either expansion or relocation.

Throughout the entire three-day conference, White swore there was no "back door" talk with the Bucs, as he repeated his mantra, "We want our team, our name and our colors."

In the end that is exactly what happened as Modell's team became the Baltimore Ravens—and Cleveland was awarded an expansion team, they were renamed the Browns when they began play again, keeping all the old records of the original Brown team.

My most memorable experience at that conference was that it was unbelievably cold, and I had to shoot a standup at the Old Memorial Stadium on Lake Erie in December. Wind whipped off the lake, heavy snow swirled all around us and the wind chill had to be about 10 below. It was so frigid that I could barely talk and get my words out correctly. When I finally got a good take, I said to photographer Kurt Beabas, who was with me on this trip, "That's a good one, let's get the hell out of here." Kurt replied, "Mike your hair looked like shit in the stand up, maybe we should do another." I shook my head and said, " Kurt, I didn't say, 'shit,' I didn't say, 'fuck,' my standup made sense, so let's get the fuck out of here before we are frozen to this spot forever!" I am sure Kurt appreciated my lack of concern about how I looked, and he agreed we should get out and go.

Although nothing was settled at that Cleveland meeting, the threat of the Bucs being the team to replace the Cleveland Browns hung over the Tampa Bay area. It ended when voters finally passed the Community Investment tax in the fall of 1996 to fund the stadium and gave the Glazer Family a sweet deal to keep the team in the Tampa Bay area.

The other highlight of that Cleveland meeting was running into the sports director of the CBS affiliate in Nashville, WTVF. Nashville stations covered the meetings because of the proposed move of the Houston Oilers to Nashville to become the Titans.

When the sports anchor (whose name I cannot remember) found out I was at WTSP, he asked me how our news director, Mike Cavender was doing. At the time Cavender was one of 17 news directors I'd had in Tampa and he and I were not overly close. He went on to become the executive director of the Radio Television Digital News Director Association (RTNDA) and we have since become social media friends. When I worked for him, however, that was not the case and I told that to the Nashville sports anchor. He told me he understood, but also had a very warm spot in his heart for Cavender.

He explained it dated back to when he was the weekend sports director at the station and Cavender was his news director. He started to describe how crazy it was doing sports on the weekend, but I stopped him because I knew all about it, having started out in sports myself at the beginning of my career. I did my share of weekend sports, including a stint in Buffalo at WGR (now WGRZ owned by TEGNA which owns WTSP).

When you're doing weekend sports at most stations, you're doing several people's jobs: writing, reporting, editing and anchoring the sports on the weekend newscasts. You are often the sole person in the sports department, and it can get crazy. In fact, reading the sportscast on TV is the last thing you worry about, the bigger problem is getting everything done in time for air.

At any rate, the sports anchor from Nashville said on one particular weekend all hell was breaking loose for the sports department. Among the items he had to cover was the Vanderbilt Football game. The anchor told me he was rushing around and did an interview with the quarterback in the locker room after the game was over. It was an interview he had to shoot while asking the questions. When he got back to the station, he had to edit the video for the 6 p.m. news, plus write all the other stories he would use.

When he introduced the taped piece about the Vandy quarterback, he didn't watch what was on the air and instead he started reading through the copy he had written because he didn't have time to review it before the broadcast. All of a sudden, the weekend anchor slaps him on the forearm and says, "There's a dick on the air." The sports director then turned to the anchor. "Quit fucking with me, I'm trying to read my copy over once before I read it on the air." The anchor then said, even more forcefully, "Look man, there is a dick on the air!"

That's when the guy looked up and said he felt "his life was over" because sure enough, standing behind the quarterback was a naked Vandy player getting ready to take a shower. Of course, when he shot and edited the interview, he concentrated so hard on getting everything done, he NEVER noticed.

"I knew my career in broadcasting was over," he told me, and of course as soon as he got into the newsroom, phones were ring off the hook. One of the callers was Cavender, who had a booming, deep voice saying, "There was a dick on the air!" The sportscaster believed he would be clearing out his desk before the night was over and said he explained to Cavender what happened. He was told, "Be in early Monday morning and we'll discuss it."

Monday came and he slowly walked into Cavender's office, expecting to be fired. His boss asked him to go over the story one more time, and he did, to which he says Cavender replied, "We can't have that happen, never do that again."

And that is why, no matter what anyone ever says about Mike Cavender, that one sports anchor will always owe him a debt of gratitude.

Meanwhile, there was another NFL winter meeting in Chicago in February of 1996 (a wonderful time to travel to Chicago). For some reason the station decided it would be wise to fly photographer Gene Yagle and me into Midway Airport on the Southside of Chicago, even though the meetings were at the O'Hare Hilton adjacent to the airport on the North side of Chicago. It apparently was cheaper to fly into Midway, but the station didn't count the cost of the van we had to rent to carry all the equipment, so by the time we drove to O'Hare, it probably was a wash or cost more.

Anyhow, when we arrived in Chicago the night before the NFL meeting was supposed to start, we stopped by to see my parents, who were living in the city on the 16th floor of a beautiful condo overlooking Lake Michigan. As I was finishing off my first drink of "Dr. Bombay" gin (as I call it) I got a page on my national pager (we didn't have cell phone in those days) saying, " Call Robin ASAP." Robin was our assistant news director, Robin Smythe, whom I generally got along with, but like most managers in TV news, she could be a bit over reactive.

As soon as I got the page, I looked at Gene, and I remember to this day my verbatim words, "This cannot be good news!" Reporters and photographers NEVER get calls from managers asking how the flight was, how the weather was, were you having a good time, so I knew this had to do with some sort of problem.

When I called the station and got hold of Robin, she said breathlessly,

"Mike I know you're not going to like this, but how quickly can you get to New York?" Although I was prepared for almost anything, that question really threw me. "That's a strange question, why do you want me to go to New York?" I think because I had finished "Dr. Bombay" number one at my parent's apartment and might have had one or two on the flight up from Florida, I was extremely mellow while Robin was close to a panic. She blurted out, "Cheryl Ann Barnes has been found in New York."

Cheryl Ann Barnes was a teenage girl who had disappeared from a small town in the Tampa Bay area on January 3, 1996. She was finally recognized at a hospital in Manhattan on February 8th. She had been in the hospital with amnesia and said she had no idea how she got there.

It was a major media story for weeks grabbing Florida newspaper headlines and dominating newscast lead stories, all asking the same question: "What Happened to Cheryl Ann Barnes?" It even made national news when she was featured on John Walsh's *America's Most Wanted* TV program.

The media frenzy continued and really spun out of control on the night she was identified. Every outlet—print and broadcast—needed to show up in New York to get the story.

Robin was hell bent on Gene and me going to New York instead of sending a crew from Tampa. Then all of a sudden, as I could hear a ton of commotion in the background, she said, "Call me back in 20 minutes."

I looked at Gene, who at least understood the craziness of the station, and my mom, who had no clue about what was going on (at the time my father was out of town on a business trip) and I said there was only one thing to do at a time like this and Gene asked, "What!" I happily replied, "We must have another drink!"

Twenty minutes later, I called Robin back as I was instructed to do, and the panic at the station seemed to have amped up even more. This time Robin said, "We're going to send a crew from Tampa to cover the NFL meeting; you and Gene will go to New York and track down Cheryl Ann."

By now it was after 9 p.m.—we had no flight booked and I said to

Robin, "So when we get to New York, where are we going to stay and what flight are we supposed to take?"

Again, I could tell the chaos in the Newsroom had ratcheted up another level and Robin, sounding hysterical said, "Call me back in 20 minutes!" I hung up the phone, smiled and said to Gene and my mom, "He's driving, I'm not, the only thing to do...is have another drink." I went to my parents' bar and poured another "Dr. Bombay" into my cocktail glass.

Another 20 minutes went by and by then I wasn't feeling any pain as I dialed the station and asked to speak to Robin again. This time, our executive producer, Dave Clegern, a bearded sort of "hippy-dippy," West Coast guy that I really got along with, got on the phone and said, "Pay no attention to anything you've heard the last hour or so and go cover the NFL meetings."

Now, although I stayed in Chicago to cover those meetings and had nothing to do with the Cheryl Ann Barnes coverage, this is how Bill Mitchel, writing for the Poynter Institute (a non-profit journalism teaching and think tank organization owned by the *Tampa Bay Times*— formerly the *St. Petersburg Times*) described the frenzy in the market:

February 7 (Wednesday): *Tampa's ABC affiliate, WFTS-Ch. 28, had a crew in New York. Channel 28 convinced its New York City ABC sister station that the story of a kidnapped girl and a missing-but-recovered car was newsworthy. A nurse in Beth Israel Medical Center's psychiatric ward recognized Cheryl as the Jane Doe amnesia victim, and called WABC, which notified its Tampa sister station. During its evening news, Channel 28 contacted the family in Bushnell, and Cheryl talked to the family by phone that evening. Its New York connection enabled Channel 28 to beat its competition on this break in the biggest story of the new year.*

Minutes after the news broke, Channel 28 news director Bob Jordan offered to charter a jet to fly the family to New York City at his station's sole expense, in exchange for 24 hours of exclusive rights to the story. Cheryl's grandmother reportedly turned down the offer, saying it wouldn't be fair to the other television stations. The Barnes family did get its Lear jet ride to New York and back, not from Channel 28, but by a cooperative arrangement of Tampa Bay media. The local TV stations arranged to pool coverage and money for the event, including the family's New York hotel (Grand Hyatt) and limousine trans-portation.

February 8 (Thursday): *Shortly after midnight, the family (father, stepmother, and grandmother) and media entourage went from the Teterboro Airport in New Jersey to Beth Israel Medical Center, where the Barnes family was reunited. The hour-long reunion was attended by immense media coverage. (The front-page headline in that day's New York Post said simply, but in massive type, "Lost and Found.") Cheryl appeared to be partially recovering from her amnesia, and recognized her father and grandmother at the hospital."* [17]

According to St. Petersburg Times reporter Andrew Galarneau in a February 11 article, *"When Cheryl came home, she was greeted by five TV satellite trucks with crews, 11 roving camera teams, and photographers and reporters for at least seven newspapers, including the New York Daily News."*) [17]

Happily, I was back covering the NFL meeting asking the Glazers at every opportunity I could if they were going to move the team, and I missed what my colleagues at the station called the complete "Butt Fuck" over Cheryl Ann Barnes.

Tampa Bay's football team saga ended in September of 1996 when voters agreed to tax themselves with a community investment tax for fire, police and of course money to build the $168.5 million Raymond James Stadium (a bargain these days) where the Bucs currently play. Speaking of bargains, the Glazer Family did extremely well with the purchase of the team. They bought the Buccaneers for $192 million—a record price at the time, which some said was a foolhardy amount to pay. Today, however, the franchise is worth more than 2 billion dollars —a great investment indeed!

FRANK RAGANO: REPRESENTING
THE MOB

ATTORNEY FRANK RAGANO grew up in Tampa's Ybor City, which is the area's "Latin Quarter" that some people compare to New Orleans's French Quarter. Starting in the early 1900's and continuing through the 40's and 50's, it was populated by Latinos, Italians and Jews. It was also an area where the mob, payoffs to police and dirty politicians, murder and corruption ran rampant. I have an affinity for Ybor City as my wife's great-grandparents had a dry goods store there and her grandfather was a dentist in Ybor City. Although they, like most in the area, ran legitimate businesses, members of organized crime were everywhere and that included Frank Ragano.

Every time I think of Ragano I imagine cuing violins to play the theme from the *The Godfather*, because it fits him so perfectly. Ragano's father was Sicilian-born and ran a small grocery store in Ybor City. His heritage might have been the reason Frank Ragano was recruited to defend several mobsters who were arrested in connection with the numbers racket (called *Bolita* in Ybor City) run by Mob Kingpin Santos Trafficante Jr., also of Sicilian heritage.

Ragano, whom I had known for years, spent several hours telling me about his life at his comfortable—but certainly not opulent—condo after he published his book, "*Mob Lawyer*" in 1993. Clearly, he was trying to promote his autobiography, but he was more than willing to share stories that made the hair on my arms stand up!

He told me that after he was hired to represent the mobsters, Trafficante took a liking to him and allowed him to pierce the veil of organized crime, not only in Tampa, but throughout the entire country and Cuba. In essence, Ragano became Tom Hagan, the *consigliere* character portrayed by Robert Duval in the movie *The Godfather*.

Trafficante, born in Tampa, was at one time considered to be the most powerful mobster in Florida. He was tapped by the Mafia to run their gambling operations in Cuba, which he successfully did until Castro came to power.

When the mob was thrown out of Cuba, Ragano alleges Trafficante was involved in several plots to assassinate Castro. Ragano added that the CIA was actually encouraging the mobster to eliminate Cuba's dictator.

Although Ragano told me several stories about his work with Trafficante, I had several encounters with the mob boss on my own, but he wasn't as talkative as his lawyer. In fact, Trafficante displayed the mob code of Omerta, which means silence, every time I tried to talk to him.

Trafficante became the focus of the U.S. Attorney's Office in the mid 80's when the feds ran an undercover operation in the Tampa Bay Area involving the Kings Court Bottle Club which was used as a front for Mob activity.

FBI agent Joseph Pistone was known to the mob as "Donnie Brasco," whom Johnny Depp portrayed in the movie of the same name. The undercover FBI agent was "working" for the powerful Bonnano crime syndicate on a number of illegal operations. As the bottle club was established, "Brasco" also established a relationship with Trafficante and his branch of the Mafia.

After six years of having an agent in an undercover role, the FBI pulled the plug and several arrests of mob figures ensued. Shortly thereafter, the U.S. Attorney empaneled a grand jury on organized crime in Tampa and throughout the state. Trafficante was called to appear several times. Attorneys are not allowed to accompany their clients into a Federal Grand Jury, however Trafficante never gave the

Grand Jury much, and over the years, Ragano was successful in keeping his mobster client from being convicted of racketeering and gambling charges.

During the Grand Jury investigation of the "Donnie Brasco" bottle club, Trafficante, then in his seventies, had the appearance of a typical Florida retiree. He was short in stature, wore a porkpie straw hat and donned thick black glasses. He looked anything but the threatening mob figure that he once was.

Each time he left the Federal court after each appearance there, I, along with a gaggle of print and other TV reporters, ran up to him and screamed, "Mr. Trafficante, Mr. Trafficante, do you have anything to say?" He never said a word but placed both hands across his chest in an "X" position and then quickly moved his arms to the side as if to signal, *Not only do I have nothing to say, but also get the hell out of my way.* Like Superman confronted with Kryptonite, everyone moved away as quickly as possible and created a huge path through which the mob boss would pass. I have rarely been concerned about pressing someone about a story or investigation, but candidly, Trafficante was not a man I, nor any of the assembled media, wanted to cross. Despite being called to the Grand Jury several times, criminal charges were never filed against him.

Nevertheless, Ragano understood how ruthless Trafficante could be. When he explained how close he and the notorious gangster had become, Ragano added, "But I knew if I ever became useless to him or crossed him, I had no doubt that he would have had me killed and not think twice about it."

According to Ragano, murder was just a regular part of business for Trafficante. As evidence, the lawyer pointed to the failed assassination attempt on Castro and the death of President John Kennedy.

While the Castro assassinations plots were unsuccessful, there were rumors Trafficante was involved behind-the-scenes with President Kennedy's death. According to Ragano, the order, or "the hit," came from Teamsters' President Jimmy Hoffa. Ragano, on Trafficante's recommendation, became Hoffa's attorney, and just as he had become close with Trafficante, he also became close with Teamsters' boss Hoffa. In fact, Ragano was standing next to Hoffa in 1964 in a Nashville courtroom when a man took out a pistol and shot at the union chief three times. Somehow Hoffa was actually able to punch the shooter.

In a matter of fact way, Ragano told me Hoffa gave him some sage advice after the incident. Apparently, Hoffa looked at him and said," Frank, remember this and maybe you'll live longer: Always run away from a knife, but charge a gun." Ragano happily said he never had to test out the theory.

Hoffa, on the other hand, was not so lucky. According to Ragano, in 1975, he was dispatched by Trafficante to warn Hoffa to beware that there might be a mob hit ordered for the Teamsters' boss, and within days of that warning Hoffa disappeared.

I had known Ragano for a long time, and before he published his book, *Mob Lawyer*, he always maintained his clients were legitimate businesspeople who were being harassed by overzealous government prosecutors. That all changed after Trafficante died and Ragano's book came out.

Ragano told me that before Trafficante died, he was extremely ill and the mob boss confessed he had arranged "the hit" on President John Kennedy. The attorney also revealed to me that *he* was the one who took the message to Trafficante and another reputed mobster, Carolos Marcello—also one of his clients—that Hoffa and the mob wanted JFK to be assassinated.

According to Ragano, and thanks to his book, *Mob Lawyer*, I can replicate the quote: Trafficante added in Sicilian, "*Carlos e futtutu. Non duvevamu ammazzar a Giovanni. Duvevamu ammazzari a Bobby*." "Carlos {Marcello} messed up. We shouldn't have killed Giovanni {John}. We should have killed Bobby." [18] Of course, he was referring to the President's brother, Robert Kennedy, who as Attorney General, made a concerted effort to go after organized crime and Jimmy Hoffa.

The rumor that the mob was behind the plot to kill JFK was not just Ragano coming up with a wild theory. In 1979, The House Assassination Committee disregarded the Warren Commission conclusion that Lee Harvey Oswald was the lone killer and instead came to the tentative conclusion that the Mob was involved in the assassination. The Committee also pointed to Trafficante and New Orleans Mafia chieftain Carlos Marcello, who died in 1992, as being heavily involved in facilitating the assassination.

Ragano also told me Trafficante had another major regret about Kennedy, in addition to "killing" the wrong brother. When Trafficante was running the gambling operations in Cuba, he set up the future president with prostitutes every time JFK came to the country. Trafficante also provided hotel rooms for the trysts. The lawyer noted that Trafficante often said he was extremely angry with himself for not taping those illicit encounters, which he believed he could have used to his advantage to get things from Kennedy when he was President.

In another wild story, Ragano revealed that Trafficante told him that in addition to the Mob ordering the hit on Kennedy, the CIA had also once asked him to have the Mob assassinate the President. Each of his stories made me feel as if I was learning about an underworld version of some of the biggest events of our time...and as unbelievable as they sounded, I believed every word he told me.

One of the more fascinating stories I heard occurred after Ragano stopped working for Trafficante. The lawyer had fallen on hard times after serving 10 months in Federal Prison for tax evasion. After he was released, he went to Trafficante and said, "Godfather, I need help." Trafficante looked at him and said, "What do you need, someone to have their legs broken or knees capped, or do you want them to be the target of a hit?"

Ragano says he looked at Trafficante and said, "No, no, Godfather, nothing like that, my problem is I am broke. I need some money." Ragano says Trafficante, who was willing to have someone *killed* at his request, looked at him, waved his index finger back and forth in front of his face and said, "When you ask for money," and Ragano told me Trafficante said the next part loudly and with emphasis, "THIS I CANNOT DO!"

Hearing those stories made me feel as if I was living inside *The Godfather* movie, but this was real life, or sometimes real death!

The final crazy Ragano story came out 15 years after he died. In 2013 the Tampa Tribune published an article that made us all try to chase after its veracity. The story said that an employee of the swank Palma Ceia Country Club, in the heart of South Tampa, overheard

Ragano talking to Trafficante and Carlos Marcello about plans for tennis player Bobby Riggs. In 1973, Riggs took on Billy Jean King in the "Battle of the Sexes" tennis match. The story was that the mob wanted Riggs to throw the match. [19]

According to the employee, he overheard Ragano explaining that Riggs owed the mob more than $100,000 and by throwing the match, the mob could bet heavily on King and more than recoup the money Riggs owed them.

I had my doubts about the story, because Ragano never put it in his tell-all book. When we sat in his condo for an extensive interview he never mentioned the Riggs incident either, yet didn't hold back as he spilled his guts about murder plots, extortion and all sorts of other illegal activities. I wish he had still been alive so I could have asked him.

Meantime, Trafficante's family not only denied the Riggs story and the assassination plots, but also claimed Trafficante never did anything illegal—he was just a hardworking businessman taking care of his friends and family.

While I was skeptical about the Riggs story, I had to check it out. it was a story that kept the local media busy for a couple of days, but neither I nor any other news or media outlet could confirm the details. At the very least, though, it certainly was good gossip and revived the memory of the man who lived the real-life *Godfather* movie and willingly shared it with me.

RAYS OF HOPE: BIRTHING BASEBALL IN TAMPA BAY

THE TAMPA BAY AREA, home to major league teams for spring training since the early 1900's, wanted a major league team. For years there were only 16 major league baseball teams, 8 in the National League and 8 in the American league. The owners as is the case with most major league sports, thought they could increase their revenue by adding teams. Once baseball expanded the American League in 1977, the area started believing baseball would expand again, and it had a shot at getting a team.

The first problem was that both Tampa, located in Hillsborough County, and St. Petersburg in Pinellas County, wanted to be the city where the major league team would locate, and competing groups formed in each city.

The quest for baseball dates to the late 1970's when Pinellas County decided to build a baseball stadium in downtown St. Petersburg instead of closer to the Tampa side of the bay as the county originally said it would.

That sparked a plan lead by auto dealer Frank Morsani for the building of *another* stadium in Tampa in order to bring a baseball team *there*. By 1984, Morsani entered into an agreement to buy the

Minnesota Twins and move them to Tampa. Although Morsani had been given assurances Major League Baseball would be supportive of the purchase, it squashed the deal and told Morsani to be patient, because expansion with a new team would bring the MLB franchise to Tampa.

Four years later, when Morsani learned the Texas Rangers were for sale he entered into an agreement to buy *that* team. But once again, MLB stepped in, killed the deal and threatened Morsani as it did with the Twins failed purchase, that if he sued, Tampa would never be considered for a team.

Meantime, the game for the Tampa Bay area changed drastically when, going against the advice of baseball commissioner Peter Ueberroth, St. Petersburg decided to build a stadium initially called the Suncoast Dome, but it eventually became Tropicana Field, when the Tropicana Juice company bought the naming rights.

Although several people in Tampa—including Yankees owner George Steinbrenner who moved to the area in the early 80's—said people in Hillsborough County wouldn't drive across "that rickety old bridge," (the Howard Frankland connecting Tampa to St Petersburg) to see a baseball game, Morsani made peace with the Pinellas County group and said they would unify their efforts to bring baseball to their backyard, so to speak.

With an empty dome waiting for baseball, it became a bargaining chip for other teams threatening to leave *their* cities unless they got a new stadium. The Chicago White Sox announced they would move to Tampa Bay in the late 80's if the Illinois General Assembly did not come up with funds for a new stadium. On the last night of the Illinois legislature meeting, Governor Big Jim Thompson stopped the "official clock" in the legislature for several minutes before the mandated midnight end of the session and persuaded lawmakers to come up with the money for the Sox to stay there.

Finally, when MLB announced it would expand in 1990, it was assumed Morsani and Tampa Bay would get one of the new teams. Major League Baseball threw the Tampa Bay area a curve ball and chose another group to represent Tampa Bay in the expansion sweepstakes. That meant Morsani was out and it looked like the fix was to give Miami the expansion team instead of Tampa Bay. MLB said the group it chose to represent Tampa Bay wasn't as financially stable as the group trying to get the expansion team in Miami, headed by Wayne Huizenga, owner of Waste Management, Blockbuster and Auto Nation. Miami was awarded the expansion team and once again, Tampa Bay was the bridesmaid instead of the bride.

Shortly thereafter, the Seattle Mariners were reportedly headed to St. Petersburg when the team's owner said he had been approached by a group from the nearby Tampa Bay area who wanted to buy the team and move it to Florida. But the deal was never consummated.

As for me, a baseball fan since I was 5 years old, a diehard Cubs fan, I had gone out and purchased Tampa Bay Twins, Tampa Bay Mariners and Tampa Bay White Sox t-shirts. Those souvenirs were long gone, but the next attempt to bring baseball to Tampa had everyone convinced it was going to happen.

In 1992, businessman Vince Naimoli stunned Tampa Bay and San Francisco when he held a news conference in the Suncoast Dome announcing he had purchased the Giants, who would start playing the next baseball season in St. Petersburg.

I remember doing a live shot about it at 11 p.m. from a local sports bar (never a good idea) and two extremely beautiful, but also extremely inebriated, women joined me and started kissing me as I walked and talked, attempting to get to the footage for my prerecorded story. If I hadn't been married—of course I had to fend them off—I'm convinced those women would have done *ANYTHING* (and I do mean *ANYTHING*) on live TV; they were really loaded!

Back then the station produced a lot of stories on location, both in and outside of our local area, and I had just spent four weeks in Hurricane Andrew-devastated Homestead which is 38 miles South of Miami and 275 miles South East of Tampa. The purchase of the Giants meant I had to pack my bags and head for the West Coast. So, after being home for a couple weeks, I was sent to San Francisco for the final two weeks of the baseball season to follow the story. After dealing with death and destruction in South Florida, I was thrilled with the San Francisco assignment. Sports stories that didn't involve "hits, runs and errors" were covered by the news division, not the sports department, and that's why I was sent.

It was a spectacular trip as my good friend, photographer Gene Yagle, and I headed to the San Francisco Bay area. When we first arrived and drove to our hotel to check in, we realized that the station had somehow booked us into a "hooker, drug-dealer haven" establishment. I said to Gene as we drove up, "There's no way we're staying here." He agreed, we didn't even risk getting out of the car to cancel the reservation and we found another "safer" spot to stay.

During those last two weeks, if there was a game at Candlestick Park where the Giants played, we did a live shot from there and froze our butts off. Our experience gave truth to the infamous conditions at Candlestick, described in *Time Magazine*'s "10 Worst Stadiums in America" article like this: *"A warm, sunny Saturday could, in an instant, turn arctic, with wind, fog and the stadium's own inscrutable design flaws giving rise to vexing mini-ecosystems throughout the complex."* [20]

Every night we did a live shot from "The Stick" as it was known. I had to wear long underwear to keep from shivering so I could get the words out. The nights the Giants weren't playing, we did live shots on the roof of KGO, the ABC network owned and operated station in San Francisco. (At that time WTSP was an ABC affiliate.)

Some said KGO stood for "Killing Guts & Orgasms" where, "If It Bleeds It Leads" was the motto for a wonderful place out of which to work. KGO was a union shop, however, which meant that Gene, one of the most talented photographers and editors in America (he had won more than 30 Emmys) couldn't edit the pieces we shot.

The union KGO editors were extremely nice and competent, but in the edit booths, they had low lights and were drinking wine...openly. I stared in disbelief. "You're drinking in the station." They laughed. "Man, this is San Francisco!" Although I love Tampa, at that point I thought of applying for job there!

The nights there weren't home games, we did a live shot for the 11 p.m. news back in Tampa, so we were finished by 8:30 West Coast time. That's when Gene and I got the opportunity to learn what the "real" San Francisco was all about, because we were on the company dime, we sampled some of the finest restaurants in the world.

Back in those days Gene had a moustache, and mine was still dark (instead of the grey it has become) so I guess we looked a little similar. Every time we walked into a restaurant, the host or maître d' would ask, "Are you two brothers?" We would say no and he'd give us a wink and smile. "Ooooh, we have a very wonderful (read romantic) table for two." The first or second time it happened we must have been in la-la land because we didn't get it, but then we realized, *This is San Francisco,* and we just chuckled from then on as we were shown the finest view at each restaurant.

By the time we were done with our work in California, it really looked as if the Tampa Bay area was finally going to get its baseball team. Everyone believed the Giants were coming to St. Pete, including the front office and the players.

I remember talking to Giants star first baseman Will Clark about the best places to live in the Tampa Bay area. The front office people asked me the same housing questions as well.

The final game of the 1992 season was painful for Giants fans. As I was quoted in this excerpt from Jonah Keri's book, *The Extra 2%*:

"Tampa news station WTSP-TV reporter Mike Deeson describes the final game at Candlestick Park by saying, "There were so many die-hard Giants fans there, and they were just breaking down. Grown men had tears streaming down their faces." [21]

That happened as a female trio sang one of the most beautiful renditions of the national anthem I've ever heard. I truly felt bad for all the fans in the seats, but on the inside, I was thrilled that Tampa Bay was, at long last, going to get its baseball team.

This was a story I had covered since New Year's Eve,1983, when the Pinellas Sports Authority voted to buy bonds to finance a stadium in St. Petersburg for major league baseball. And now it seemed like it was a reality that the Giants were coming to the Tampa Bay Area. In fact, I remember buying some tickets in San Francisco (even though I got into the game on a press pass), a scorecard and anything else I could get my hands on showing it was the final game, which would make a great souvenir years later.

As the final game of the season ended, the fans wouldn't leave and they sat in Candlestick Park for what they thought was the last time, watching their beloved San Francisco Giants.

Freelance Photographer Brad Mangin describes it best:

"By the time the game ended I was emotionally exhausted. The Giants were really moving. Fans waited around watching the grounds crew tear up the pitching mound with pickaxes to get the field ready for a 49er game the following Sunday, I sat down on the grass behind home plate and cried. I could not believe this was happening." [22]

Mangin was not alone. The fans in the stands were at a mass funeral for their team. It was like the break-up of a long-time marriage where one partner wants to leave and the other is begging for him or her to stay.

But once again, Major League Baseball interfered and would not allow the sale of the Giants to go through; Instead it found another buyer for the team at a *lower* price than Naimoli and his group had offered. The owner of the Giants Bob Lurie was not happy with the lower price, but any sale and move of a baseball team had to be approved by the commissioner and MLB, so he was stuck with taking the offer on the table or not being able to sell the team. It didn't seem fair, but baseball isn't always fair, as Tom Hanks said in *A League of Our Own,* "There is no crying in baseball."

Once again, the Commissioner and MLB told the powers that be in the Tampa Bay area that if they sued, they would never get a baseball team. The tactic didn't work, however, and Naimoli sued MLB for "tortious interference" with his contract to buy the Giants. The threat of the lawsuit prompted MLB to announce it was going to expand again. It cut the field of finalists for this expansion to four areas: Northern Virginia, Orlando, Tampa Bay and Phoenix.

So, three years later, in March of 1995, the major league owners met at the Breakers Hotel in Palm Beach, also a favorite meeting spot for the NFL, to decide which two cities would get the expansion teams. When we got there, like every other station in Tampa Bay and reporters from the three other cities hoping to get a team, we were trying scoop on where the two teams would be. I was at a disadvantage because the head of the Tampa Bay baseball group, Vince Naimoli, wouldn't talk to me. Naimoli was irate because on the way to the baseball expansion meetings in Palm Beach a source beeped me on my pager (this was before cell phones were part of our arsenal) and told me to call immediately because he had a major tip for me.

We pulled over to a pay phone and I called my source who told me the name of the Tampa Bay team would be the Devil Rays. Up to that point it was a highly guarded secret and a major coup if it was true!

Although my source was reliable, I had to know how he found out the name of the team and could be sure it was right. My source explained through a lucky happenstance he had been at a major t-shirt factory which was in the process of printing thousands and thousands of Tampa Bay Devil Rays shirts.

At that point I was convinced we were on to something, but I had to get more confirmation. As cars were whizzing by me on State Road 60, I used the pay phone again (reporters didn't have cell phones those days) and called John Higgins, the Tampa Bay baseball group's senior Vice President and General Counsel, who is a truly nice man.

Higgins and I got along really well and when he picked up the phone I said, "John, Mike Deeson here. How does the name Tampa Bay Devil Rays sound?" Remember this was a closely guarded secret and I counted to myself as the phone was silent for 10 long seconds and Higgins gained his composure and said, "Mike don't run with the name or you will embarrass yourself on TV tonight." I told Higgins, his silence told me all I needed to know, and we broke the name of the team that night.

Years later when the Rays (by that time they had dropped the Devil from their name) made the World Series in 2008, I sat in center field before the game and did an interview with Higgins who was going to throw out the first pitch that night. I asked him if he remembered that call and Higgins told me, "Mike I will never forget that moment as long as I live."

It wasn't so much that I called him with the name of the new team, but rather that he would have to go tell Naimoli the cat was out of the bag. Higgins said that was "Not one of my favorite conversations that I ever had with Vince."

Naimoli, who had a terrible temper, was livid that I had "let the cat out of the bag" and that's why he wouldn't talk to me at the baseball meetings. Although, when he walked into the Breakers Hotel he did look straight into my eyes and said, "Short term gain, long term pain!"

Another singular characteristic about Naimoli was that he had a terrible stutter. When he confronted me in the press room in front of all the other reporters, he had trouble getting his words out, screaming as he stuttered, "Y-y-you, had, had, n-n-no right to tell the world the-the team name."

When I replied I had ever right and that my station was pleased with what I did, he got even angrier, screaming loudly, "Y-Y-You, spoiled it for everybody!"

I politely said that I may have spoiled it for him, but I was doing exactly what I was paid to do and that I was sorry he didn't like it.

With that, the guy stormed out of the press room and all the New York sports writers, in cruel mockery, put their fingers on my chest as they stood around me and screamed, "Y-y-you, had n-n-n-no right!" It was cruel, but also came off as a bit comical.

While Naimoli had an explosive temper, he also had a short memory. In fact, he was angry with so many people at one time, he quickly forgot who he was mad at.

My friend Rick Nafe, who left the job as Executive Director of the Tampa Sports Authority—which managed the stadium where the Buccaneers play—to become a vice president of the Rays told me after his career move, "I thought I'd made a terrible mistake." One of the reasons he'd left the Sports Authority was that he had 11 bosses who were on the board of the public agency. He thought it would be easier to deal with just one boss. He was wrong.

As soon as Nafe started getting the so-called "nasty-grams" several times a day from Naimoli, he had second thoughts. He soon realized, however, that *everyone* in the front office was getting "nasty-grams" from Naimoli each day, and that Naimoli couldn't possible remember what he was pissed off about from one minute to the next. Nafe decided to ignore most of the emails and only deal with the ones where Naimoli had a valid point.

Meantime, back to the week the Tampa Bay area was awarded the baseball team at the Breakers in 1995. Everyone was trying to get the scoop as to which cities would get the franchise and we pumped all our sources as hard as we could.

When Marge Schott, the owner of the Cincinnati Reds, checked into the hotel, I happened to be near the front desk, along with my photographer Larry Perkins. That was fortunate, because Larry, a great guy that everyone immediately liked, had worked in Cincinnati before coming to Tampa. Also, luckily for us, Larry had taken part in a regular show with the Reds that often included Marge Schott.

Marge had a gravelly, sand-paper voice and was a chain-smoking, hard-drinking woman who inherited the team from her husband and managed to be politically incorrect almost every time she opened her mouth, insulting homosexuals and all minorities with complete and equal abandon. So, she was somewhat of a "loose cannon" (to say the least) but nevertheless, we walked up to her. She had a cigarette hanging from her mouth and once she saw Larry, her eyes lit up. She looked at him, opened her arms and said, with her husky voice, "Hello Honey!" (She called everybody, "Honey.") "Give me a big kiss."

It was one of those moments where Larry took one for the team as she planted a big smooch on his lips. I had to control my laughter because we were trying to find out who would get the two expansion teams and I knew he didn't want to do or say anything to offend her, one of the "insiders."

Happily, Larry didn't pass out. Instead, he was quick on his feet and said, "Marge, I'm in Tampa Bay now, do you think we have a chance of getting the owners to vote for us?" She gave him a big smile. "Honey, I like Tampa Bay, they are at the top of my radar." That didn't guarantee a win for the area, but it was something we could report on.

As we continued to try to get some source to tell us which cities would get the two expansion teams, we couldn't get a verifiable sense for how the owners were feeling until the night before the vote was about to go public.

Larry and I stood in the lobby of the Breakers trying to figure out what we were going to do for our 11 p.m. piece when New York Yankees owner, George Steinbrenner walked through like he was floating on air.

"The Boss" who could be crazy, vindictive, and at times, a real son-of-a-bitch, also had a soft side. He walked up to me, I'm assuming because I was the only Tampa Bay Reporter in the area, and said with tears in his eyes, "We've got it!" It took a second for that to register. I said, "The vote is final?" Steinbrenner, clearly on a euphoric high, said, "Yes!" That meant that at long last Tampa Bay, where Steinbrenner had lived, would be successful in its long quest for baseball. I immediately asked if he'd be willing to do an interview. Steinbrenner was in a great mood. "Of course," he said. And we had a great scoop for the 11 p.m. news.

To this day, I am convinced the George Steinbrenner whom, as I said at the top of this story, was convinced that no one would ever cross "a rickety bridge" to see a baseball game in St. Petersburg, was as much responsible for bringing the Rays to Tampa Bay as anyone else.

While Steinbrenner loved the Yankees, and had a huge ego that could rise higher than Mt. Everest, he also loved the Tampa Bay area, where he permanently moved in 1983 and wanted to see baseball come to his adopted beloved city.

So, in 1995 Naimoli and his group were awarded the Tampa Bay Devil Rays. As Naimoli announced what we had already announced 2 days earlier, the team would be called, "The Tampa Bay Devil Rays," his stutter got him again as he explained, "A Devil Ray is a gentle fish that eats p-p-p-plankton." Once again, the New York sports writers, who had witnessed his previous meltdown with me, became their cruelest as they mocked Naimoli saying over and over, "A Devil Ray is a gentle fish that eats p-p-p-plankton."

Despite everything the area had to go through to get Major League Baseball, the team signed an ironclad lease that said there would be irreparable harm and damages for anyone who tried to move the team from Tropicana Field until 2027.

Finally, on March 31st, 1998, the Tampa Bay area got its baseball team, as the Tampa Bay Devil Rays played their inaugural game at Tropicana Field. It was a momentous day for the Tampa Bay area and every station sent their reporters there to cover the first game.

For me, it was a moment I will never forget. I was standing in the bleachers in centerfield doing a "stand-up" (that's where you see the reporter on camera). As I started, future hall-of-famer and Tampa native Wade Boggs was at the plate.

Just as I started my stand-up, Boggs swung, and I did play-by-play as the ball traveled out...and out and out over the right field wall for the first home run in Devil Rays history! It truly was a thrill. What a topper for a quest I had followed for fifteen years.

BLOW WIND, BLOW

"ANYONE WHO SAYS they are not afraid at the time of a hurricane is a fool or a liar or a little bit of both." —Anderson Cooper

California has earthquakes, people who live in Northern cities have to deal with snow, ice and freezing temperature, living in Florida means hurricanes are a way of life. And in the news business, when there is a threat of one hitting the state, we go "balls to the wall" with hurricane coverage.

My first real encounter with a hurricane was Labor Day weekend, 1985, with Hurricane Elena. When I had previously lived in Virginia, we had minor brushes with winds from tropical storms, but nothing like a hurricane. Hurricane Elena never got closer than 60 miles from the Tampa Bay area, but caused major damage ($1.3 billion) as it swirled in the Gulf of Mexico all weekend long. Elena also caused a massive evacuation along the east coast and, at the time, was the largest peacetime evacuation in history.

It was a crazy weekend as the station was scheduled to host the Jerry Lewis Labor Day Muscular Dystrophy Telethon, and I was supposed to be one of the on-air talent. But instead of wearing a tuxedo all weekend staying awake for the 20-plus hour telethon, I spent the weekend in jeans, wet clothes, wet socks (the worst) and I lost sleep covering the hurricane.

Although we'd been tracking the storm all week long, it looked like it was going to pass Florida, make for a wet weekend, and then hit Biloxi, Mississippi. However, on Friday afternoon, our chief meteorologist, Dick Fletcher—a consummate professional and one of my closest friends at the station—called us all together and said, "There's been a wobble." I asked Fletch what the hell that meant and he said that the storm had slowed, picked up winds, and was churning in a circular motion without moving forward off the coast of Florida.

Fletch explained that if the storm continued circulating as it was at the moment, it was going to be a wet and potentially dangerous weekend for everyone in our area. Clearly that was an understatement, as eventually nine people died as a result of the storm.

Our station, as did every station the in the Bay area, went into full "Hurricane Mode" as we suspended regular programming and did round-the-clock coverage of the impending storm. I can't remember much about the early part of the afternoon on that Friday, except it didn't seem like we were in the path of the hurricane, but the truth was I had no idea what to expect.

By the 11 p.m. newscast, the weather was still relatively mild, considering what was going to hit us. There was a slight drizzle and the winds and waves had picked up at Clearwater Beach, where I was with photographer Bert Moreno for a live shot.

Before every live shot, the photographer gets what is called a "white balance," where a sheet of white paper is held up to the camera and the camera is then able to discern all colors from that "white balance."

Bert asked me to give him a balance and I put down the microphone on the edge of the beach so I could reach under my rain gear and get a reporter's notebook out of my pocket. As I put the microphone down, the next few seconds went by as if we were in a slow-motion movie. I saw the panic on Bert's face as a huge wave came up on the beach and washed over the microphone, ruining it forever.

There was an immediate problem, however, as we were supposed to be live in 45 seconds and the closest microphone was back in the live truck, almost a football field away.

I have never seen Bert run so quickly. Fortunately Fletch went long with his forecast off the top of the show, which gave an exhausted Bert enough time to get back to me with a new microphone that I plugged in right before the station came to us. We warned people along the Pinellas beaches that people in Clearwater, St Petersburg, anyone living along the Gulf of Mexico may have to evacuate; we had no idea how extensive the evacuation would be.

Nevertheless, the excitement of the destroyed microphone was not the most memorable thing that happened that night.

After we finished the live shot, we packed up the gear and headed back to the station. We had a radio station blaring in the background when all of a sudden, we heard the familiar tones of the emergency broadcast test come on the radio. Most of you are accustomed to hearing that loud, obnoxious signal on your radios or televisions, followed by a voice saying:

"This is a test of the Emergency Broadcast System. The broadcasters of your area in voluntary cooperation with the Federal, State and local authorities have developed this system to keep you informed in the event of an emergency. If this had been an actual emergency, the Attention Signal you just heard would have been followed by official information, news or instructions. This concludes this test of the Emergency Broadcast System."

This time, however, we heard the voice of Guy Daines, the Emergency Operations Director of Pinellas County, which made us realize the seriousness of the situation.

Daines (as he told me later) took a deep breath before announcing, "This is not a test. We are activating the Emergency Broadcast Network."

To hear the words, "This is not a test." was chilling. Perhaps it was a carryover from growing up in the Cold War 50's when air raid sirens were tested every Tuesday in Chicago, and many of my friends and I lived in constant fear of the "Russkies" launching a nuclear attack. As it happens, the system was never used for a nuclear emergency, though it was activated more than 20,000 times between 1976 and 1996 to broadcast civil emergency messages and warnings of severe weather hazards.

But now Guy Daines was declaring an actual emergency and ordering everyone along the Pinellas County Beaches to evacuate. About 325,000 people spent several nights in evacuation shelters across the Tampa Bay area, unsure of when they could go back home. More than 113,000 of those were from Pinellas County. Nineteen nursing homes and three hospitals were evacuated. At the time, it was the largest medical evacuation that had taken place anywhere, according to Daines.

Elena had become a tropical storm on Aug. 28th, 1985 near the eastern tip of Cuba and grew into a hurricane a day later. After wandering in the Gulf for a few days—at times packing 125 mph winds —it finally came ashore near Biloxi, Mississippi on Sept. 2nd. Tides of six feet above normal pounded the Pinellas beaches for days. Those levels were seven feet above normal in the waters of Tampa Bay. Sustained winds of 60 to 65 mph also battered the shoreline. The rotation of the winds built up the tides.

"The water and the waves just kept getting higher and higher," Daines told me, as we talked about the storm on its 10th anniversary. He explained the frustration experienced by him and his staff as they helplessly viewed the damage caused by the circumstances. "The water could not get out. It just kept building, tide after tide after tide."

As is the case in most evacuations, not everyone left their homes willingly. The one constant that I encountered in each subsequent hurricane I've ever covered, is to a person, everyone I ever talked to who tried to ride out the storm said something to the effect of: "*I was a damn fool, I put myself and my family's life at risk and I would never do that again.*" That was *after* the storm, however.   .

The problem *now* was getting those out who were willing, even if begrudgingly so, to go, and time was the enemy. There was wide-spread fear, which turned into reality when the evacuation routes became blocked by high winds and rising tides.

As the storm churned, it would go from unbelievably high winds and torrential rain to complete calm. By Saturday and through Sunday, the churning hurricane had taken its toll on the area. The storm surge was the biggest problem. Because the hurricane was stalled off the coast, the water had nowhere to go, destroying 265 homes along the beaches and severely damaging more than 7000 homes in the area.

Meanwhile in Tampa, Bayshore Boulevard, lined with million-dollar homes on the West side and Tampa Bay on the East, was engulfed with water. In fact, a balustrade that ran four miles along the road to downtown couldn't stop the water as it spilled over the structure and onto the street at shoulder level.

One of the fears was the scenario where the hurricane might shift its path and hit at the mouth of Tampa Bay. Fletch, our Chief Meteorologist, had shown me models, where in worst case scenarios the water in the bay could push into downtown Tampa at a height of 15 feet, causing massive destruction to the city core. Fortunately, that did not happen.

The TV station, however, was in a flood zone surrounded by the bay and the authorities ordered everyone who was still manning the fort to evacuate because they thought a storm surge could destroy the building. The station was actually forced off the air, but not without a fight.

Fletch, who had been on the air nonstop for hours (his eyelids kept closing so he only had little slots to see through) vehemently argued with authorities that there were enough volunteers at the station who were willing to keep it on the air to inform viewers about the impending storm. He lost that battle for about eight hours as I recall, and then he later convinced the authorities that the station was no longer in danger of being destroyed by the storm. I'm not sure that was exactly true, but considering his vast experience and his desire to calm those who still had power and were watching our station, the authorities let a skeleton crew sign the station back on.

I was nowhere near the station because I was out in the elements getting soaked to the bone. I can't even count how many live shots I did that weekend, but I was soaked each time I stepped out of the live truck, even though we had rain gear. We would sort of dry off in the truck between shots and then go back into the storm and do another live shot.

Because that was my first experience covering a real hurricane, I didn't know the most important thing a reporter needed during such an event: towels, dry socks (lots of them) and several changes of clothes.

When I finally made it back into the station on Labor Day afternoon, by which time the hurricane had stopped its circular motion and headed for Mississippi, the parking lot was empty.

We'd all left the keys to our cars at the station so our vehicles could be moved to higher ground as we expected the parking lot to be flooded, which, indeed it was.

After dumping my raingear at my desk, I took the least damp clothes I had and headed for a bathroom to change, and there it was in the prop room, a jet-black Jaguar that belonged to the General Manager, Larry Clamage. Larry had a love/hate relationship with the Jag which was in the shop so often he told me he had visiting rights on Wednesdays.

Anyway, Larry wanted to protect his "precious baby" from the storm and figured putting it inside the station was the perfect fortress, even though we were in the hurricane destruction zone.

I was so tired, so wet and so amused by the ridiculous thought of the "come hell or literally high water" proviso that the Jag had to be protected, that I burst into uncontrollable laughter when I saw it and had a hard time composing myself.

Although the storm was gone, in many ways the work for the TV station was just beginning. People's homes had been destroyed, their lives turned upside down and this was a major story we would cover for weeks. It happens that way in any community touched by a hurricane.

When we were finally permitted to go back to the Pinellas Beach communities, it was heartbreaking to watch homeowners as they viewed their damaged homes. I was struck by the wide-spread devastation. I saw stilt houses collapsed and roofs caved into the living area of homes.

One of my most vivid memories was a live shot on Indian Rocks Beach where we started with a tight shot of a woman cleaning the chaos created in her kitchen; then we pulled out and showed sand engulfing the entire living area of the house and then we pulled out more to show no back wall, and me standing on the beach looking straight into the family home.

Hurricane Elena changed me in two ways. First, I would never apologize for telling people to evacuate even if the storm ended up bypassing their area. I saw the problems of evacuating our water-surrounded communities and knew how important it was to get people out, especially when you take into account that it takes a massive amount of time to evacuate a hurricane-prone area.

Second, and more importantly, I developed a powerful fear of hurricanes, just seeing the devastation from Elena when you consider it never got closer than 60 miles from Tampa Bay. While that hurricane was considered a Category 3 out of 5, and the winds in our area never got more than 75 miles an hour, the water kept rising and rising to more than seven feet above sea level.

I couldn't imagine what a more powerful storm with a direct hit would do, but unfortunately, I got to learn that seven years later when I was introduced to Hurricane Andrew and found myself close to the center of the storm.

In mid-August of 1992, forecasters started following a tropical storm that was forming off the coast of Africa and building in strength. While meteorologists don't want their communities to experience damage or death and destruction, they always get excited when they start tracking severe weather. This is what they live for.

As Andrew was growing in strength, all the news organizations in Florida started paying more and more attention as it was obvious this was no ordinary storm. Compounding the interest in the story was the fact that while there had been some hurricane activity such as Elena, Florida had been relatively lucky and quiet during subsequent hurricane seasons (June 1st through November 30th) for several years.

Forecasters initially thought the storm, which was now building to a Category 5 (the strongest hurricane) with winds up to 175 miles an hour, was going to hit further north on the Florida Peninsula, but early on the morning of August 25th, the storm roared into Homestead, which is at the southeastern part of the mainland before the Florida Keys.

More than a million people evacuated South Florida and the devastation was overwhelming. On the day of the storm in Tampa, 300 miles away, we knew it was going to be bad in South Florida but didn't know how bad.

The station decided this was a storm of epic proportions(*duh*) and we had to send several crews to cover it. Somehow, the news gurus at the station decided it would be a great idea for my crew to get to our destination by taking U.S. 41, Tamiami Trail, which ran across the state above Alligator Alley all the way from Tampa to Miami. They assigned photographer Mike Dietrich and me as the duo that would make the trek. I voiced my reservations about driving into this killer storm, but my bosses said since it had already hit, the worst I would encounter would be the lingering remnants of the backside of the storm and it wouldn't be a problem.

Wrong!

As we drove south across the Sunshine Skyway, South of St Petersburg, to get to the west-to-east portion of US 41, the rain and wind kept picking up, blowing our news truck back and forth across the road, and making visibility almost zero.

Before we started heading east, I decided to update the station on the conditions, using a payphone from a 7-Eleven (remember this is 1992 and cell phones were a rarity) and again they said they didn't think it would be a problem, because we were on the back end of the storm.

Again: wrong!

The more we drove east on what is a two-lane rural road that cuts across the state like a thin ribbon, the sky got darker and darker, the rain came down harder and harder, and the wind kept gusting strong enough to shake the truck, making it hard to keep on the road.

We kept driving, though, and then about halfway across the highway, we started encountering downed power lines and telephone poles, as well as trees that had fallen, blocking either the eastbound or westbound lane. Essentially turning US 41 into a one-lane highway.

I remember getting out of the truck, being pelted by stinging rain while trying to move trees or fallen poles that scraped the exterior of our vehicle as we went by.

By this time photographer Mike Dietrich who was driving, turned to me in the passenger seat. "Should we turn around and head back to

Tampa?" Quite honestly, we were both freaked out a bit and definitely scared, but I told him that we seemed to be at least halfway across, and we might as well push on in hopes of getting to safety.

We finally reached a semblance of civilization when we arrived at the Krome Detention Center, one of the most famous immigration detainee facilities in the country. It opened in the 80's and housed Cuban and Haitian refugees trying to get into the country. It was often criticized for its horrible conditions and abuses.

By the time we reached Krome, it was dark and most of the 200 inmates had been transferred to other jails or detention facilities. Krome was being used as a staging area for local police, and fire and rescue workers who were going to have to cope with the aftermath of Andrew.

Although I knew of Krome's reputation, I was never so happy to see it, because there were other people and rescue workers all around. Somehow, we had all made it across the state safely.

I still had no firsthand experience of how bad the storm actually had been, other than the reports we were listening to on the radio, and we really wouldn't see the full effect until the next morning.

I found a pay phone and called the station to tell my bosses about our peril-filled journey, but they didn't want to hear about it and instead told us to drive to the ABC affiliate in Miami (WPLG) so we could do a live shot for the late news.

WPLG was north of downtown Miami and north of where the eye of the storm hit, but on the way there, we saw cracked windows, downed trees and damaged homes.

Arriving at WPLG, we saw a damaged microwave receiving tower that had collapsed at the station under the fury of the storm. The station that was running on a generator as the electricity was out and the toilets wouldn't flush.

In all, more than 1.4 million people lost electricity as a result of Andrew and, besides the darkness, it also meant no air conditioning and no fans during the ungodly hot and humid Florida August that people had to endure.

After the live shot, we drove to Ft Lauderdale where the station had booked rooms for the crews. The hotel was utter chaos. Ft Lauderdale, which was 63 miles from the center of where the storm hit, was the closest place people could find to get running water and electricity. The lobby at the Marriott where we had reservations was filled with local people who had to abandon their homes, and they too were looking for shelter with hot water and electricity.

Fortunately, the station had paid in advance for the rooms for the three or four crews we had in South Florida, and while it took forever to get checked in because of the gaggle of wet, tired, angry, scared people in the lobby, we actually got into our rooms with no problem. In the ensuing days, however, getting back into our rooms was not always that easy. Since we were coming back late each night, the hotel more often than not gave our rooms to someone else, but they didn't tell us.

Several times I'd open the door to my room and there would be people sleeping in there who would scream as I walked in. I'm not sure who was more frightened when I walked into "my room" or at least I thought it was my room.

Apparently, the hotel would remove our luggage and put it at the front desk when we hadn't come back to our rooms after 10 pm. I guessed the hotel assumed with all the chaos we weren't coming back.... I thought it was bizarre, but candidly everything in South Florida seemed out of control and there was no normal. Usually I was able to bunk with someone else from the station who had an extra bed in his room.

The craziest night was after returning to the hotel extremely late, because we had done something for Ted Koppel's *Nightline*, which kept us in Homestead well after midnight. After packing up all our equipment and driving 63 miles back to the hotel, it was well after 1 a.m.

Again, they had given away our rooms. At that point, there was only one room left in the entire hotel with one king-size bed and there were three of us: satellite operator Jeff Newman, photographer Mike Dietrich and me.

We were exhausted after an uncomfortable day spent crawling through the hot and humid debris to get our stories in Homestead. To make matters worse, we were scheduled to be back into Homestead at "o'dark-thirty" the next morning so we could do something live for *Good Morning America.*

Jeff and Mike looked at the one bed in the room and both said, "What the Fuck!" I looked at them. "We have about three hours to get some sleep. I advise we all sleep lengthways, and I promise I won't play spoons with either of you." I climbed into the bed lengthwise and they looked at each other and agreed it was the only thing to do. Nobody "played spoons."

While we were inconvenienced in covering the aftermath of Andrew, it was minor compared to what the people of South Florida were going through. I realized the enormity of the damage from the storm the first morning after Andrew hit, when we drove into Homestead—which they were already referring to as "the war zone."

Before leaving Ft. Lauderdale, we loaded the truck with a cooler full of ice, drinks, and some food, because there was no place to get any of that in Homestead. Traffic moved slowly on the highway as we made a trek to "ground zero'. We came around a curve and I saw a Holiday Inn that was still standing, but one side was ripped away so that you could see into each room as if you were looking into a child's doll house. We drove to Cutler Ridge Mall where the second story had collapsed and destroyed what had once been a thriving shopping center. Homestead Air Force base was destroyed: the control tower collapsed, hangers were twisted wrecks, two giant C-130 transport planes were smashed on the runway, and the base housing was gone.

The several mobile home parks in Homestead were reduced to slabs, as the mobile homes were either blown away or looked like the Jolly Green Giant had stepped on them and crushed them like a beer can.

Then there were the looters. Despite a 7 p.m. to 7 a.m. curfew, those trying to take advantage of the situation were out in force. The National Guard patrolled the area with riot gear and guns and made arrests. People took on a frontier mentality, armed with shotguns and putting signs on their homes saying, "Looters will be shot on sight;" "You loot, we shoot;" "You try, you die." Daily survival became a major task as people felt as if they were living in a third world country.

Water that was running had to be boiled and homeowners were using their grills to heat the pots full of water because there was no electricity, no air conditioning, money machines didn't operate, gas stations which weren't destroyed were not able to dispense gas, and because there was no refrigeration, food and ice were a scarce, but valuable, commodity.

When people learned that rescue workers would be bringing ice to a location, folks would form an endless line in hopes they could get some but supplies often ran out.

I remember being at a shopping center doing a live shot for WPLG, which was broadcasting around-the-clock, although the majority of their audience had to listen on a simulcast through battery-operated radios. During the live shot, the truck distributing the ice ran out and there was a near riot.

I was live for a good 20 minutes and when things finally calmed down, I finished my live shot and pitched back to the studio to legendary South Florida Anchor, Ann Bishop, and said I would hunt down those in charge to find out when more ice was coming and then report back to them.

Ann said in my earpiece, "Mike, go ahead and see what you can find live on the air, we'll stay with you, we've got all the time in the world." Which they certainly did.

I was walking and talking during the live shot and finally tracked down the county official in charge who told me live on the air that another two trucks were on their way with more ice and food supplies.

Those who ventured north to buy a one-day supply of perishable food would cook their meals on barbeque grills, which after the sun went down also provided a source of light to the darkened neighborhoods.

It was eerie at night because there were no electric lights, street signs were down, and it was hard to navigate the area safely. Neighbors huddled together like villagers block-to-block to protect each other from looters and express their anger, frustration and fears like a group therapy session. Tempers were short because of the situation as well as the thick, humid hot air that hung-over South Florida like a cruel blanket thrown over someone who can't cool down.

And while the worst place was in Homestead, all of South Florida was a wreck. Electricity was out for days; damage was extensive, and the combined psyche of the area was total shock and disbelief.

Governor Lawton Chiles was in disbelief as well. After touring the area by helicopter, the Governor held a news conference on the ground and said, "It was devastation. Devastating. It's hard to come up with a word. What we saw was far worse than any of us ever expected." Chiles added, "If you look at Homestead, it looks like an atomic bomb went off over it and flattened it. I've never seen damage like that and neither has anyone else I have talked to."

In Coral Gables, a charming upscale community with older homes and tree-lined streets that formed canopies in many neighborhoods, it was heartbreaking to see the trees uprooted and streets that were almost impassible.

The storm changed the face of South Florida and forced the state to institute new building codes. As bad as it was, Andrew could have been worse. While windows blew out of some buildings in downtown Miami, because the eye of the storm was 25 miles away in Homestead, the damage downtown was much less than originally feared, and the huge storm surge initially predicted for Miami Beach never materialized.

One of the more chilling perspectives on the storm came when I did a story on the 10th Anniversary of Andrew. I talked to Homestead City Manager, Curt Ivy. When Andrew had hit, Ivy was the Police Chief in Homestead.

He said that after the storm, a group of officials from South Carolina came to Homestead to explain how they rebuilt after Hugo hit their area. "It will take you a full 10 years to recover," the South Carolina contingent told the officials from Homestead.

After the South Carolina delegation left, Ivy said the Homestead officials laughed and said, "10 years, no way! This is South Florida, not South Carolina. We will recover much quicker."

Then I got goosebumps as he added, "However, they were right, we were wrong!"

Although no one should ever die as the result of a hurricane, because there is plenty of time to evacuate, the long-term effects of being at ground zero can be devastating to a community for years and years.

While Andrew was the worst hurricane I've ever encountered, the 2004 Hurricane season was almost as challenging because we dealt with *four* hurricanes in the state: Charlie, Jeanne, Francis and Ivan.

August 13th is the date that Charlie hit, and for the next several weeks we were covering an impending storm or the massive cleanup afterwards. Charlie was probably the most frightening, because it was on track to hit Tampa Bay. The damage would have been massive, and the aftermath would have changed the area forever.

The day before the storm we did stories about precautions, storm preparations and the massive evacuations that were going on in the area. I did a live shot for the 11 o'clock news adjacent to a major highway which was an escape route out of the area, but the highway had become a parking lot as people tried to evacuate.

I arrived home at midnight, slept for an hour, took a quick shower and then got ready for work as photographer Larry Perkins was picking me up at 1 a.m. Our station, like all the other stations, was doing wall-to -wall, around the clock broadcasting, so we were basically working almost 24 hours a day.

As I left my house that morning, I looked around and figured it would be the last time I would see it looking this way because we had several oak trees. If the hurricane hit, I was sure they would crash through the roof and the storm would destroy the interior. I'd seen it before with other homes that I'd done stories on for work. For some reason, I wasn't too upset and said to myself, *That's what insurance is for.* I knew my family, which had evacuated, was safe and I figured that was the price you pay for living in Florida.

We continued doing live shots all night and then through the next day as we prepared for Charlie to destroy our area. I remember being on location for a live shot at a Publix Grocery store a few blocks from my house around noon where I'd heard a forecaster from the national weather service say, "The two worst and hardest hit spots will be Longboat Key in Sarasota and South Tampa," where I lived. I got a sick feeling in my stomach, but powered through the live shot, and then heard our chief meteorologist, Dick Fletcher, say in my earpiece that there had been a wobble (this time I knew what he meant) and it looked like the center of the storm would move South, which it did, destroying counties about 45 minutes from Tampa Bay.

That entire summer of 2004, it seemed like I was soaked most of the time. I remember doing a live shot for the CBS *Morning News* during one of the storms and a friend from Virginia who saw it asked, "Who was the person throwing buckets of water in your face every 20 seconds"? That's the way it was covering hurricanes.

Speaking of doing coverage for the network, during hurricanes they wanted live shots from local reporters to show the rest of the country what was going on. The problem was the network producers took advantage of local reporters whom they thought would "bow down" to the network in hopes of being discovered.

I knew that no one ever gets discovered doing a hurricane story, nor did I ever have a desire to work for the network, so I made sure they understood my ten-minute rule.

Whenever I was asked to do a live shot for the network, I told the producer to tell me the exact time they expected to take my live shot, and I would agree to stand out in the rain and wind for ten minutes. I warned them, however, that if they didn't put me on the air within that ten-minute window, and the anchor in New York introduced me at ten minutes and ten seconds, I wouldn't be there. Instead, I would be inside of our live truck getting ready for the next live shot I had to do for *my* station.

The network producers couldn't believe a local reporter had the audacity to tell them he wouldn't be there for the network live shot, but as I always explained, it was just another live shot where I was going to get soaked and not discovered and I didn't give a damn about being on network TV. The good thing about "my rule" was they never wanted to test me and always put me on the air as soon as they could.

One final thought about the 2004 hurricane season. During that time, I developed a rash on my arms that was more irritating than poison ivy. I couldn't quit scratching myself, so I went to my daughter's dermatologist.

The doctor ran all sorts of allergy tests and couldn't find anything that I was allergic to. Then she asked, "Is there any chance you've been in wet clothing?" I looked at her. "Doc, do you know what I do for a living and what we've been through this past hurricane season?" She laughed. "Oh, I get it now—you have the equivalent of diaper rash on your arm!" She gave me an ointment and the itching stopped.

Bottom line, I hated covering hurricanes. Any of us who've been around a long-time despised hurricane coverage as well. Reporting those kinds of stories, however, was part of the bargain of being a reporter in Florida. I wouldn't have traded a moment of it to work in any other profession in any other place.

THE ROAD TO THE SUPER BOWL

PART of the Karma and rewards from the Gods for covering the arduous road to keep the Buccaneers in Tampa Bay and the vote to build the new stadium was that I got to cover Bucs playoff games. Although it was hard work with long hours and tight deadlines, it was a dream assignment in many ways, because I have been a Bucs season ticket holder and major fan for years, even during their horrible, ugly "Creamsicle" phase. They got that moniker because in the early days they wore orange and white uniforms and looked like Good Humor Creamsicle bars; they didn't play well, either.

The team, which had been the laughingstock of the league prior to the Glazers buying them, turned into a winner with the hiring of Tony Dungy as head coach. Under general manager Rich McKay, the son of the Bucs first head coach, John McKay, the Bucs were able to put together a group of eventual NFL hall of fame players: Derrick Brooks and Warren Sapp, and NFL pro Bowl players, Mike Alstott, Ronde Barber, John Lynch, Simeon Rice and many other above-average players.

The first playoff appearance since 1982 was the final game in the Old Tampa Stadium, which ESPN's Chris Berman nicknamed, "The

Big Sombrero," and it stuck. On December 28th, 1997 The Bucs
defeated the Detroit Lions for their first playoff win since 1979.

The atmosphere in The Big Sombrero was electric that night as the
Bucs became the darlings of Tampa Bay. That win meant the team was
headed to the "Frozen Tundra" of Green Bay to play the Packers for
the division championship and, lucky me, I was going to be part of the
coverage.

New Year's Day, 1998 the station sent a six-man crew including me
off to Green Bay for the NFL Division Championship Game. Our
flight was at "o'dark thirty" and we all figured the airport would be
empty on New Year's Day. Were we ever wrong!

Tampa airport was packed and with all the equipment we had to
check in, we worried we'd miss our plane. The air seemed chilly while
we tried checking in all our gear at the outside checking stand. The
weather was balmy, however, compared to the cold we would feel as
soon as we stepped off the plane in Green Bay, Wisconsin. The
problem there was not only the cold, but our entire Florida news
team didn't have the proper clothes to keep our balls from freezing
off!

So, after checking into our hotel, our first stop was Target—which,
thankfully, was open on New Year's Day— and we bought (or should I
say the station bought) down jackets, long underwear and heavy socks.
I still froze my ass off each night during our live shots, which we did
for the six and 11. By then in January, the sun set around 4:30 p.m., so it
was unbelievably cold, even for my first shot.

Most of the trip, I worked with photographer Fred Scherer, a great
guy who loved Chapstick (I don't know why, but he was always
applying it like lipstick) and was just a "salt of the earth" nice guy. He
was from Pennsylvania and didn't mind the cold. In fact, he eventually
left our station in Tampa to go to work in Philadelphia. Quite frankly,
the number of people who leave Florida to go back to Pennsylvania can
only fill a very thin book.

Nonetheless, Fred was kind to me, because being the weather
wimp that I am, I didn't want to get out of the truck to do the live
shot each night. Instead of my standing in front of the camera and
doing the mic check and setting up the shot for the director, Fred

would stand in front of the camera shot he set up for me and acted as my stand-in.

Every night, about a minute before we hit the air, Fred would say, "Mikey, (everyone at the station called me "Mikey" or "Mikey-D") it's time for you to get out of the truck, put the microphone on and stand in front of the camera." Most nights it took me about 30 seconds to get into place, so we cut it pretty close to being ready out there for our live shot.

Besides the down jackets we (the station) bought, we also got stocking caps to keep us warm. I thought I also had another secret weapon against the cold.

Two weeks before the Bucs got into the playoffs I had been on vacation and didn't shave the entire time. I thought the beard would not only keep me warm in Green Bay, it also made me look pretty good, too. And since I'd been away from work for two weeks before flying to Green Bay, no one back at the station had any idea I'd grown a beard.

The night after our first live shot in Green Bay, however, our assistant news director Dave Clegern, who had a beard himself and sometimes seemed like a leftover from the 60's—which meant we were kindred souls—called me. "Okay, Deeson," he said, "with the down coat, the stocking cap, and the beard, you look like a homeless guy we hired and sent to Green Bay to get the downtrodden view of the play-offs." He paused for effect. "Lose the coat, lose the stocking cap or lose the beard." I laughed and decided the beard was the least likely thing to keep me warm so by the next live shot, I was back to my mustached normal self.

Green Bay has to be the most unusual major sports city in the country. It has a population of around 104,000 people and has one of the most revered franchises in the world, the Packers. Everything in the town revolves around "The Pack." You see Packers memorabilia and signs everywhere: Gas Stations, convenience stores, drug stores, and everyone is the "official" gas station, drug store or whatever of the Packers. I imagine that if there's a local house of ill repute there, I'm sure they would call themselves, "the official whore house of the Green Bay Packers."

People were extremely nice, very Midwestern and down to earth. While looking for features to do about our location, the first thing everyone asked was, "Have you been to the Packer's Hall of Fame?" Next to Lambeau Field where the Packers played (and was considered "holy territory,") the Packers Museum was the next most revered spot in town. In fact, most nights we did our live shots from there and got to know the museum inside and out.

The best response we got when we were trying to find out what made Green Bay special came from a grizzled old guy in a winter-camouflaged hunting outfit who looked at me and said, "Son, all you need to know about Green Bay is we drink, fuck, hunt, eat cheese and live for the Packers, not necessarily in that order!" I got the impression that what he said wasn't far from the truth.

After being there for 7 very cold days, game day finally came. We arrived at Lambeau field at 8:30 in the morning for the game which started at 12:30 p.m. When we drove up, the parking lot was already filled with fans who'd been tailgating for who knows how long, and most were feeling no pain.

Packer fans were among the most hospitable in the world, shouting to us as we approached the press entrance, "Hey, Tampa Bay, want a brat, want a beer, want a shot?" They were sincere and when we thanked them and explained we had to work, many said things like, "The game is more than three hours away, a shot will keep you warm!"

It was cloudy and cold with a game time temperature of 32 degrees at kickoff, and that might have been the *warmest* part of the day. As I walked into the stadium and onto to the field where the Bucs were warming up, the wind was swirling, and it felt much colder than what Wisconsin natives probably considered a "balmy" 32 degrees.

I was freezing my butt off and at any time could have gone inside into the warmth of the press box, but this was the iconic "Frozen Tundra of Lambeau Field," and I wanted to soak it in as long as I could. While standing on the field before the game, I chatted with some Bucs fans who'd made the trip to Green Bay from Tampa Bay and they concurred with my assessment of how hospitable the folks in Green Bay had been.

While Bucs fans were hopeful the team could beat a much

seasoned and better team led by Brett Favre, most were just thankful the team was in the playoffs.

The odds were against the Bucs, which had never won a road playoff game, nor won a game when the temperature was freezing or below at kickoff. That streak would stay intact until the Super Bowl Season in 2003 when the Bucs won their first road playoff game in Philadelphia with a 26-degree game time temperature.

But back to that night in 1998: the Bucs lost the game 21 to 7 and the Pack truly dominated. The disappointment wasn't overwhelming because we truly didn't expect to get much further. The next time the team went to the playoffs, however, it was a different story.

After missing the playoffs in 1998 the Bucs, once again, were back in the hunt in the 1999/2000 season. The team won the old central division, giving the Bucs a bye for the first round of the playoffs. That meant they didn't have to play in the first round of the playoffs, and it would take only two playoff wins instead of three to get into the Super Bowl. This time, the fans, the media and the Bucs all thought the team had a good chance, as ESPN sportscaster Chris Berman says, "To go allllll theeee way!"

Tampa was Bucs crazy and, even though the team wasn't playing in the first round, our coverage was intense. We did a special that ran Saturday or Sunday night of the Wild Card weekend. My assignment was to do a story about Bucs tight end Dave Moore.

Dave, who went on to be the color man on the Bucs radio broadcast, was knowledgeable, articulate and an all-around nice guy. He invited me to his house for the interview and he was great. His four or five-year-old daughter, however, who was cute as could be, fell in love with our camera. She was a little shorter than the lens, but she made up for that by standing close to the camera and jumping up about every 10 seconds, screaming into the lens, "HI, HI!"

My good friend John Barlow, who was shooting the interview, poked his head around the camera and gave me one of his looks that instantaneously translated to: "*What the fuck are you going to do about that little girl and if you don't do something quick, I will.*"

John, who was a great guy but could be very intimidating, looked a little like Bluto from the Popeye comics, minus the beard. I didn't want Dave Moore's little girl to go running from the room screaming, "Get the scary man away from me!" (meaning John), so I turned to Dave and said, "Do you think she might like to join us on the couch for the interview?"

Her eyes lit up and I was congratulating my wise solution to what seemed like a big impediment to getting the interview, until she sat down next to the family dog—I believe it was a golden retriever—who was between Dave and her.

As we started the interview again, Dave's daughter started patting the top of the head of one of the sweetest and calmest dogs I've ever seen. The little girl kept saying "Nice doggy, nice doggy, nice doggy" with her "love pats." Even though she was small and meant to show her love for the dog, she kept patting him harder and harder, and I was concerned not only that she would hurt the family pet, but also that it was hard to do an interview with "Nice doggy, nice doggy" interspersed with Dave's answers. It was almost worse than her jumping up into the lens and screaming, "HI, HI!"

Fortunately, before John could give me another one of his looks, Dave said to his daughter, "Sweetheart, we don't want to hurt the nice doggie, so let's sit here quietly or go into the other room with mommy." His daughter was truly enthralled by the camera and decided to sit with us, and for the most part, she was quiet and we got a really nice interview with Dave for our special.

For the 1999/2000 season, the Division Championship was in Raymond James Stadium against the Washington Redskins.

The game was a nail biter as the Skins blew a 13-point lead with 1:17 left on the clock. Washington was trying to kick a game winning 50-yard field goal, but the snap from center was low. Holder Brad Johnson tried to pick it up and throw a pass to keep the drive alive, but it fell short. (Ironically, this was the same Brad Johnson who would lead the Bucs to a Super Bowl Victory three years later).

Now, the Bucs won and were off to St. Louis to take on the Rams for the conference championship and a trip to the Super Bowl in Atlanta. It was a totally different feeling from the Green Bay trip, because this time, the anticipation and expectation was high.

Going to St. Louis was in some ways like old home week for me.

Not only did I spend four years at the University of Missouri, two hours outside of St. Louis, I had a lot of friends who lived there, so I had spent a lot of time in that town.

The station sent a crew of six and we got there on Thursday before the game. From the get-go it was a "goofy" trip.

I drove one of the rental cars we picked up at Lambert Airport and when we got to the hotel where we were staying, I parked behind our sports photographer/producer Chris Tilley, a wonderful guy who always had everything organized. Chris also worried about everything as well. He was sort of a Jewish mother. As we were unloading the equipment, I somehow neglected to put my car in park, took my foot off the break and slowly bumped into the car Chris was driving.

I thought he was going to have a heart attack when he got out of the car and looked at the minor damage I'd caused. He started shaking his head. "The rental company is going to charge us a fortune! What are we going to tell the station?"

I tried to calm him down. "Chris, it's a nick, a little love tap." But he was apoplectic. "Someone else has to drive this car for the rest of the trip!" Which was fine with me, because that meant I didn't have to worry about how much I drank when we went out after our 11 p.m. live shots.

We did live shots for all the newscasts and we also shot a big special the Saturday night before the game. At the time when we were on location in St. Louis, it was before we had the technology to edit on computers and use digital tapes. So, this meant we had to schlep bulky editing equipment wherever we went.

Back in those days the station spent a lot more money when we went on location, so we rented an extra room at the hotel to use as an edit suite. Everybody who was editing had to share the equipment, which meant we were all crammed into the room for a lengthy period.

Although I had worked with John Barlow for most of our Bucs playoff stories, photographer Tom Walters was also on that trip, and on Saturday I worked with him for the early and late shows, as well as whatever piece I did for the special.

Tom was a wonderful, talented photographer with a great sense of humor. He worked at the station twice and the first time he left, on his final night at the station he took all the live trucks and the photographer vehicles and moved them one-by-one into the manager's parking spaces (back then each manager had a parking space closer to the building). Those of us who were not in management thought it was hysterical; managers, not so much. Even though management didn't like their spaces blocked, it was a testament to Tom's talent that they hired him back again.

As I said, Tom was one of the more talented photographers I ever worked with, though on occasion he could be temperamental or, as we called it (and Tom would agree), "an Asshole." There was "Good Tom," who was wonderful and then there was "Bad Tom," who was very scary. Luckily, Bad Tom didn't appear too often but when he did, he was really, really bad.

On the day before the playoff games, we were in a crunch to edit stories for the 6 newscast and the special. The equipment, as it sometimes did, (usually at the worst possible time) wasn't editing correctly. It clearly had something to do with the fact that it was not built to be shipped around the country and for some reason didn't like the atmosphere in the St. Louis Hotel room.

Once the stories were edited, we had to feed them back to Tampa via satellite and we had tight deadlines to get them back to the station.

As the equipment kept screwing up, Tom got angrier and angrier, and I could see the transition like Bruce Banner turning into the Hulk. Tom started throwing tapes, swearing, hitting the equipment and becoming "Bad Tom." I didn't think much about it because I had seen it before and knew the thing to do: keep quiet, sit back and he would get the story done on time—as he always did.

Sports photographer George Albright, however, who was waiting in the hotel room to use the equipment, had never seen this type of behavior before and started freaking out. George, a talented photographer who was an enthusiastic, hard-working guy, cowered in the corner as Bad Tom was going crazy. As Tom went downstairs to feed our story, George turned to me. "That guy is psycho, we need to do something." I explained it was just Bad Tom and, like the Hulk, he would turn into Bruce Banner in short order.

We fed our pieces, did the 6, did the lives for the special, did some new stories for the 11, did our live shots and Tom was no longer "green" like the Hulk and back to being Good Tom. All of us went to several bars near our hotel and as each one closed, we found another close by that was still open, so we could have another round of drinks. By 2 a.m. we were all walking or staggering back to our hotel, arm-in-arm singing very loudly songs like "We will Rock You!" and feeling no pain. By then Bad Tom, was long gone, and Good Tom was back.

The next day, we decided to meet for breakfast at 9 o'clock before heading to the stadium, because the game was at 3 p.m. Central time, which gave us the morning to get ready.

As I recall, everyone met for breakfast except photographer John Barlow. I asked, "Where is John?" and no one had any idea, until he wandered downstairs, looking greener than the Green Giant. He had a doozy of a hangover and still had to shoot a loud football game inside the TWA Dome where the Rams played. John, always the professional, worked through it and shot some great video of what was one of the most bizarre championships in NFL history.

There we were at half time, the Bucs trailing 5 to 3 (sounded like a baseball game) with a field goal for the Bucs, and a field goal and safety by the Rams. The Bucs scored another field goal in the 3rd quarter, to go ahead 6 to 5 and then the Rams —with less than 5 minutes left— scored a TD and went ahead 11 to 6 as they missed the two-point conversion.

Although time was running out, the Bucs were on the move and clicking. They were at the 22-yard line with 47 seconds left. Quarterback Shaun King completed an 11-yard pass to receiver Bert Emanuel, and you could feel the momentum swing— everyone, even Rams fans, "knew" the Bucs were about to score.

I sat in the press box next to our sports director, Al Keck. "Al, we are going to win and we're going to the Super Bowl." He looked at me, a big grin on his face. "I agree, destiny is on our side."

The next thing we knew, however, one of the officials called a time out that seemed like an inordinate amount of time and everyone in the press box was asking what it was all about. The people from Tampa Bay and media folks from St. Louis had no clue.

Then the officials announced that after reviewing the play, the clear catch was an incomplete pass. That ruling led to the NFL "Bert Emmanuel Rule" the next season, saying if a player makes a catch, maintains possession and controls the ball, it is a catch even if the ball hits the ground.

For this championship game, however, the rule was not in effect, the catch was declared incomplete and for all practical purposes the game was over. Shaun King threw two incomplete passes and St. Louis headed to the Super Bowl while Tampa Bay headed home.

Throughout my career I have been in many locker rooms following a game, but that was without a doubt the most downtrodden and depressed locker room I have ever been in. Everyone from general manager, Rich McKay, to coach Tony Dungy and the players, the PR people, the trainers—all had thought the Bucs were on their way to the Super Bowl and now the long season was over.

While the Bucs were packing and headed home, we still had to do our 11 p.m. show, which (although it was only sports, and no one died or was injured) was still one of the more depressing shows I've done.

By 11 p.m. it was 11 degrees in St. Louis, it was snowing and all of us huddled up together outside the stadium to try to keep warm from each other's body heat. I ended up snuggled next to our main anchor, Sue Zelenko, a beautiful, talented, down-to-earth, really nice woman, but it was so cold, I couldn't appreciate it—who knows whether or not she did.

Somehow, we shivered through the show. We went back to the hotel and left the next morning, hoping that next year the Bucs would be in the Super Bowl. There were several disappointments ahead before the team would reach the promised land. The Philadelphia Eagles became the Waterloo that the Bucs never thought they would conquer.

Finally, in 2002, victory in the NFL Championship against the Eagles. Although I didn't cover that game, I knew if the Bucs won, I, along with 17 others from the station, was going to San Diego for the Super Bowl. As a season ticket holder and longtime Bucs fan I had seen the team fall to Philadelphia in the playoffs two times before, but I was hopeful that the 3rd time would be a charm.

We had a bunch of friends over to the house to watch the game and it looked as if it was going to be the same old story. The Eagles ran the opening kickoff 70 yards and less than a minute later scored with an early touchdown. The Bucs turned things around, however, and were leading in the 4th quarter, 20 to 10, with less than 4 minutes remaining, but the Eagles were driving, and we were all nervous.

The Eagles were at the Bucs 10-yard line and we all were afraid a big collapse was coming when Bucs defensive back, Ronde Barber, faked a blitz, dropped back into coverage and Eagles quarterback, Donovan McNabb threw the ball into Barber's arms. It turned out to be a 92-yard touchdown interception to seal the deal.

As Barber was running down the field for the greatest play in Bucs history, I was screaming at the top of my lungs, "I'M GOING TO THE SUPER BOWL, RUN RONDE RUN! I'M GOING TO THE SUPER BOWL."

In all, the station sent out 18 people to cover the 2003 Super Bowl as did all the other Tampa Bay stations. This was a big deal for the area, and it dominated all the coverage from the moment Ronde Barber intercepted the Donovan McNabb pass and brought us to victory.

The station staggered the crews going out to San Diego. The first crew, photographer Gene Yagle and reporter Virginia Johnson, left almost immediately after the Eagles Game so they could do stories for our morning and noon shows all week.

I'm pretty sure my good friend, Dave Wirth, who by that time became sports director, and sports photographer Chris Tilley left straight from Philadelphia. Another sports crew left Monday and I believe it was the Tuesday after the playoff game when the rest of us flew out.

When our group arrived in San Diego, we immediately went to the convention center even before we checked into the hotel, in order to get credentials for events the next morning and throughout the week.

Our group was in extremely good spirits (it could have been from the excitement of being in San Diego, or because we were covering the Bucs first ever Super Bowl trip, or —and this was what my money was on—it could have been the massive amount of alcohol we consumed on the two flights we took from Tampa to get to San Diego).

Anyhow, we were all feeling great and extremely happy, and then we got to the convention center. In a hallway we had to pass through, there was our very own, Virginia Johnson, wearing a "Buccaneer Ship Hat" that looked like the Bucs ship in the stadium, sprawled out on the floor, crying uncontrollably. Gene, one of the nicest and most easy-going guys in the world and a good friend, had this look on his face that screamed, "*What the Fuck?*"

Apparently, the station had just told Virginia, an extremely bright, educated and talented woman, that they didn't like the stories she'd been doing. WTSP hired Virginia to do offbeat stories, and that's exactly what she did. Sometimes she hit homeruns; sometimes she struck out and apparently the station decided she was swinging and missing with everything she did in San Diego.

After we got our credentials, we convinced Virginia and Gene to come with us to the hotel. We decided things would get much better with alcohol. Despite the fact they had to be on the air at 6 a.m. EST, which was 3 a.m. in San Diego, Virginia went with us to "experience" (translation: drink our way) through San Diego, and for some reason that did the trick. I don't think she got any sleep that night, but after we arrived, the station quit complaining about her stories and everyone seemed happy.

The week flew by as we did all sorts of Super Bowl stories about the Bucs, San Diego, fans from the Tampa Bay area who came out for the game and anything else we could think of. We did live shots every night at 5, 6 and 11, but just like when I was in San Francisco to cover the Naimoli purchase of the Giants, it meant we were done by 8:30 California time, so that left plenty of time to party.

I remember one night after our live shots, we were all planning on going to dinner and I was riding back to the hotel with our operation manager, Eric Burks, a great fun-loving guy, and our special projects executive producer Melissa Liberman Rancourt.

On an organizational chart Melissa was technically my boss because I worked for special projects at the station, but we were also good friends. She was without a doubt and through my entire time at the station, the most competent person in the newsroom. When the shit hit the fan, everyone—news directors, general managers, reporters

—EVERYONE turned to Melissa. She was level-headed, smart, understood TV, was willing to work hard and knew how to get the job done.

Melissa was also very opinionated, passionate about what we did and not shy about voicing her opinion. In many ways that could be a description of me. And while Melissa always had my back, there were times we disagreed and had public "Fuck You" shouting matches. Newsrooms are not like normal businesses: people are noisy, outspoken and often speak with profanity-laced sentences.

The wonderful thing about Melissa was that after one of those *Fuck You* arguments, she never held it against me. In fact, usually after such an incident, I would call her on my way home and ask, "Is the makeup sex at your house or mine?"

While our respective spouses clearly would object if I literally meant what I has asked, it actually meant the argument was over and we would get back to work the next day as if no disagreement had ever happened. In today's atmosphere that could never happen, but Melissa knew I wasn't serious and was never offended.

Anyhow, on that night I was going back to the hotel with Eric and Melissa and Eric conveniently had beer for all three of us as we were driving to the hotel. Eric, in the driver's seat, only had had a few and was clearly under the legal limit, however he wasn't paying close attention to the path back to the hotel.

We were all talking, and I looked up from the back seat and mentioned to Eric, who thought we were in a line to pay a toll booth fee, that he was mistaken. We were not in a line for a toll booth, but somehow, we had gotten into a line to cross the border to go to Tijuana.

While it might have been tempting to go into Mexico, we all decided we could get into a lot less trouble in San Diego and got the border police to allow us to turn around and find our hotel.

We made it there safely and once again explored the bars and restaurants of San Diego. We got back to our hotel, caught up with the rest of our station colleagues and did the only logical thing, hit the bars! There might have been some food involved, I can't remember if that was the case that night. And while I certainly had my share of alcohol, particularly because I wasn't driving, I didn't go crazy. Unfortunately, my good buddy, photographer John Barlow wasn't as moderate as I was. We worked with all different crews throughout the week and the next day I was scheduled to work with John.

When we got in the car the next morning, he had the same look as he'd had in St. Louis after we had closed down several bars the night before the Bucs playoff loss to the Rams. There was a new added feature, however, to John's hangover. I only drink Bombay Gin and usually it doesn't affect me much, while John usually drinks beer. Unfortunately, I had to learn about a phenomenon I never knew before: "The Beer Shits."

John explained that along the way as we were shooting our story, we might have to make several stops so he could find a bathroom. So that day we ended up going to various places in San Diego so John could use "the can".

Eventually, we ended up back at the convention center, which was "media central" as all the sports radio stations from around the country were broadcasting live from what was called "radio row." TV stations were doing their live shots from Qualcomm Stadium where the game would be played or some location in San Diego. As soon as we got to the convention center, John looked at me and said," I'll be right back." For the third or fourth time of the day, he disappeared.

Meanwhile, every promoter worth their salt tried to get free airtime during one of the most watched and listened to events of the sports calendar (and there was a lot of airtime to fill). Various PR guys came to radio row to try to get their client on the radio or interviewed by the TV stations, which were hanging out in that general vicinity, as well.

So, of course, right after John left, the promoter for the "Miller Light Twins," two well-endowed, scantily clad women wearing a Miller Light banner, asked if I would like to interview them. "Well yeah," was my response, but John was nowhere in sight.

Fortunately, they didn't have any other pressing interviews set up, so I was forced to talk to these women for an inordinate amount of time. It was "painful," but I took one for the team. Oh, the sacrifices I make for my job.

While it was fun trying to make eye-contact instead of looking at the cleavage assembled before me, it was tough to make small talk, because it was clear the two lovely women were not hired while having lunch at Cape Canaveral, because they certainly were not rocket scientists. Finally, John arrived back from the john (sometimes I can't help myself) and we did a truly forgettable interview.

It was clear if anyone our audience wanted to see the interview all they cared about was the scantily-clad, cleavage-enhanced women so it didn't matter what they said—which was good, because I don't think anyone cared how honored each of them was to have been chosen as one of the Miller Light Twins.

In truth, everything the week before the game was really a distraction and, particularly if your team was playing the Super Bowl, it was game day that meant everything. The city of San Diego, which has unbelievable public transportation, wouldn't allow cars to drive to the then-called Qualcomm Stadium on the actual day of the game, so we had to get all our equipment stowed there the night before.

On Super Bowl Sunday at 11 a.m., we crowded onto the San Diego trolley prepared for a long day, but with our hopes high that the Bucs would prevail. Journalistically speaking, we were supposed to be objective in our coverage, however when the hometown team, which at one point had been the laughingstock of the country, was in the biggest football game in the world, it was impossible to be objective.

As Jeff Gluck explained in SB Nation: *"The cardinal rule of sports writing is simple: No cheering in the press box. Along with "No autographs", this is the unbreakable, non-negotiable standard by which all sports writers must abide. It doesn't matter whether you're writing for the New York Times, The Podunk County Weekly or you operate a web site out of your parents' basement.*

*If you are credentialed as media at a sporting event, **YOU DO NOT CHEER IN THE PRESS BOX**. It's very simple, really.*

Sorry, but when you apply for a media credential at a sporting event, you give up your right to cheer. You want to cheer? Buy a ticket and go sit in the stands." [23]

So, there I was, sitting in what was the auxiliary press box, along with my executive producer Melissa, Fox 13 anchor Kelly Ring and several other media people from Tampa Bay. Every time the Bucs made a great play, we tried to hold our enthusiasm in, but it was impossible. In fact, the press box PA announcer had to read an announcement reminding people, "the National Football Press Association prohibits cheering in the Press Box."

I knew those were the rules, I knew it was wrong to cheer, but I rationalized, I am not a sportswriter, I was there covering the game from the fan's perspective, and I wasn't in my normal role as an investigative reporter. I was thrilled beyond compare for the team that I had followed for so long as a fan.

As the 4th quarter began, and with the Bucs having a commanding 34 to 9 lead, I was feeling pretty confident and didn't mind the fact I had to leave the press box and go to a tunnel outside the playing field to get ready for the interviews and postgame show.

The NFL, for some reason, not only wants everyone who steps onto a Super Bowl field to have their credentials prominently displayed, but the league requires the working media to wear NFL issued vests. All of us in the tunnel waiting for the game to end were wearing deep purple, hideous looking vests (I still have mine today). However, when former NFL quarterback and ESPN/ABC commentator Ron Jaworski came into the tunnel and tried to walk onto the field, the security guard wouldn't let him pass.

Jaworski, who was dressed in a suit and tie, was extremely diplomatic as he tried to explain that ABC was covering the game and he was expected to be on the field at the end so Al Michaels and John Madden, who were doing the game in the broadcast booth, could throw to him on the field for his analysis.

The security guard was not impressed or moved. He kept saying, "I'm sorry sir, you don't have a purple vest on, so I can't let you on the field." In the politest terms, Jaworski said, "ABC is paying a lot to cover this Super Bowl and they are also paying me to be there on the field when the game ends." The Security guard was steadfast. "No purple vest, no admittance to the field."

Jaworski was getting exasperated when an NFL VP walked through the tunnel, saw Jaworski and yelled, "JAWS, (that was his nickname) HOW'S IT GOING?" Jaworski. who at this point was somewhat frustrated, explained everything was fine except that the security guard wouldn't let him on the field without the vest, to which the NFL VP looked at the security guard and screamed, "ARE YOU CRAZY? THIS IS RON JAWORSKI! LET HIM ON THE FIELD NOW! HE DOESN'T NEED A DAMN PURPLE VEST!!!!"

Jaworski got on the field, and as soon as the game ended, so did all of us in the tunnel so we could watch as the Vince Lombardi Super Bowl Trophy was presented to Bucs owner Malcolm Glazer. Glazer then handed it to the ebullient head coach, Jon Gruden, who lifted the trophy up in the air to the cheers of the crowd at Qualcomm Stadium. The team was bursting with pride and joy as well.

As the Bucs headed to the locker room, a bunch of us were dispatched to get as much audio as we could that would run in its raw form for an extended 11 p.m. newscast. One of the first people I encountered was Bryan Glazer, one of the Bucs' owners.

I got to know Glazer well covering the long road from the purchase of the team, to the threats to leave, to the vote for the new stadium to the Super Bowl. As I saw him, I said, with a huge smile, "Congrats!" Bryan looked at me, grinning broadly. "Is it all right for an owner to give a reporter a hug?" I responded, Absolutely!" And he gave me the biggest bearhug of sheer joy; it was wonderful.

As a side note, at training camp the next year when I saw him, one of the first things Bryan showed me was the Bucs Super Bowl ring. As I was admiring it he asked, "Want to try it on?" Again, I responded, "Absolutely!" And for a minute or two, he let me wear the ring of the team this big fan had covered for so long.

I always thought Bryan was a decent guy and felt his family didn't get the credit they deserved for the things they brought to Tampa Bay, including the Super Bowl. And while he was obviously a multi-millionaire, I would sometimes run into him shopping at Publix Supermarket, because we both lived in South Tampa. We would stand there in the aisle like two football fans talking about our favorite team.

While some people felt the Glazer family lost some interest in the Buccaneers once they bought the storied United Manchester Soccer team in England, I can attest to the fact that whenever I ran into Bryan in Publix after a loss, you could see it had emotionally killed him. If I saw him after a win, it was like the happiness of that bearhug on Super Bowl night. Luckily for both our reputations, however, he didn't repeat the embrace in the supermarket aisle.

Back to the night of the Super Bowl victory in San Diego: our 11 p.m. news went on forever as we played the tape some of us got in the locker room, and we had live interviews with several of the Bucs players who were more than happy to talk on TV to the hometown folks about the victory.

When we finished up our coverage, we still had to help one of our sister stations in Sacramento, which was Raider territory. Although we were on the West Coast, most of us were working on East Coast time, because we had to service our various shows, and the Sacramento station's 11 p.m. newscast didn't hit air until 2 a.m. Eastern Time. Needless to say, when *that* broadcast was over we were all exhausted. In fact, there's a picture of me somewhere nodding out in the satellite truck.

And then of course, before heading back to the hotel to get some much-needed sleep, we had to have several beers and then head to an all-night Denny's where now it was after 2 a.m. *West Coast* time.

Next day we slept in, caught our flight back to Tampa and another Super Bowl was under my belt. Although I've been fortunate to cover five Super Bowls, none of them will ever compare to the thrill of being in San Diego when the Bucs became Champions of the World!

THE OTHER SUPER SUPER BOWLS

DURING SUPER BOWL WEEK, everybody in the media does strange interviews. I learned that during four Super Bowls held in Tampa.

That first Super Bowl held in Tampa in 1984 was the most important to the city. Although Tampa, which John Naisbitt in his 1982 book *Megatrends* predicted would be "America's next great city", there was plenty of doubt not only around the country, but in the city itself about its future.

People were especially concerned that if the Super Bowl and the festivities surrounding it did not come off well, Tampa's image would be damaged forever. All the politicians and those on the Super Bowl committee worked hard to make sure everything went well, but you could always see the fear in their eyes that this was going to be a "make or break" event. Even those involved weren't sure they could pull it off.

Tampa's first Super Bowl was clearly a major victory for the area, however, as Stephen Birnbaum wrote in the *Chicago Tribune* following the game: *"Seldom has a city acquitted itself more admirably or left visitors with a more pleasant memory of its generosity and welcome...and the kudos are bound to pay big dividends in the years to come."* [24]

To say there was a collective sigh of relief after that first Super Bowl week came and went is a mild understatement. Things went exceedingly well, at least for the city, but certainly not for the Washington Redskins, the defending Super Bowl Champs with the best record in football, who were expected to run all over the Los Angeles (that's where they were at the time) Raiders.

I had an inkling earlier in the week that the Redskins might be having too much fun and too much confidence after their win the previous year against the Miami Dolphins.

One of my good friends and former roommate from Norfolk, Mike Springirth, was in Tampa covering the Redskins for WJLA in Washington.

Mike and I had worked together at WAVY in Norfolk. He was the weekend sports anchor when I was the weekend anchor at the station. At the time, Mike and our weekend meteorologist, John Bulatawicz, rented the upstairs of my house and when we were all together in the family room I always sat in the middle, like a did on the anchor desk on the weekends with John on my left and Mike on my right.

Well, not actually, that's not true, but that's what I told everyone when they learned the weekend anchor team was living in the same house. It was sort of like The Beatles in the movie *Help,* but we didn't have separate doors. The truth is, I didn't spend much time at home in those days (it was following my first divorce; it took me three times to get right) and I tended to find other places to sleep. I saw Mike and John more at the station on the weekend than I did at the house.

At the time, besides being the weekend anchor, I was also the weekend assignment editor and producer, which was crazy. When we were on the air each time a taped piece would run, I'd pick up the phone to the control room and ask the director where we were in terms of time left in the newscast.

Often, he would say, "You are 30 seconds over," and I would turn to John and Mike and say, "Each of your segments has to be cut by 15 seconds, and if you don't like it, the rent goes up 10 bucks a month." Anyhow, Mike and I went way back and he was slammed most of the week leading up to the Super Bowl doing stories for his station. One night between the 6 and 11 broadcasts, he was able to get away and we grabbed some dinner.

When we got back to the Tampa Westshore Marriott where the

Redskins were staying and where Mike and his crew were going to do an 11 o'clock live shot, we saw the team's star running back, John Riggins, in the hot tub in the gym. The only problem is he was passed out and wearing a full white suit that looked like he was an escapee from the John Travolta movie *Saturday Night Fever*.

Riggins was the same NFL star who, just a year later, according to the *Washington Post*, consumed an unknown amount of Scotch at a fancy Washington Dinner and did the following:

"'Come on, Sandy baby, loosen up,' Riggins told tablemate, Supreme Court Justice Sandra Day O'Connor. 'You're too tight.' He then walked over to O'Connor's husband and knelt beside him and put his arm on John O'Connor's shoulder. Then he dropped to the floor and fell asleep.

Guests at the table of 12 — which included Virginia Gov. Charles Robb and senior editors of People magazine — said Riggins slept for about 45 minutes, often snoring during the program, which included a humorous speech by Vice President George Bush. When the program was over, Riggins' wife Mary Lou awakened him. Two editors with People, which had invited Riggins to the dinner, helped him out of the Sheraton Washington ballroom to his waiting limousine." [25]

So, it was not completely out of character for Riggins, who had been the Super Bowl MVP the year before when the Skins literally ran over the Miami Dolphins, to enjoy himself in a way that wasn't the most appropriate.

As we looked at Riggins, (a future NFL Hall of Famer who was inducted in 1992) passed out in the hot tub, I remember turning to my friend Mike and saying, "It looks like the Skins may be having too much fun leading up to the Super Bowl. I don't know if this looks good for their chances to repeat."

With that inside knowledge, I should have placed a heavy bet on the underdog Raiders, but never did.

As predicted, however, the Raiders destroyed the Redskins 38 to 9, with Marcus Allen helping the team wrack up the biggest victory margin in Super Bowl history at the time. The blame for the loss couldn't be pinned on Riggins, who was actually the leading rusher for the Redskins and had twice as many yards gained as the rest of the team combined. Riggins also scored the team's only touchdown, however the rest of the team whose members might not have been as adept at partying and recovering without a problem stunk up the place.

On the night of the Super Bowl we had both a 6 and 11 p.m. show because the game was covered by CBS and at that time, we were still an ABC affiliate. The 6 p.m. show was a huge waste because the ratings showed everyone was watching the Super Bowl, but nonetheless we had to fill a half an hour. I was assigned to do a live shot from the private airport hangar across from Tampa International where all the big shots had flown in their private jets. It went without a hitch and then I had to scramble over to Tampa Stadium for the game.

Because of traffic, I didn't make it in time to hear Barry Manilow sing the national anthem, but I really didn't have to get any sound until after the game. My assignment was to find out how fans enjoyed Tampa and how the area did.

As the game ended, we tried talking to screaming fans coming out of the stadium and somehow through the frenzied crowd I was pushed up against the Raider's Cheerleader bus which had pulled up right outside the stadium. The young women on the bus were more than excited about their team winning and because I was pushed up against the window of the bus I was "forced" to watch them jump up and down as their "pom-poms" went up and down with them— Oh, the humanity!

Anyhow, after what seemed like a slow-motion pleasant eternity, I came back to reality and realized I had to finish getting interviews with people coming out of the stadium and then head to Tampa International Airport.

There was a huge concern that the airport would have a tough time getting fans on all the commercial flights scheduled that night, and I was assigned to cover all the chaos for the 11 p.m. news. The scene at Tampa International Airport was like a good news/bad news joke. The good news for Tampa was that everything at the airport worked perfectly and all the airlines were able to get people on their flights with no problem.

The bad news was that by 10:45, the only people in the main terminal at the airport were the photographer I was working with,

Nelson Jones, a cleanup man running an Oreck vacuum cleaner and me. Not exactly what you would call an exciting live shot.

Meantime at 10:50 out, our competitors ran a tease for their 11 p.m. show and had the chaos going on across the field where the private jets were trying to get out. I got a call from our 11 p.m. producer, Liz Crane who knew the situation where I was, saw what the competition had and was in a panic. Liz said, "All the action is across the field, you've got to do the live shot from there."

I calmly, or maybe not so calmly replied something like: "Are you out of your fucking mind? We can't tear down this live shot, drive to the private jet terminal and set up another live shot there before the 11p.m. newscast is over." I explained she had two choices: Kill the live shot or come to me with the Oreck vacuum cleaner guy in the background, which is exactly what she did, because producers hate killing a live shot 10 minutes before the show, as it throws off their timing completely.

I think I started my live shot saying something like, "Imagine giving a party and nobody shows up. That's sort of what we have here, except for George (I made up his name) and his Oreck vacuum. I can report, however, that people who came to Tampa loved Tampa," and we went to my prerecorded piece with the fans. I came out of the tape piece, gave kudos to Tampa International for handling all the passengers so well and put a ribbon on my first Super Bowl coverage.

The success of that first Super Bowl in Tampa got the area into the Super Bowl rotation. and three years later the league awarded the city Super Bowl 25, or as the NFL likes to say, "Super Bowl XXV" in 1991.

The game was played January 27, which was just 10 days after the United States and U.N. forces began the all-out assault on Iraq in Operation Desert Storm.

The entire Tampa Bay area was focused on the war effort because it was being directed and lead by Central Command at MacDill Air Force base in Tampa and several local troops were deployed. In fact, less than a month earlier, I had been in Saudi Arabia with American troops and understood the focus on the war and the concern of families in our area.

At that point in the year, because of concern for loved ones in a

War zone, for many the Super Bowl almost was an afterthought. But it was still the biggest sports event in the world and the show had to go on, even during war time. And because this was the biggest televised event in the world and MacDill was located in Tampa, there was a huge concern about security and the fear of a terrorist attack at the game. This was ten years before 9/11 and the country wasn't used to high level security measures and the scanning of people walking into a stadium that has now become commonplace.

For this Super Bowl, however, everyone who walked into the stadium had to pass through a handheld metal scanner. There was a major concern by the NFL that the scans would delay fans who had paid big bucks to get into the stadium in time for the opening kickoff.

I remember making a private joke in the piece I did for the 6 o'clock, because the manufacturer of the handheld scanners was a company called Garrett, which was imprinted on each unit. I said in the story, "The Garretts were in full force, prominent everywhere at the entrance to the stadium." That was absolutely true, but I got a private chuckle out of it because my wife's maiden name is Garrett and I was pleased I could give her family a little plug as I was journalistically honest about what was going on.

Once inside the stadium for the game featuring the Buffalo Bills, who were favored over the New York Giants, it almost seemed as if the football contest was secondary. Lee Greenwood's "God Bless the USA" played over the speakers several times and each time the song ended; the crowd cheered with patriotic vigor.

Then it was time for the national anthem. With 155 million viewers in the United States and a global audience of 750 million people, Whitney Houston, along with the Florida Orchestra, brought chills to the entire crowd of 73, 813 fans who were surely focused on our troops half a world away. Especially when fighter jets from MacDill Air Force Base flew over the stadium the moment the last note rang out. That Whitney Houston rendition of the Star-Spangled Banner during America's new-found patriotism resulting from the Gulf War, became one of the most revered versions in history and became a pop hit when it was released for radio air play. Two weeks later the song made it onto Billboard's Top 20.

A couple of notes (music pun intended) about Whitney Houston singing the national anthem. After the game, it came out that the song was prerecorded, and lip synched. But that fact didn't take anything away from the beauty, the goose bumps and the magic moment created as everyone in that stadium and across America who heard it were united in supporting our country.

Another interesting piece of behind-the-scenes info came from one of the pilots of the F-15's who did the flyover right after the national anthem. I had a chance to meet him a few weeks later and asked how he and his colleagues were able to time it so perfectly to hit the south end zone just as the last note rang out. He laughed and explained that they'd practiced a couple of times and had the timing down pretty well. On the night of the actual game, however, their commander was in the press box at Tampa Stadium, singing along with Whitney Houston on a two-way radio connected to the jet fighters. The pilot told me they were able to gage their flight through his singing which he said was so terrible, that they had a rough time keeping their thoughts on the flyover as he warbled along with Whitney Houston.

The game turned out to be one of the best in Super Bowl history. The Giants were leading the favored Bills 20-19, but with 8 seconds left, place kicker Scott Norwood had a chance to win the game for the Bills with a 47-yard field goal. The tension in Tampa Stadium was probably the highest it had ever been in the life of the Big Sombrero (as it was called), when Norwood kicked the ball that had plenty of distance but was wide right and the Giants won.

My assignment that night was talking to fans about their experience in Tampa Bay, and once again people gave the area and the Super Bowl rave reviews. I had what was called an "all stadium" press pass, which meant I could wander just about anywhere during the game except for the press box, which was filled with out of town media, and on the field once the game started.

When the first half ended, I had to use the facilities and happened to go into one of the bathrooms in the high-price seating area. I was astounded as the fans from New York City and upstate New York, whom all apparently had been drinking a lot of beer, lined up as well, but in addition to using the urinals, they were lined up to relieve themselves in the sink! Yuck! I saw one guy actually do that, then turn on the water to flush it down. Several fans behind him screamed in thick New York accents, *"Heeeey whataya doing? Flushin' the fuckin' sink? Move your ass outtathere! I gotta pee!"*

I decided to wait until *after* half time to use the facilities but couldn't get the image of New Yorkers peeing in the sink out of my head.

I had to get back to work and do some interviews after the game as people left the stadium, which I did. We had some extra time, however, because the game was carried by ABC; at the time we were an ABC affiliate. That meant there would be a network post-game show and then the network would run a new program that it hoped would be exposed to the huge audience watching the game and become a runaway hit.

So, after the all the sports programming that night, ABC premiered a new sitcom, *Davis Rules*, with Randy Quaid. The timing and exposure didn't help, though, and the series was cancelled after one season.

For me and my colleagues, however, it meant we had plenty of time that night to put our stories together for the late newscast, which ran more than an hour-and-a-half after the game ended. I was thankful for that because it meant I was able to stay in the stadium to see that last wide right kick instead of being in a live truck feverishly working to put my 11 p.m. story together. It all went smoothly with another live shot around the pre-recorded package where out of state fans gushed about how wonderful Tampa was and Super Bowl 1991 was done and put to bed for me.

And I have to say, while the game was a thriller, the Whitney Houston national anthem was a moment frozen in my memory. The patriotic feeling in the stadium was palpable, and that experience engraved itself even more than all that occurred at half time and during the entire game.

It was another ten years before the Super Bowl came back to Tampa, Super Bowl XXXV (that's 35 for those of you not into Roman numerals) in 2001 was a big one for the station, which by now was a CBS affiliate and for CBS, which hadn't broadcast a Super Bowl since 1991. It was also the first time the Super Bowl was held in the Buccaneers new home, Raymond James Stadium which was constructed adjacent to the old Tampa Stadium.

Both the network and our station pulled out all the stops. We did our broadcasts Super Bowl Week live from a special set constructed for the game and we broadcast from the NFL Experience which was a football-based theme park built next to the stadium.

There were two major problems though, The NFL Experience drew huge crowds which made it extremely noisy on the set, forcing our anchors to wear headset microphones so they could hear each other and be heard by our audience. The other problem was that in January, even in Tampa, the temperature can dip drastically at sundown.

By the 11 p.m. newscast it was in the 40's. Everyone on the set was freezing and had to wear coats and gloves to do the broadcast. Although the weather the week before the game was extremely cold, Super Bowl Sunday was glorious with the temperature at kickoff 65 degrees—perfect football weather and wonderful for a late January night.

My assignment for that night was the easiest Super Bowl duty I ever had. The station wanted me to talk to people who were fans of Baltimore Raven's quarterback Trent Dilfer. Dilfer, who'd spent six years in Tampa Bay after being the Bucs 1st round draft pick in 1994, had six up and down seasons with the Bucs, but while he was in Tampa, he won more games than any other Bucs quarterback at the time. He went to the pro bowl in 1997, was the first Buc quarterback to do that, and lead the team to its first playoff win in 15 years.

Dilfer drove fans in Tampa crazy, because he would show moments of brilliance, but then would look just terrible in other games. The lasting impression I had when he played for Tampa was that he was an extremely nice man. We used to do a live interview with him during the 6 p.m. newscast on Mondays after the Sunday game.

On one Monday, a sports producer who was supposed to be at One Buc Place, the Bucs training facility, was sick. I'd been doing a story in the area and volunteered to go over and help out. It so happened that also on that day my babysitter got sick and asked if I could get my three-and-a-half-year-old son so she could go home early. At the time, I was a single parent, so after I finished the story I was shooting, which didn't have to air that night, I got my son and we headed to One-Buc for the story with Dilfer.

The day before, he'd had one of his ugliest Buc games, threw several interceptions and in general "stunk up the place." I was impressed, however, with how warm and nice he was to my son Andrew, a rambunctious kid who I was concerned would make loud noises during the broadcast. He didn't, thank goodness, and Dilfer really stepped up to the plate, saying without hesitation, "Put that loss on me, I was terrible."

So, here was a guy who was truly gracious on and off the air, I remember thinking a couple of months after I'd interviewed him when his first child, Trevin, was born, what a great dad he would be. Unfortunately, in 2003, Trevin lost a battle with heart disease and passed away. Two months later, when Dilfer made his first comments about Trevin and his family's loss, he openly wept in the news conference. It was heartbreaking.

Whatever I thought about Dilfer as football player, I respected him as man and was delighted to have this latest assignment Super Bowl night to talk to his fans. Clearly, I didn't want to bother people during the game, so I walked around Raymond James Stadium with photographer Tim Kania as people were coming to their seats well in advance of kick-off and approached anyone with a Dilfer Jersey on.

Before the game started we had more than enough soundbites for the story and all we needed to do was a "stand-up" in the middle of the piece which we would shoot during the game, once we knew how Dilfer had performed.

Because so many people cover the Super Bowl, the media passes to the press box were limited and Kania and I didn't have one. Once again, we had an "all-stadium" pass, so we could roam anywhere throughout the stands during the game.

Since we had everything we needed except for the stand up in the middle of the story (which is called a bridge piece) and some game footage, Tim and I took a seat in the club seat area to relax and we figured as soon as the ticket holder came we would move and roam through the stadium.

When the two people who had the tickets to the seats we were occupying came in, we got up, prepared to move out of the club seats; the usher, however, pointed to another two unoccupied seats four or five rows back. We plopped ourselves down, once again waiting for the ticket holders to take our place when they arrived. No one ever came and we later learned that the seats we sat in sold for more than $1,000 a ticket.

One of the people who had claimed her seat earlier was Tyne Dailey of *Cagney and Lacey* fame. So, she sat several rows ahead of us and seemed to be enjoying the game until the Ravens began to dominate the Giants.

By the second half it was obvious the Ravens were easily going to win the game which they eventually did 34-7. So, I could do my "bridge stand-up" talking about Dilfer's triumphant return to Ray Jay (what we locals called the Raymond James stadium). We watched the game until the beginning of the 4th quarter, went to the live truck to put together our story for the 11, watched the end of the game in the truck, did a live shot and another Super Bowl was under my belt.

The fifth and last Super Bowl I covered was in February of 2009 as the Pittsburg Steelers defeated the Arizona Cardinals 27-23 in what was one hell of a game. Pittsburg took a big lead into halftime; the Cardinals came back and took a lead with 2:35 left in the game. Then with 35 seconds left, the Steelers scored a TD on a six-yard pass to win the game.

Although I wasn't covering the sports angle of the game, it truly was a thriller to watch, particularly because I didn't have a preference for one team over the other. It certainly wasn't as nerve-wracking as watching the Bucs in the Super Bowl in San Diego.

Besides the game, two incidents stand out from that week that I'll never forget. We, like all the other Florida stations, were doing Super Bowl specials every night from various places around the area.

On this particular night, I was at one of the "hot night clubs" where many of the celebrities hung out. I was doing a live intro to an investigative piece tied to the Super Bowl about how the Public Transportation Commission was bending its rules for some big money, out-of-town limousine companies and squeezing out some of the little local companies.

Before my live-shot hit, one of our reporters, Preston Rudie—a truly wonderful journalist who'd won several Emmys for beautiful features and many awards for his political coverage—was doing a live shot. (Preston later left the biz to go to work for Congressman David Jolly who served one term and then was defeated by former Governor Charlie Crist.) Anyhow, Preston, a good friend of mine, was a Green Bay Packer and University of Wisconsin diehard fan, which we liked to rub in anytime the Packers or the Badgers lost a game.

Preston sometimes intimated he knew everything there was to know about football which is why, on that particular evening, he recounted Lynn Swan's acrobatic 53-yard catch in Super Bowl X that is considered one of the top five plays in Super Bowl history. Preston was interviewing people going into the night club and as he recounted that story to the man whom he thought was Lynn Swann, he wanted to know how it felt to relive that great moment.

Unfortunately for Preston, "Lynn Swann" turned out to be former Dallas great Tony Dorsett, who'd won the Heisman trophy in college and was a member of the NFL Hall of Fame, not Lynn Swann.

I remember hearing the exchange in my earpiece while I was waiting to go live, when Dorsett realized Preston didn't know who he was talking to and said, something like, "Who do you think I am, Lynn Swan?" Preston sort of gulped and nodded yes. Dorsett replied, "No man, I'm not Lynn Swann, I'm Tony Dorsett." To Preston's credit, he not only admitted his mistake, but wrote about it on a blog, and Dorsett was nice enough to finish the interview as Tony Dorsett instead of playing the part of Lynn Swann.

My other favorite moment that week was about 45 minutes before kickoff when I was walking along the field near the tunnel on the north end of Raymond James stadium where the players for the visiting team come out. As the players were going through their warmups, I ran into Tampa Mayor Pam Iorio. Pam had led a charmed political life as Hillsborough County's youngest commissioner, which lead to her being elected supervisor of elections and the state president of the Florida Supervisors of Elections.

Pam had always enjoyed great media coverage and praise for her skyrocketed during the debacle of the 2000 election when things went relatively smoothly here. She was the voice of reason for the state supervisors, many of whom were in disarray. My stories as an investigative reporter, however, were never "warm and fuzzy" and usually dealt with problems happening in the city during her administration. She didn't deal well with that, particularly in the beginning of her tenure.

The truth is, our relationship thawed over the years as she understood "it was just business" when I did those harsh stories. She even admitted when I was the first reporter granted to do an exit interview at the end of her term, that I actually toughened her up and was good for her. Pam broke down in tears as I asked, "What advice would you give to your successor?" I was shocked as her lip quivered and the tears flowed as she said, "Love the city." It was clear to me Pam truly did.

Final footnote on Pam, who became the national president and chief executive officer of Big Brother and Big Sisters. Whenever I run into her, I get a big warm hello and she laughs and says something like, "I can't even remember the things you gave me a rough time about as Mayor; I guess it was just part of the job."

But on this particular night she was thrilled for what was happening in "her" city. I was somewhat surprised that when she saw me, she called out and screamed "Mike, Mike, we must have a picture together!" I always kept that picture on the bulletin board at my desk, along with a picture of Pam giving me a huge hug the night she was reelected. That picture came as I stopped into her victory party to get a quick interview for the 11 p.m. news. Pam was surrounded by several happy supporters and again she called out, "Mike Deeson, my favorite reporter, give me a kiss and a hug."

Fortunately for me, to sum it all up, when a Super Bowl comes to town, all the reporters are called into action, and as a huge sports fan I was able to cover five Super Bowls—the four in Tampa and the one when Tampa played in San Diego. It was always a week of long hours and hard work, but the truth is, I almost felt guilty getting paid to cover one of the biggest sports events in the world. They were all sheer joy!

TERRI SCHIAVO-NO HAPPY ENDINGS

THE TERRI SCHIAVO SAGA was one of the most gut wrenching and on-going stories we covered. It captivated national attention and when it finally ended, our newsroom and I'm sure all the newsrooms in Tampa Bay were relieved.

It was a story that began Feb 25, 1990 when Terri Schiavo suffered massive brain damage and went into a coma after cardiac arrest and it lasted 15 years.

Two and half months after the incident, Doctors concluded that Schiavo wasn't responding to therapy and said she was in a permanent vegetative state. Her parents, as well as her brother and sister refused to accept the diagnosis, but Schiavo's husband Michael disagreed.

I covered several emotional court hearings where Michael Schiavo testified his wife told him after her grandmother was placed on a venti-lator in a nursing home, that she would not want to be kept alive in that condition. He advocated removing the feeding tube which was keeping her alive.

During each hearing Terri Schiavo's family looked on with disgust as they contended, she was not brain-dead and could recover. At some hearings they would play video of Terri lying in bed with her mouth open as her parents were desperately calling her name or having her track a balloon that they moved back and forth in front of her face.

In some of the videos Terri would groan or move her head, but most doctors concluded those were involuntary movements and not a response to her parents or the balloon. Regardless, it was hard to watch, not only the video, but also the raw emotion that was palpable from all the participants who were looking at a shell of what was once a vibrant, beautiful woman.

Although I was convinced by the testimony of several physicians that Terri would never recover and was brain dead, as a parent I understood her parents, Mary and Bob Schindler, were looking for a miracle that would have Terri recover and become the woman she once was.

In addition to the trauma of losing his wife, Michael Schindler was subjected to unmerciful attacks by Right to Life groups which called him an accessory to murder.

That spawned a series of court battles and intervention by Right to Die with Dignity Groups, Right to Life groups, President George Bush, his brother Florida Governor Jeb Bush and State and Federal Courts.

After covering several court battles where Michael Schiavo was granted permission to let his wife die with dignity, the feeding tube was removed in 2001 but then through a series of appeals, a judge ordered the tube to be reinserted

Over the next 4 years there were several court battles and again in February of 2005 a Circuit Court Judge ordered the tubes to be removed, but President Bush signed an order moving the issue to Federal Court. At a hearing that went late into the night and that attracted national attention, Federal Judge James Whittemore, a well-respected jurist, whom I knew well from when he was an attorney, agreed with the circuit court ruling and the tube was removed March 18th, 2005.

During the final court battles, and particularly after the tube was removed, protesters lined up outside the hospice where Schiavo would spend her final days. They chanted, prayed and held signs supporting keeping Schiavo alive. Every station in Tampa Bay as well as network outlets went onto "death watch".

Clearly it was ghoulish, but it was a big story and as sick as it sounds, no one wanted be scooped on her death. Every night at 5, 6 and 11 either another reporter or I would do a live shot on the death watch from the hospice where Terri eventually died.

It was a story shrouded in sadness as we would report, "She is still alive!" The reports were complicated by the hundreds of protestors who held signs berating the judges involved, Michael Schiavo and anyone in favor of pulling the feeding tube.

The protests were not always calm. In fact, 47 protestors including many children were arrested, mostly for trespassing as they tried to bring a bottle of water to her. One protestor actually slipped past the police and got into the hospice before police tazed him and arrested him for burglary and resisting arrest.

Terri actually lived 13 days after the court ordered her feeding tube removed. Before she finally passed away there were two bizarre incidents.

The first happened on a day when I was not at the nursing home where Terri was spending her final days. I was in the newsroom working on another investigative story when I looked up at the row of monitors which were always individually tuned to every station in the area, as well cable news outlets, and I saw one of our competitors run what's called a crawl, were the words go across the screen, saying Terri Schiavo had died. I screamed out, "Holy Shit, Terri Schiavo is dead."

Just as all the news managers were about to have a heart attack because we weren't the first to report it, that station ran another crawl saying it was a mistake and she was still alive. I'm assuming they had preloaded the information into the machine that does the crawls and a director hit the wrong button. I can't imagine the screaming and yelling at that station after they prematurely killed Terri - at least on the air.

The other incident took place with a drop-dead gorgeous reporter Kim McIntyre who never seemed to get along with managers at the station.

Kim had worked as a model in Europe and she told me she was known as the "poor man's Julia Roberts" because she looked like the famous actress but didn't charge as much to be in a commercial shoot.

One of the ending days of the Schiavo ordeal, Kim was assigned to cover the protests and when she came up live at the scene there was Kim in the middle of the protesters holding a sign in support, that said something like, "Keep Terri Alive"

I could hear the groans in the newsroom, particularly from the managers who couldn't understand how Kim could support one side or the other in this controversial story where we were supposed to be objective.

Apparently after the live shot, managers called Kim and expressed their displeasure, or I should say DEEP displeasure. When she got back to the newsroom after the live shot, Kim came to my desk upset that she was chastised.

I asked, "Kim, why did you hold a sign in support of keeping Teri Schiavo alive?" She told me with an answer that made perfect sense to her. "The managers told me I looked too stiff in my live shots," Kim explained, "So I thought if I waved a sign it would give some movement, but they yelled at me for it."

Although Kim sometimes had a rough relationship with the managers at our station, she ended up going to work for Fox News and became a national reporter and then went to work in media relations at the Heritage Foundation, a conservative think tank.

Kim's sign waving was the only "light moment" in a tragic story. However, it didn't end with Terri's death.

More than five years after Terri Schiavo died at a Pinellas Park hospice, which was the scene of protests, lawsuits and even Congressional action, her family was still working to keep her name alive, with the Terri Schiavo Foundation. But according to IRS records we obtained, they also profited off of her name.

In the IRS report that all non-profits must file, we discovered, in the 2008 filing, it showed the Terri Schiavo Foundation took in $91,568 dollars and paid Terri's dad Robert Schindler Sr., her brother Robert Jr. and her sister Suzanne Vitadamo $59,275 or 64 percent of the money they raised.

Charity Navigator, a respected Charity Rating organization, says any charity spending more than 30 percent on salaries gets a zero rating. The foundation didn't come close.

Meantime, since the IRS report was filed, the salaries had increased to $80,000 a year, but the Foundation says one salary is in arrears causing some family members to work without pay

Schiavo's widower, Michael Schiavo told me with disgust in his voice, "The family should be ashamed of what they are doing. He added if Terri ever knew this was happening, she'd be horrified not only about the Terri Schindler Schiavo Foundation, but also how the money was being distributed.

While Terri Schiavo's brother Bobby said the organization was set up to help families in similar situations, widower Michael Schiavo says he doesn't believe it. He says he has not seen them do anything for anybody. Instead Schiavo says they are using their deceased sister's name to make money.

I called the Foundation but neither sibling wanted to talk to me and, instead, they referred me to their attorney David Gibbs. Gibbs who first said he would set up a meeting, then called me back and said there were scheduling problems and the interview wouldn't be possible.

I wanted to confront her bother, Bobby Schindler and her sister, Suzanne Vitadamo on camera and ask about how they could profit of their sister's death, so I stopped in the office with cameras rolling.

The look on their faces was priceless, however Schindler didn't tell me anything including how the organization spent $34,000 more than it collected in 2008; about the money it raised from a concert with country stars Randy Travis and Colin Ray; why, as it told the IRS, the Foundation doesn't have a conflict of interest policy; and why it is using the name Terri Schiavo. A court document gives Michael Schiavo intangible rights to his wife's name.

Schiavo says that means no one can use Terri Schiavo's name without him granting permission. Schiavo also told me he did that to protect anyone from exploiting Terri Schiavo's name and sent a letter telling the Foundation it is in violation of Florida law. He added it is unfortunate he had to do that, but he couldn't stand by and watch the family make money off Terri's name to support their lives.

In the meantime, the Foundation's Attorney, David Gibbs, sent us a letter saying, "They are shocked and disappointed we would participate in attacking the organization under the guise of investigative reporting." Without seeing our story Gibbs said, "Our attack on this well-respected foundation is unfounded and unjustified."

Meantime, Terri Schiavo's siblings wouldn't answer any questions on camera. And while they're wouldn't talk, the family made thousands of dollars from a foundation named after their sister who died embroiled in controversy and whose name continued to live even after her death.

The attorney for the foundation maintains the high percentage of revenue going to salaries is because of the lack of money the foundation raises.

Gibbs says the Schindlers are doing their nonprofit work cost effectively and it should be viewed as an accomplishment.

The Foundation also says the use of Terri Schiavo's name is proper because she is a public figure and Michael Schiavo has no right to challenge them.

The foundation, according to its latest filing with the IRS, spent more money on fund raising and expenses including almost 30 percent of the $260,000 it collected in 2016 going to Schiavo's brother Bobby Schindler and Schiavo's mother Mary, almost 60 percent spent on salaries. Add in other expenses, and the foundation spent 89 percent of the money it took in before it could start "helping" people in similar circumstances as Terri. The father, Robert, died at the time the report was filed.

It was an investigation that dredged up the raw emotions from a tragic story that had a second sad ending.

SWITCHED AT BIRTH

WHILE I ALWAYS FELT BAD for Terri Schiavo's parents because of their misguided belief that their daughter would miraculously recover and become the woman she once was, I had nothing but complete distain for another set of parents, Earnest and Regina Twiggs, whom I encountered in several hearings and trials.

The Twiggs had a baby daughter born in December of 1978 in a rural county about an hour and a half away from Tampa. The little girl, whom they named Arlene, appeared to be a healthy child. That's what doctors told her parents when she was born, but three days later, before they left the hospital, the Twiggs were told their baby had a serious heart defect.

Over the next nine plus years the Twiggs, along with their seven other children, had to deal with Arlene's illness, which included repeated trips to the doctor and long nights at home sitting up all night comforting the little girl.

When Arlene was nine and hospitalized in anticipation of heart surgery, the couple was shocked to learn that her blood type was B positive, which neither of the Twiggs were, leading a doctor to tell them she almost certainly couldn't be their biological daughter. Further tests confirmed that to be the case.

Three months later Arlene underwent heart surgery which was supposed to fix her defective heart. It appeared she came through the surgery fine, but the next day she died from complications.

The Twiggs were not only stricken with grief, and for that I feel deep sympathy, but because of their efforts to find out what happened to their biological daughter and the way they subsequently handled it, I developed a deep anger and dislike for the couple.

Initially the Twiggs believed someone at the hospital had maliciously switched their healthy biological daughter so that she could be adopted by another couple hoping to get a baby. That was not the case, however, as it turned out that at the same time Arlene Twiggs was born, another little girl was born at the same hospital who went home with her proud parents, Bob and Barbara Mays. They named their little baby Kimberly.

Years later, a nurse at the hospital claimed Kimberly's maternal grandmother paid a doctor at the hospital to switch the babies, but that has never been substantiated and to me seems unlikely.

Unfortunately, Barbara developed cancer and died when Kimberly was two and half. Her father met and eventually married someone who worked in the hospital where Barbara died, but the marriage didn't last, and after seven years they divorced.

That meant that at nine years old, little Kimberly had lost two mothers, the one whom she believed was her biological mother and the woman who had raised her—but the worst was yet come.

After an extensive investigation, including complaints to the FBI, the Twiggs found that another little girl was born in the hospital four days before their biological daughter and they surmised *she* was the one sent home with them by mistake.

Eventually the Twiggs were able to find Bob Mays and his daughter, Kimberly. They wanted the little girl to undergo tests to prove she was in fact *their* biological child.

So, when Kimberly was nine and a half, Bob Mays faced the unenviable task of telling his daughter, who had essentially lost two mothers, that she may not be his biological child. Mays brought home some ice cream after school and after sharing it with Kimberly, he broke the news to his little girl. In a story I did about the situation, he said her reaction was, "Daddy I don't want to move away, you're my daddy, is anything going to change?" Mays assured her nothing in her life would ever change, but unfortunately that was not true.

The world learned about Kimberly when Mays held a news conference to say that she was probably the little girl the Twiggs had been searching for. I remember Mays saying, "I will fight to keep Kimberly even if genetic tests show she is not biologically related to me." That hit me right in the gut as my son Andrew, one of my two children, is adopted. And while I am not his biological father, he is as much my child as my biological daughter, Megan.

While the Twiggs wanted Mays to have Kimberly tested to see if she was biologically their daughter, Mays insisted on several conditions, including a promise that they would not seek custody if the tests proved positive.

The talks broke down and there ensued a series of court hearings, the first of which was to force Kimberly to undergo genetic testing. The stakes were raised as the attorney for the Twiggs said they were going "all in", and if the genetic tests proved the little girl was biologically theirs, they would seek custody. The attorney added that they didn't see any reason not to do so.

Once the Twiggs said they wanted to seek custody, my hatred—and I will admit it was hatred—for the couple was a visceral feeling that tested my ability to be objective on the story. I could certainly sympathize with them for having lost a child whom they believed to be their daughter, who was not biologically theirs, but she was in every way their daughter for the first nine and a half years of her life. Now they wanted to destroy the life of the little girl they professed to love, and whom they believed was theirs.

I remember the look in Regina Twiggs' eyes at every court hearing. In my opinion she looked like a crazy woman with blinders on, intent on taking back what was rightfully hers, even if it destroyed the little girl.

Eventually the test proved Kimberly was in fact the Twiggs' biological daughter and, because the case moved slowly, five years later when she was 14, Kimberly went to court to try to "divorce" them.

The thin little girl took the stand and told the judge, "I don't want anything to do with them." Regina stared at Kimberly with a frightening gaze as the child was on the stand, and Kimberly ran through a gamut of emotions; sometimes crying, sometimes speaking out in anger - particularly toward the woman who was her biological mother — and sometimes looking perplexed as if she was in total disbelief this was happening to her.

"She intruded into my life," Kimberly said of Regina. "I don't like her, and I want my life back!" At one point she said she felt like her life had become a Jerry Springer show.

It was heartbreaking to hear Kimberly explain her reaction when the only father she had known told her about the possibility that she had been switched at birth. She remembered saying, "Daddy don't let them take them away and—" she couldn't finish the sentence and then broke down in tears. All the while Regina stared intensely at the little girl. I remember thinking, *how could this woman say she loved Kimberly when here she was in a courtroom destroying her life.*

Eventually a Sarasota judge (where the trial was held), ruled the Twiggs had no right to Kimberly, including even visitation rights, stating that they officially were a constant source of danger to her and her father, so forbade further contact. He added that the man who raised her was her legal father and Kimberly would never have to deal with the Twiggs again.

Not surprisingly, Kimberly had problems adjusting to a normal life and when she was 16, she said she had an identity crisis and actually moved in with the Twiggs for a short time to try to establish a relationship with her seven biological siblings. It didn't work out though, as she said they seemed to resent her and all the attention she received.

Both families won multimillion-dollar settlements from the hospital where the two girls were inexplicably switched at birth. The repercussions for Kimberly, however, were quite damaging. She married her high school sweetheart at 18, had a child whom state child protection workers took away and then returned; she was twice divorced; ended up having six children with four different fathers and, after blowing through her portion of the settlement, turned to stripping for a short time to feed her kids.

At age 36 Kimberly was part of a Barbra Walters special where, to no one's surprise, she said her life was not normal. When I saw that all I could say was, "No shit!" She also admitted she'd had an identity crisis in her teen years, clearly caused by her biological mother.

Meanwhile, in 1996 Regina Twiggs filed for divorce to end her 29-year marriage with Earnest Twiggs and Robert Mays died in 2012. It was a gut-wrenching, heartbreaking, hard-to-cover story that unfolded like a Hollywood movie script that was eventually made into a TV Movie called, "Switched at Birth."

TAKE AWAYS

AFTER ALMOST 50 years in Journalism I believe I have learned several things through the stories I have done that can help make any organization or person better.

1. No matter what Business you are in, your number one product is people and the focus should be on those people - not you. I have found that businesses, charitable organizations and particularly politicians get themselves into trouble when they forgot the customer, the people they are supposed to help or their constituents are number one. It's not about you, it is about them. McDonalds "You Deserve a Break Today" was one of the most successful ad campaigns the company has ever run. The reason for the success is that it focused on the customer and their needs...a good thing to remember no matter what business or organization you are involved in.

2. Spend more time asking people about themselves than telling them about you and you will own the world. People love to talk about their own lives more than they want to hear about you. That lesson came home in the Bill Clinton story I shared where he wanted to know about me (at least he said he did), rather than Clinton telling me about him. In that encounter Clinton not only remembered my question, but also remembered my name. I always made it a point to ask the people

I dealt with about their families, their hobbies and what they did away from work. When I would ask them about it the next time and remember something they told me weeks or months ago, I became their instant friend. It is not only helpful, but also nice. One of the most successful land use attorneys in Tampa is Harvard Educated Attorney Ron Weaver. As the Tampa Tribune wrote. *"Weaver amazes with his ability to recall the names of contacts, their spouses and their children even weeks or months after meeting someone."* [26] Everyone likes Ron and it is obvious why. He genuinely seems concerned about the people he meets. He is always nice as well as charming at every encounter, not just when he is trying to get something for his clients. It is a great life lesson. Investing in other people's lives and interests will pay back more than you can imagine.

3. Everyone has setbacks, disappointments and disasters. Successful people grieve for a moment and then move forward. Colonel Sander didn't let all his failures stop him. He got knocked down and tried and tried again until he hit it big with KFC. Norman Schwarzkopf's career could have come to an end following the friendly fire incident, but he pushed on and didn't look back...determined to have a successful military career which he obviously did. Bill Clinton is another example. Long before he was impeached as a result of the Monica Lewinsky episode, Clinton had his share of political setbacks, but he labeled himself the "Comeback Kid" because he always bounced back... from losing his first congressional race to becoming Arkansas Attorney General then Governor, then losing his Gubernatorial re-election bid in Arkansas. However, Clinton, didn't mope or go away with his tail tucked behind his legs (maybe that's a bad analogy for Bill Clinton), but he turned around figured out what he did wrong and ran again against the man who defeated him and was reelected as Governor of Arkansas. Clearly the Monica Lewinsky scandal didn't slow him down at all as he finished his presidency and then went out to start the perhaps controversial, but highly successful Clinton Foundation and now is paid almost a quarter of million dollars a speech. The best philosophy may be from Pop Singer Taylor Swift in her song "**Shake it Off**".

4. You can't always replicate the success from a previous victory,

new situations often need new solutions and new thoughts. This was obvious to me from several situations throughout my career. Perhaps the two most notable: when General Manager Elliott Wiser, who was the driving force behind an extremely successful all-news cable channel in Tampa Bay that was much his brainchild, came to our station. Many of us felt he tried to replicate his success from a 24-hour cable news network, with shorter stories, particularly the investigative pieces and institute the success he had on cable at our station a network affiliate where viewers wanted something other than "headline news".

It also was obvious when the news management at our station tapped into the number one station's computer and tried to replicate the story order so our news cast would mirror the number one station. It failed miserably, and the News Director and Assistant News Director were arrested and fired to boot.

5. Like sailing, you can't overtake the leader by following the same course. Perhaps the best example that I saw of that came from two News Directors, Mel Martin and Lane Michelson. Both of them said to turn off the monitors and don't pay attention to what the other stations are doing. In every newsroom throughout the country there are monitors throughout that, not only have the programming from its own TV station, but also monitors are tuned to the competition, to the cable networks and almost any source of news that is available.

Mel Martin always said if we do compelling TV it doesn't matter what the other guys are doing, eventually people will watch us because we are providing something worthwhile.

Lane Michaelsen synthesized it even better when he instituted a new way of telling stories that wasn't dependent on crime and blood and guts, which is easy, but lazy journalism. Putting a reporter in front of crime tape provides a clear visual and helps fills the news hole, but a 2-minute report about a murder, unless it is highly unusual or spectacular, has no relevance in anyone's life, except for the victim, the victim's family, the perpetrator, the perp's family and a 4-block radius of where the crime occurred. Too many TV stations, however, think that is the key to doing local news and the newscasts across the country are filled with stories like that.

Lane's philosophy is that we were not going to do that, but instead tell stories that affected people's lives and tell it through their eyes. It was a different approach and worked wonderfully. As Lane put it, while the other stations are playing baseball, we are going to play football. He once told me, "Not everyone wants to watch Football, but for those who do, if we are the only ones playing football, they will watch us!"

The station zoomed to number one under that philosophy until our corporate "boneheads" came in and said, "Research shows people don't turn to our station for 'breaking' or 'spot' news." Lane would reply, "Ok, but we're number one in the ratings." And then the corporate geeks would scream once again "But research shows people don't turn to us for 'breaking' or 'spot' news."

With pressure from the corporate geniuses, the station changed course, and started "playing baseball" so to speak just like the other guys and guess what, the ratings went into the tank. It drove home the point; you have to set your own course and you cannot overtake a leader by following the same path.

6. Learn from others' mistakes and experiences. As I learned through my entire career, everybody screws up! Some of the most successful people I have ever encountered told me they learned more by their failures rather than successes. Certainly, it helps to know what works and how someone or a plan became successful, but perhaps even more importantly it is powerful to learn why something that seemed destined for success failed! Knowing why something failed can help you plan and have your company or organization avoid those pitfalls, give you the opportunity to make your own new mistakes and learn from them.

The 2016 Presidential Election is a prime example. The Democrats thought they had it in the bag, and that Hillary Clinton was destined to become the first woman President. Clearly, they were wrong and until they figure out not only what went wrong, but also how to correct it, the party will have problems for years.

7. Talk and, more importantly, listen to everyone. Value what they say and know and their perspective regardless of what they do. This is one of the strongest lessons I learned throughout my career. I talk and try to listen to everyone! Sometimes I learn more from the mainte-

nance people than I did from the CEO of an organization. Everyone who knew me was aware I would stop and talk to everyone. Photographer Paul Thorson would threaten me if we had to go to some governmental office close to deadline to pick up documents by saying, "Don't talk to anyone. Just get the document and come back to the car so we can get the story on the air." Then he would add, "or do I have to strap you to the seat and pick up the documents myself, so we won't miss our deadline?"

I was aware talking to everyone sometime could slow things down, but it is the reason stories felt as if they were "jumping out of the walls" every time I would go into a government building and get the "real scoop" from "real people". So, no matter what you do talk to people who will give you the real story and an honest opinion.

8. Never assume you are the smartest person in the room- I have seen more organizations fall apart because the man or woman at the top thought he or she was the smartest person in the room. People like this often are smart, but they have a "My way or the highway" mentality and think they are the only ones with the correct answer or solution to a problem. Sometimes they get it right, but nobody hits it out of the park 100 percent of the time. The organizations that I've seen that have continued success don't depend on just the thoughts of the top person all the time.

9. Surround yourself with people smarter than you. That is a key to success. One of the smartest General Managers I ever worked with, Jim Saunders told me his job was to hire great people, let them do their jobs, run their departments and make the station a success. He told me his job was to get out of the department heads way and let them be the best they could be. He also added, "but if they fuck up my job is to fire their ass before they completely fuck the TV station." Like I've said, TV people use colorful language.

10. Don't expect everyone to work just like you. If they can accomplish the goal by going down a different road who cares that you would have done it differently. I have seen too many organizations fail or chase away good people because they want all their people to use a formulaic approach to the way they approach tasks. I had an executive producer once who was extremely anal and orderly in the way he did

things. That is the opposite from the way I work. He used to get on my case about my process versus his. Sometimes he would say, well the way I would do it is very different. Finally, one day when he was giving me shit about the way I went about putting a story together I had enough and said, "Do you like the way my stories turn out?" He admitted he did and no problem with my stories. So, I looked at him and said, "Who gives a fuck how I get there. As long as my stories are on time, factual and compelling the process doesn't mean shit!" It was like a lightbulb went off in his head and he said, I guess you're right. He never bugged me about my process again, and I think it made him a better manager as well.

11. Great leaders have to have at least one person who can say "That is the dumbest idea you have ever come up with." And they can tell you without fear, that you are going down the wrong path.

You must allow those people to tell you, your idea is full of crap. Clearly that's why Robert Kennedy was such an asset to JFK, because he could look at his brother and say, "What the Fuck are you thinking!" I thought one of the downfalls of Jeb Bush, whom I admired, but didn't often agree with, was the fact that he seemed to surround himself with a group of people who would always say, "Governor, that's brilliant!" Truth was, not all of Jeb's ideas were brilliant and he needed someone close to him and whom he respected to be able to say it to his face

12. When there is bad news, don't hold back, admit the mistake, tell it all, explain how you will correct it and promise it will never happen again. And keep that promise. First off, people are willing to forgive a mistake if you admit you made one, because as I said earlier, everyone makes mistakes. A prime example involved one of Tampa's best-known television figures, Hugh Smith, who was the anchor at WTVT, at that time the CBS affiliate, from the 60's until the 90's. During that time WTVT had tremendous ratings and Hugh Smith was the main anchor and news director of the station and essential was the Walter Cronkite of the Tampa Bay area. However, in 1982 Smith was arrested for soliciting a prostitute during an undercover sting. I covered his news conference the next day on the steps of the Hillsborough Court House and he was unbelievable. Smith looked at the

cameras and told the TV and print reporters, "I have stood for truth in this community for more than two decades and I'm not going to start lying now" He went on to say, "I'm not going say I was doing a story, or was trapped, I'm going to tell truth. I did it, it was stupid, I will never do it again."

Smith offered a similar apology on air, was suspended for a week and came back with stronger ratings than ever, case closed! Except he did it again in 1991, this time soliciting a 15-year-old prostitute. He couldn't survive the second mistake.

As UPI reported Smith issued this statement the second time.

"I have devoted my life to telling the public the truth about the news. I have now been asked to answer to the public about some personal and private conduct of mine.

I have been confronted with that once before. I could not deviate then from the truth and deny it, and I cannot deviate and deny it now. I am guilty and therefore, in the light of the integrity of WTVT, I have resigned from WTVT this morning.'

David Whitaker, the station's president and general manager, accepted the resignation 'with deep regret'." [27]

The other reason to give all the bad news at once is because it blunts story after story after story. Former Investigative Reporter and now Crisis Management Consultant, Clarence Jones, calls it the "Big Dump Strategy."

Jones explained an Investigative Reporters Conference that he tells his clients if they get the bad news out in one "big dump" it may be a painful story for a few days. If they hold back information, however, something that might not have been covered in the "big dump" can turn into a front page or lead story night after night after night. It also can give the appearance that something is being covered up.

The public always thinks the cover-up is much worse than the original sin. Case in point, Richard Nixon. If he had said regarding Watergate, "Ya we did it, it was stupid, we will never do anything like that again," he probably would have survived the incident. His downfall was the cover-up not the break in.

13. Honesty and Integrity are the best way to operate, however if you are going to do something, illegal, unethical or immoral, treat your

employees wonderfully, because it you don't they will be the first ones to throw you under the bus and expose you. I can't tell you how many tips I get from people who hate their boss, their department head or owner. Usually these anonymous sources either point me in the right director or leak critical documents. Often, they end their call by saying not only is "so and so a true son of bitch and treats people terribly, but also he or she is breaking the law, violating the rules or doing something unethical."

14. Never Forget your number one product is people. This one is so important I wanted to start and end with.

THE FUTURE OF TV

THERE WILL ALWAYS BE a need for journalists who can gather facts and put together meaningful, impactful and important stories. I'm not confident, however, the vehicle for delivering those stories will be over what we have known a TV set.

Today's generation gets its news online via their handheld devices. My kids and their friends are never going to sit down in front of a TV to get news at a time scheduled by a TV station. They want news when they want it and will find a source to give it to them...And clearly new technology that we haven't even thought of will change the paradigm even more.

As I said at the outset, I worked in the golden age of local news... I was uniquely blessed to have a job I loved that hopefully made a difference and made my community better. Hope, you enjoyed reading about it as much as I enjoyed living it and writing about it.

ARTICLES CITED

1. Smith, A., Kruse, M. & Caputo, M. (2014, October 20).
    *Knowing Charlie Crist as manager and as politician. Tampa Bay
    Times*.

2. Deggans, E. (2002, June 10). Department of Children and
    Families. *St. Petersburg Times*.

3. Associated Press, (1993, April 22). Florida Executes Killer of
    12. *New York Times*.

4. Catalanello, R. (2008, February 12). Deputy dumped man
    from wheelchair. *St. Petersburg Times*.

5. (2008, February 13). Sheriff apologizes to man dumped from
    wheelchair. *CNN*

6. Thrash, R. & Catalanello, R. (2008, February 16). Deputy in
    video accused of abuse: Dumping a man from a wheelchair
    brings felony charges. *St. Petersburg Times*.

7. Poltilove, J. (2008, February 29). Committee to review
    county jail procedures: Abuse allegations spur actions.
    Tampa Tribune.

8. Hove, S. (2009, October 1). Sheriff's office cuts off Channel
    10: Reporter is accused of berating civilian employee. *Tampa
    Tribune*.

9. Belcher, W. (2009, October 2). Deeson won't stop reporting

on sheriff: Gee says contact with Channel 10 will resume. *St. Petersburg Times*.

10. Graham, K. & Testerman, J. (2005, January 25). Ex-official accused in domestic case. *St. Petersburg Times*.

11. Jones, T. (2011, February 17). Most Indefensible. *St. Petersburg Times*.

12. Lush, T. (2012, August 20). Tampa's strip club king weighs in on RNC. *Associated Press*.

13. Manning, S. (2012, August 30). How Joe Redner Invented The Lap Dance, Built A Strip-Club Empire, Became A Model Citizen, Fought For Your Rights, And Beat Cancer. *Deadspin*.

14. Denton, J.A., (1976). *When Hell Was In Session*. WND Books, Inc.

15. Chawkins, S. (2014, March 29). Jeremiah Denton dies at 89; POW who blinked 'torture' in Morse code. *Los Angeles Times*.

16. WND Staff. (2014, July 24). We do have heroes...Adm. Jeremiah Denton. *World Net Daily*.

17. Mitchell, B. (2002, August 25). Media Feeding Frenzy: The Cheryl Ann Barnes Chronology. *St. Petersburg Times*.

18. Rangano, F. & Raab, S. (1994) *Mob Lawyer*. Scribner.

19. Times Staff. (2017, September 21). Account of famed Riggs-King match heightens Tampa mob intrigue. *St. Petersburg Times*.

20. Gray, M. (2012, May 9). Top 10 Worst Stadiums in the U.S. *Time Magazine*.

21. Keri, J. (2011). The Extra 2%: How Wall Street Strategies Took a Major League Baseball Team from Worst to First. *ESPN Books*.

22. Magnin, B. (2011, January 20). Black Sunday: The day the Giants almost moved to Tampa Bay. *The Washington Post*.

23. Gluck, J. (2011, February 23). No Cheering In The Press Box – Ever. *SB Nation*.

24. Birnbaum, S. (1984, January 23). Tampa's First Super Bowl. *Chicago Tribune*.

25. Steinberg, D. (2012, October, 29). John Riggins' Big Sleep: He Came, He Jawed, He Conked Out. *The Washington Post.*

26. (2008, April 26). Deciphering Property Tax Changes with an Expert. *Tampa Tribune.* Tampa, FL.

27. (1991, March 14). TV anchor admits soliciting teen prostitute. *UPI.*

DEESON MEDIA

Deeson Media is a multimedia company specializing is Investigative Documentaries.

Founded by 12 Time Emmy Winning Investigative Reporter Mike Deeson, the only broadcast journalist in the State to be honored by the Society of Professional Journalists as the Florida Journalist of the year. In all Deeson has been nominated for more than 40 Emmy Awards

Deeson who was also honored with the life time achievement Silver Circle Award from the National Academy of Arts and Science (NATAS) is a Six time winner of the Green Eyeshade Awards (the oldest journalism competition in the Southeast sponsored by the Atlanta Chapter of SPJ); a two time winner of the Edward R Murrow Award; and winner of more than 50 Associated Press and United Press International Awards including Top Broadcast Journalist of the year at least once in 4 decades. He also was chosen the Outstanding Broadcast Reporter in the Southeast.

In 2015 Influence Magazine named Deeson one of the 100 most influential people affecting Florida Politics

Deeson Media is a full-service organization, shooting, writing, editing and providing talent and music for documentaries. Mike Deeson is also an Emmy nominated BMI songwriter who spent 15 years as the regional coordinator for the Nashville Songwriters Association International (NSAI). He has more than 500 songs in his catalogue.

A graduate of the University of Missouri School of Journalism, Deeson has been a working Journalist since the 60's spending 35 years at WTSP TV the CBS Affiliate in Tampa Bay.

Contact Info: Deeson.media@gmail.com